THE THERAPEUTIC REVOLUTION

From Mesmer to Freud

The Therapeutic Revolution

Revolution

From Mesmer to Freud

by

LEON CHERTOK

and

RAYMOND DE SAUSSURE

*Translated from the French
by Dr. R. H. Ahrenfeldt*

BRUNNER/MAZEL, *Publishers* • **New York**

Library of Congress Cataloging in Publication Data

Chertok, Léon.

    The therapeutic revolution, from Mesmer to Freud.
    Translation of Naissance du psychanalyste, de Mesmer à Freud.
    Bibliography: p.
    Includes index.
    1. Psychoanalysis—History.   I. Saussure, Raymond de, 1894-1971, joint author.
II. Title. [DNLM: 1. Psychotherapy—History.   2. Psychoanalysis—History.
3. Psychotherapy—Biography.   WM11.1 C522n]
BF175.C5213   616.8'917'09   79-13123
ISBN 0-87630-208-8

French edition copyright © 1973 by Payot, Paris
English edition copyright © 1979 by Léon Chertok

Published by
BRUNNER/MAZEL, INC.
19 Union Square, New York, New York 10003

MANUFACTURED IN THE UNITED STATES OF AMERICA

Foreword

THE FOLLOWING LINES bear my signature alone. For Raymond de Saussure was denied, because of his untimely death, the satisfaction of seeing in print the product of our close collaboration.

Scion of an old Swiss family—which was related by marriage to such persons of distinction as the 18th century French minister, Necker, and his celebrated daughter, Madame de Staël—and son of the linguist, Ferdinand de Saussure, the young Raymond soon turned his interest to the study of medicine and psychiatry. In 1920 he went to Vienna, in order to attend Freud's lectures and be analysed by the master himself. Henceforth won over to psychoanalysis, he was untiring in his efforts to further its propagation in his own country as well as in France. In this way he was brought, almost exactly half a century ago, to expound its principles in his book, *La Méthode Psychanalytique* (published by Payot in 1922). To this work Freud personally contributed a preface, in which he stated that it was "especially well calculated to give French readers a correct idea of what psychoanalysis is and what it contains."

Raymond de Saussure was one of the founders, in 1927, of the Paris Psychoanalytical Society, as also of the *Revue française de Psychanalyse*. He subsequently became vice-president of the International Psychoanalytical Association and president of the European Psychoanalytical Federation.

We had been friends for many years. In fact, we first met in 1955 in Geneva at the 19th International Psychoanalytical Congress. I had at that time only just completed my psychoanalytic training, while he already had a brilliant career to his credit. We found that we shared a common interest in the study of the origins, so often unrecognized, of psychotherapy from the end of the 18th century to the advent of psychoanalysis. The neglect of these sources is no doubt attributable to the fact that this period is associated with the development of animal magnetism and hypnosis—both subjects which still today frequently arouse resistances in psychoanalytic circles.

With his passion for history, Raymond de Saussure believed that, for a science to be thoroughly apprehended, it had to be studied *synchronically* as well as *diachronically* (to borrow terms introduced by Ferdinand de Saussure). I can still see him as, in 1955, he showed me around his library, which comprised an extensive collection of works relating to the prepsychoanalytic era. In the course of further encounters in the ensuing years, we gradually conceived the idea of retracing the history of this period in a new perspective; we wished to rediscover, among so many concepts and experiments, those which had paved the way for the emergence of psychoanalysis.

It took a long time to realize this project. As will be apparent from the appended bibliography, the literature which it was necessary to analyze was indeed vast. Moreover, we both had other professional commitments; and in view of the fact that one of us practiced in Geneva, and the other in Paris, it was obviously not easy to arrange meetings. And finally, for the last three years Raymond de Saussure was obliged, for reasons of health, to moderate the tempo of his work. It was then that he entrusted me with the editing of the final draft. I can but hope that I have succeeded in acquitting myself of this task to the best of my ability, while adhering faithfully to the line of thought that together we had laid down.

I cannot conclude these preliminary remarks without some reference to the man himself, who on so many occasions gave me proof of his friendship. This "Genevese patrician," of tall and straight bearing, was the soul of simplicity. With this he combined unfailing courtesy, and I well recall the warm cordiality which he was able to impart to our working sessions in his fine old house in the Rue Tartasse where he received so many psychoanalysts from all corners of the earth. And often we then gathered around the table where Madame Janice de Saussure, herself an informed psychoanalyst, extended to us the most charming hospitality.

Raymond de Saussure suffered with great courage his painful and fatal illness. He maintained to the very end his actively inquiring mind and his devotion to intellectual pursuits. I remember that in July, 1971, in Vienna, three months before his death—and I was not to see him again—he still urged me to go and see one of Mesmer's manuscripts whose existence had come to his knowledge.

It is my sincere hope that the psychohistorical work which follows is worthy of the wish expressed by Raymond de Saussure.

LEON CHERTOK

Contents

Introduction

THE PURPOSE OF THIS BOOK is to retrace the origins of Freud's earliest fundamental discoveries, while placing them in the perspective of the history of psychotherapy from the late 18th century through the 19th century. Such an undertaking is certainly not without precedent; but we believe that we can throw new light on these origins and define more clearly the originality of the ideas of the inventor of psychoanalysis in relation to those prevalent in his day.

While Freud was, needless to say, influenced by the German writers and scientists, French culture and science in some respects exerted upon him a determining impact. It was in Paris in 1885-1886 that the first seeds of his discoveries were implanted in his mind, and it was there that he arrived at the crucial decision to abandon physiology for psychology.

We shall, therefore, concern ourselves with this influence insofar as psychotherapy, which, as we shall see, was introduced in France with "animal magnetism," arose out of the realm of the "esoteric" and, gathering in that country its true impetus, emerged on an experimental plane.

We propose, however, to examine the obvious and fundamental correlation between this French influence and the whole body of investigations from which it is derived. The names and (sometimes decisive) works of many researchers of other nations will in fact be seen to constitute landmarks along these lengthy and complex lines of "filiation of influences"—the heritage of an entire century.

In adopting such a working perspective, our aim is to contribute to a better understanding of the contrast between the psychotherapy introduced by Freud and that of his predecessors.

It is interesting to note that, in Bachelard's (1965) view, the beginning of the 20th century marks the point of transition from the period of the "scientific state" characterizing the preceding century to the "era of the new scientific spirit." Bachelard suggests that, following Einstein's discoveries in 1905, the physical sciences did in fact undergo a real revolution, and "in the course of twenty-five years there appeared ideas, any one of which would alone suffice to distinguish a century—a sign of a remarkable maturity of mind" (1965, p. 7). It would seem that, thanks to Freud, a similarly eventful change occurred about the same time in the field of psychology; indeed, we commonly speak of "the psychoanalytic revolution."

In the 19th century the scientist remains an "observer" placing himself "at a distance," or at least "apart," from the experiment which he is undertaking. But, in the 20th century he becomes directly "implicated," even in the realm of the purely physical sciences. This is especially true in the science of psychology, where the study of intersubjectivity becomes an essential element. It is consequent upon the discovery of the transference and counter-transference phenomena that research subsequently became centered on the exchange, in every psychotherapeutic act, between the two persons subjectively involved.

The psychoanalytic revolution has radically transformed and given operational significance to the concepts of the unconscious and the object-relationship, which are in fact closely connected. We shall endeavor to show how, starting from data accumulated throughout a whole century, and owing to Freud's genius, there occurred a veritable mutation which, far from being restricted in its effects to the field of medicine, came to exert an influence in every area of contemporary culture.

In our research, we have made use of historical and psychobiographical material. We started from established facts, to which we were obviously obliged to give a personal interpretation, but with the greatest possible degree of scientific accuracy and objectivity. We are, however, under no illusion as to the fact that absolute objectivity, always difficult to attain in history whatever the aspect studied, is even more elusive in the history of psychotherapy —for instance, when it is necessary to deal with certain psychobiographical aspects. This difficulty notwithstanding, we have not relinquished our intention to study Freud's personality at one particular stage of his life history, inasmuch as, in the genesis of a discovery, apart from the individual's creative genius and his cultural heritage, the emotional factor plays a considerable part. This is especially true in the case of the master of psychoanalysis.

This book does not purport to be a complete history of psychotherapy. It is concerned only with the period which witnessed the decisive transition from a prescientific era to a scientific one, and prior to which experimental psychotherapy was unknown. We shall refer in this context only to the fundamental aspects of the work undertaken during this period, albeit in sufficient detail to provide a general idea of the lines of research which preceded those pursued by Freud.

Our efforts have been directed towards the production of a book that is both clear and concise. We have so far as possible avoided the use of unduly technical phraseology. A chronological table is appended for convenience of reference.

It is our hope that this work may provide some basic data which will prove of particular value to young psychologists, psychiatrists and psychoanalysts, as well as to historians of psychotherapy, medical students, and the medical profession generally, and finally, to all those concerned with the evolution of ideas in the human sciences.

THE THERAPEUTIC REVOLUTION

From Mesmer to Freud

I

The Object Relationship in Animal Magnetism

THE TERM "OBJECT RELATIONSHIP" is employed to describe the relationship which develops between a patient and his therapist.* The expression "therapeutic relationship" is also employed but is less specific to psychotherapy.**

The scientist observes natural phenomena "from the outside," avoiding so far as possible all subjective interpretation. This is a difficult attitude to maintain in psychotherapy, as the doctor finds himself involved in the therapeutic process. While this involvement had been vaguely perceived in earlier years, it is Freud who deserves the credit for studying it scientifically and elaborating the concepts of transference and countertransference, which we shall have occasion to consider more closely and which constitute the basis of analytical treatment. These two ideas are taken equally into account in the majority of present-day psychotherapeutic methods.

Freud's discovery has clearly demonstrated the importance of the affective forces which come into play in the psychotherapeutic process. For a long time physicians tended to be reserved in the

---

* The accepted sense of the term "object relationship" is in fact wider—and still the subject of controversy. The reader is referred to *The Language of Psycho-Analysis* by Laplanche and Pontalis (1973, pp. 277-281).

** The doctor-patient relationship has been studied from the psychoanalytical and anthropological aspects by Valabrega (1962).

3

face of this intersubjective relationship and, in attempting to circumvent the difficulties presented by an emotional, if not indeed an erotic, attachment, they endeavored to treat the illness and not the patient. This mode of procedure could not but influence the concepts proffered in explanation of the illness and might provide the key to certain setbacks that would perhaps have been obviated by a more personal relationship. Viewed in this perspective, it will be easier to understand the vicissitudes and gropings of the investigators throughout the 19th century, as also the radical change brought about by Freud's discoveries.

In practice, psychotherapy entered the experimental stage, under the name of "animal magnetism,"* at the end of the 18th century, with the appearance of Mesmer.** The originality of Mesmer's theories was called into question and already at that time became a highly controversial subject in medical and scientific circles (Thouret, 1784). These polemics have been well summarized in Jean Vinchon's (1936, 1971) book on Mesmer. Before mesmerism, the therapeutic relationship was often linked with religious concepts, as also with magic and even witchcraft—hence the undisguised contempt evinced by the medical profession.

MESMER (1734-1815)

Franz Anton Mesmer graduated as a Doctor of Medicine at the University of Vienna, but was obliged to leave Austria because of the eccentricity of his doctrines and practices. No sooner had he arrived in Paris in 1778 than he proceeded to promulgate his theories on the existence and action of a universal fluid (ideas inspired by the esoteric masonic doctrines). According to him, illness was caused by an uneven distribution of this fluid. The magnetist, through his action on the patient, and especially by inducing convulsive attacks or "crises," brought about a harmonious redistribution of the fluid, which accounted for the curative effect. Mesmer thus believed that he was propounding a physiological theory,

* Later known as "hypnotism" or "hypnosis." The most recent detailed history of hypnosis in France is that by Barrucand (1967).
** A selection of Mesmer's works, edited and annotated by R. Amadou, has recently been published (Mesmer, 1971).

related to those of·electricity and magnetism (as this term is understood in physics) which were a focus of interest in scientific circles at the time. It may be noted that the idea of a curative "crisis" is in fact a very old one.

Mesmer operated through direct physical contact (stroking and magnetic passes), or else by indirect procedures. In his group sessions he made use of the famous *"baquet"*—a covered vessel or tub filled with water, in which were placed glass splinters, stones, iron filings, bottles, and iron rods, the ends of which emerged so as to touch the patients who were linked together by a cord to facilitate the "circulation of the fluid" between them. In his contacts with the patients, he sometimes employed glass rods so as not to touch the subject directly, but this in fact he could not avoid entirely, especially when establishing the initial relationship. He effected "rapport"* by various means, for example by pressing his knees against those of the patient or rubbing the latter's thumbs against his own, while in magnetic passes his fingers lightly stroked part or the whole of the subject's body with a view to inducing a "crisis." Imbued with his theory, Mesmer saw the magnetic fluid as the sole agent in the relationship between therapist and patient. Indeed, his works contain but one single allusion to the part played by feeling. In his own words, animal magnetism "must in the first place be transmitted through feeling. Feeling can alone render its theory intelligible. For example, one of my patients, accustomed to experiencing the effects that I exert on his mind, possesses one more faculty than other men, with which to understand me" (Mesmer,

---

* Mesmer appears to have selected, from among others, the word "rapport" to indicate the *effective* contact, the physical contact between individuals. Psychotherapist before his time, he did not suspect that he was at the same time describing the *affective* contact.

Today, for French-speaking therapists this term no longer retains any specialized meaning. In English, *rapport*, which suggests the idea of "affective harmony," has its place in the vocabulary of psychotherapy as well as in current usage. In Russian, it is noteworthy that the word *rapport*—simply taken over from the French—is the one which is used exclusively to designate the psychotherapeutic relationship. The cognate Russian word, *ráport'*, is only employed in administration, the army, etc. In German, *Rapport* is fairly widely used to describe the relationship of mutual trust between the hypnotist and the hypnotized subject. Freud employed it in this sense—but also to indicate the transference relationship between the analyst and the patient undergoing analysis (1913, p. 139).

1781, p. 25). From this isolated remark, surprising from his pen and which he never elaborated, it is justifiable to infer that Mesmer showed little inclination to enter into an affective relationship; the fluidist theory at all events provided him with the means of avoiding any personal involvement. By forbidding the "verbal dialogue," he forced the patient into a deep regression where the "somatic dialogue" was alone permitted.

Mesmer had witnessed manifestations of induced somnambulism during which the subject remained perfectly calm in his behavior and retained throughout the ability to converse with the therapist (phenomena which, as we shall see, were to be first described by Puységur in 1784). But Mesmer had neither derived benefit from what he had observed, nor appreciated its therapeutic potential. He was moreover little inclined to allow the patient the slightest initiative. This is why he later minimized the import of Puységur's work and regarded induced somnambulism as but a side effect of animal magnetism, which he termed "critical sleep."

Mesmer believed that his theory was both physiological and rational; to him the fluid was as real and "tangible" as the action of a magnet. He had, therefore, never given any thought to the question of the psychological relationship which developed between himself and his patients; without his ever having in any way sought to establish it, it developed nonetheless inevitably.

Inasmuch as this relationship and its management today constitute the basis of all psychotherapy, we must attempt to define its nature in terms of mesmeric procedures. What strikes one above all is that it is a one-way relationship. It is Mesmer who operates and it is he who speaks—and should the patient "reply" to him with some symptom, his first care is to abolish this symptom by giving authoritarian orders. He brings the patient back to a preverbal stage and "dominates" him. This mode of treatment, howsoever rationalized and elevated to the status of a theory, is not only the product of his thought, but the expression of his temperament as well. It is necessary therefore to recall here certain relevant biographical data.

Shy as an adolescent, Mesmer did not assert himself until after his marriage, which gave him an introduction to the Austrian Court and provided him with a substantial fortune, soon squandered on the building of a palace where one lavish entertainment succeeded another. His shyness was then compensated by grandiose and paranoid attitudes. Concerning this period of his life, we need only recall here his conviction that he had made a revolutionary medical discovery and that he believed himself to be the future benefactor of humanity. Although compelled to leave Vienna, this in no way deterred him from asking Louis XVI to place at his disposal one of the royal châteaux in which he might treat his patients. He showed a compulsive need to dominate the latter—albeit while maintaining a certain distance. By and large, he succeeded in asserting himself through the omnipotence with which he firmly believed himself to be endowed.

It is not easy to assess the part played by eroticism in Mesmer's life; few data are available concerning his sexual life.* After a belated and childless marriage to a woman older than himself, within a few years he had left her and was on his way back to Paris. Although in that city the apostle of animal magnetism was not spared his share of malicious gossip, no charge of sexual misconduct was ever, even remotely, levelled against him. Was he, in fact, totally abstinent—possibly due to sexual inadequacy? Magnetism would, in that case, have served him, as it were, as a defense mechanism; conscious of his impotence, he would have wished to assert himself over others, at times with paranoiac violence, as when he thought himself betrayed by his friend D'Eslon who had founded his own school of magnetism (Chertok, 1966a), and at times by the kindness which he showed his patients (especially in the last years of his life, spent for the most part in Switzerland). But, assuming that his own sexual conduct was "irreproachable," it may well be supposed that the same could not be said of all magnetists.

Numerous, indeed, were those who, once they themselves had been magnetized, felt that they were thereby entitled, in their turn, to magnetize others. It had, so to say, become a drawing-room pastime. The magnetist neophytes induced convulsive attacks, as well as transference-love to which they responded on occasion by forms of acting out, some amateur therapists even going so far as to have sexual rela-

---

* A reappraisal of "Mesmer's character" was recently published by one of the authors (de Saussure, 1971, pp. 9-19).

tions with their female patients.* These facts were known to the police, and were in conflict with the conventions of the aristocratic and bourgeois establishment. Thus, it would seem that when Louis XVI decided to appoint the commissions to which we shall presently refer, he did so not at Mesmer's request alone, but in all probability under pressure also from these sectors of society. The question of "erotic complications" received particular attention on the part of one of the commissioners, Bailly, whose "Secret Report" (Rapport, 1784c), as we shall see, emphasized the dangers of eroticism in the practice of magnetism.

These complications, about which Mesmer kept silent but which were being discussed all around him, only served to strengthen the resistance of the scientists and the unconscious motivations of the fiercest opponents of mesmerism. A century later, the same sexual fears were to foster the intense antagonism to the discoveries of Freud who, discussing sexuality openly, would be accused of pansexualism. The controversies surrounding Freudian ideas were, however, nothing to those which raged against animal magnetism.

Unconscious motivations also influenced Mesmer's followers, inasmuch as pre-romantic sensibility (as opposed to the rationalism of Voltaire, who died in 1778, the year that Mesmer arrived in Paris) provided a favorable medium for the development of ideas (such as that of a fluid) to which mystical qualities could be attributed. Moreover, former patients of Mesmer's, such as the attorney Bergasse, retained toward their benefactor a very strong attachment (positive transference) and became dedicated propagators of his ideas (Bergasse, 1784). As the object relationship induced, in addition, an identification with the therapist's omnipotence on the patients' part, the latter, having themselves become magnetists and practicing grandiose methods, sought to compensate for their personal inferiority feelings and could thus in some cases find relief for their own disabilities.

It is, as always, difficult to apportion the part played by rational and irrational factors in the motivation, respectively, of the opponents and the followers of Mesmer, as well as of postmesmeric mag-

---

* In this connection, we will subsequently refer briefly to a certain theory of "love treatment," elaborated some two centuries later by one of our contemporaries.

netists. Some of the latter, however, medical men and others, were at all events seeking the truth in a rational and scientific spirit. Among the most responsible in this respect may be mentioned D'Eslon, Puységur and Deleuze.

The famous reports of 1784 (Rapport, 1784a, b, c) clearly show how rational and irrational components coexisted in the minds of serious investigators. While controversies were raging on the subject of Mesmer, Louis XVI had decided to appoint two commissions of enquiry on animal magnetism, whose members comprised eminent scientists. The first commission consisted of five members of the Academy of Sciences, including the astronomer Bailly, a future mayor of Paris who was later beheaded; Benjamin Franklin; and the chemist Lavoisier (also subsequently beheaded), and four members of the Faculty of Medicine, including the chemist D'Arcet and the humane Dr. Guillotin, professor of anatomy and inventor of an all too celebrated apparatus. The second commission consisted of five members of the Royal Society of Medicine (later, the Academy of Medicine), includnig the botanist Jussieu. Each commission issued a public report (Rapport, 1784a, b).

Both reports condemned animal magnetism, denying the existence of any kind of fluid. They described in minute detail the magnetic (or, as we would now say, hypnotic) phenomena, and even recorded some curative effects of magnetic procedures. But having undertaken the task of detecting the fluid, the commissioners, after a fruitless search, proceeded to draw their conclusions without attempting to look any further or gain a clearer view. So far as Bailly and his colleagues were concerned, all these phenomena were simply attributable to the imagination: "The imagination without the magnetism produces convulsions, and . . . the magnetism without the imagination produces nothing" (Rapport, 1784a, p. 77). The commissioners were not aware that they were thus observing the reality of interpersonal psychological interaction—quite specifically, the object relationship, nor that they had in fact drawn up the very first scientific documents on experimental psychology.

The fluid was nonexistent; such was the commissioners' verdict. As to the fluidists, their interpretations differed: a physical reality for some, a metaphysical concept for others, and even, for a few, a simple metaphor (Chertok, 1966a). Whatever the truth might be, one fact remained certain: magnetic treatment transmitted "something" from the doctor to the patient, who in consequence now found his equilibrium restored. The dynamic nature of this treatment was in radical contrast to the medical practice prevalent at that time, in which the patient was treated as an inanimate object. An exchange was taking place between doctor and patient, foreshadowing the interpersonal relationship.

By ascribing the cause of the phenomena to "imagination" (and thus to something that to them was unreal and non-existent), the commissioners were in effect refusing to study it. This probably represents an unconscious resistance on their part to having anything to do with such phenomena as were liable to give rise to complications—the very same phenomena described by Bailly in his Secret Report to the King, which he drew up simultaneously with the Public Report.

The Secret Report contains the following statements: "The women are always magnetized by men;* the relations then established are no doubt only those of a patient towards her doctor, but this doctor is a man; whatever the nature of the illness, it does not divest us of our own sex, nor does it entirely remove us from the power of the other sex; illness may weaken the impressions caused by the latter, without ever abolishing them . . ." (Rapport, 1784c, p. 279). "They [the women] possess charms enough to affect the doctor; they enjoy good enough health to be liable to be affected by the doctor: thus the danger is mutual. The long-continued proximity, the inevitable physical contact, the transmission of individual heat, the glances exchanged, are Nature's well known ways and the means that she has ever devised to bring about unfailingly the communication of the sensations and the affections. The man who is magnetizing generally has the woman's knees clasped between his own; the knees and all the lower parts of the body are, consequently, in close contact. The hand is applied to the hypochondriac regions, and sometimes lower down, to that of the ovaries..." (1784c p. 279).

The Report continues: "It is not surprising that the senses are in-

---

* There were, however, women who did, in fact, practice magnetism.

flamed. . . . The crisis continues, however, and the eye becomes glazed; this is an unequivocal sign of the complete disorder of the senses. This disorder may be unperceived by the woman who experiences it, but it did not escape the observant eye of the physicians. As soon as this sign has appeared, the eyelids become moist; the respiration is shallow and intermittent; the chest rises and falls rapidly; and convulsions set in, together with precipitate and sudden movements either of the limbs or the whole body. In lively and sensitive women, the last stage, that ends the sweetest of emotions, is often a convulsion. This state is followed by lassitude and prostration, a kind of torpor of the senses which provides a necessary rest after severe agitation" (1784c, pp. 279-280). "Since the emotions experienced are the germs of the affections and inclinations, one can see why the magnetist inspires so great an attachment—an attachment which must needs be more marked and more intense in women than in men, so long as the practice of magnetism is entrusted to men alone. Many women, doubtless, have not experienced these effects, while others have been ignorant of this cause of the effects they experienced; the greater their modesty, the less must they have suspected it. It is asserted that several of them have become aware of the cause and have withdrawn from the magnetic treatment; but those who are unaware of it are in need of protection" (1784c, p. 280).

The conclusion reached in the Secret Report is that "the magnetic treatment cannot but be a threat to morality" (1784c, p. 280). There can be little doubt that a moral condemnation such as this dissuaded investigators, for a whole century, from studying the psychological influence of one individual on another, and acted as a bogeyman which haunted, whether on the conscious or the unconscious plane, those who had undertaken research of this kind. More than that, some were thereby encouraged to deny the existence even of hypnotic phenomena, although these had been observed and described by the commissioners. In this way, reports, favorable or unfavorable, and impassioned debates succeeded one another before the Academies until such time as the learned bodies had, in 1840, once again arrived at the conclusion that animal magnetism was nonexistent and decided to have no more to do with it (Burdin and Dubois, 1841, p. 630).

Having left France in 1784, soon after the verdict of the Royal commissions, Mesmer only occasionally returned there. His disciples, however, were by no means discouraged and continued to pursue their activities in that country. Were they aware or not of the "erotic hazard" and the affective bond between magnetist and patient? Whatever the truth may be, we shall endeavor to ascertain how they envisaged their own position within this relationship, what were the defense mechanisms by which they neutralized the risks of personal involvement, and to what extent rationalization entered into their theoretical explanations.

The works of the period contain relatively few passages useful in compiling a history of the object relationship. For indeed, most of the authors who were then inquiring into the nature of the magnetic fluid had no idea that they were in fact dealing with *feelings*. There is an extensive literature restating the discussions on the nature of the fluid: an element of a universal force, according to Mesmer, or another name for the will, the attention, or indeed the soul. Might it not be that, as a reaction to the romantic period which was imminent, physicians were distrustful of "feelings"—which they generally referred to, if at all, as "passions"?

PUYSÉGUR (1751-1825)

In the 19th century, right up to Charcot's time, the aim of the magnetists was to improve the patient's condition, and generally speaking treatment was free of charge. The fluid was manipulated with a view not only to curing the subject, but also to "developing his soul." This led some magnetists of the period to assimilate the fluid with a spiritual principle which would allow glimpses of the hereafter.

The most renowned of Mesmer's pupils, Puységur, had, through the discovery of "magnetic somnambulism" (i.e., induced or artificial somnambulism), profoundly altered the process of applying the magnetic theory. His method excluded the induction of the convulsive attack in the patient, who was, as it were, "disconnected"; the subject, on the contrary, assumed a state of submissiveness, without, however, ceasing to take part in the dialogue. In consequence, the object relationship became more variegated and required certain "adaptations."

Puységur in actual fact remained a fluidist—without, however, impugning the importance of such secondary factors (which we may describe as "psychological") as the will to cure a patient and giving some consideration to the latter's personality. He also took into account the value of purely emotional factors: "The salutary effect of a direct physical contact," he wrote, "when the will is directed toward the patient's welfare, is so obvious that many people will, on due reflection, be aware of having often produced it unwittingly. How many loving mothers have instinctively saved their children's lives by clasping them with feeling to their bosom at times of unforeseen suffering! How great is the peace and comfort conveyed by the presence of a loved one in the ills that we experience! I am convinced that, knowledge and experience apart, it cannot be a matter of indifference to be cared for in our illnesses by a Doctor and a Nurse who become attached to us" (1785, p. 252) .

Puységur was aware of the possibility that erotic factors might intervene: "As to the sequelae consequent upon the feelings of mutual affection which are invariably aroused between persons of opposite sex, by the care provided, on one hand, and the sense of gratitude felt, on the other, it is sufficient to give due warning that these feelings will always be intensified by the magnetic action, so that whosoever fears its dangers shall expose himself neither to communicating nor to receiving its influence" (1807, p. 217).

In order to guard against these "erotic deviations," Puységur made use of the patient's regression to a stage literally of infantile dependence: "A patient in a magnetic crisis," as he stated, "must respond to his magnetist alone, and must not suffer any other person to touch him; he must be unable to tolerate the proximity of dogs and of all animate beings; and if, perchance, one of these should touch him, only the magnetist can relieve the pain that this will cause him" (1807, p. 171) .

This last quotation clearly indicates a state of total regression; just as the small child tolerates physical contact only with its mother, so does the magnetized patient tolerate only that which occurs with his magnetist. It should be noted that the reproduction of this regression may be equivalent to mothering and, as such, of potentially curative value.

As far as the object relationship is concerned, it is seen to be independent of any other relationship. But it sometimes happens that the patient proves refractory, like a child towards its mother: "This influence is absolute in all that may have a bearing upon the patient's welfare and health . . . but were one to demand of him anything liable to displease him, he would then be much annoyed, and would not obey" (1807, p. 172).

The relationship may even be severed: "Were one to persist in trying to get him to carry out that which did not suit him, what would be the outcome? The patient, after experiencing considerable distress, would suddenly emerge from the magnetic state, and the consequent harm thus caused him would be difficult indeed to remedy" (1807, p. 172).

In Puységur's view, verbal communication with the patient must remain on a purely therapeutic plane, and he refrained from making use of the somnambulistic state to ascertain the patient's past conflicts. He stated: "One must not in the first place overwhelm him with questions, still less try to move him to action in any way. The state in which he finds himself is new to him; one must, as it were, let him become acquainted with it. One's first question must be: *How do you feel?* Then: *Do you feel that I am doing you good?* After that, tell him what pleasure it gives you to be able to help him. From there you gradually come to the details of his illness, and your first questions must not extend beyond the subject of his health" (1807, p. 174). It would seem that this limitation was imposed because of the critical attitude of public opinion. Puységur wrote: "All the greatest abuses, I was told, may follow from this influence which you acquire over your patients. An unscrupulous person will therefore be able to uncover secrets, take advantage of his friends' confidence, and take vengeance on his enemies" (1784, p. 40).

One important point, at all events, did not escape Puységur: the somnambulistic crisis proved more effective if, in the relationship, the patient's role was confined to the presentation of symptoms and to taking such medicines as were proposed to him.

He was likewise aware of the variety of attitudes and feelings which could enter into the one-to-one therapeutic relationship (transference and countertransference) : on the patient's part, fixation on the person of the therapist; on the latter's part, inordinate interest or lack of self-confidence. Let us see what advice Puységur proffered in these situations.

In reply to a letter from Madame de R., who had inadvertently induced in one of her female patients a fixation on her own person, he wrote: "It is necessary that you bring your patient [in the magnetic crisis] entirely into subjection; I will go so far as to say, she must not even be capable of having a will of her own" (1807, p. 430).

It is, therefore, clearly through total regression and the subsequent cure of the psychosomatic symptom that he dealt with the manifestations of transference. It is relevant to take note here of his advice to Madame de R. in this connection: "I would urge you, nay, even beg of you, for the sake of your own happiness, that you do not pursue the treatment of your interesting patient; by your withdrawal, you have caused her less harm than would be the case, were you once more to magnetize her while entertaining doubts. If however, on the contrary, armed with confidence in your abilities, you have the will solely and absolutely to alleviate and to cure, with no other aim than the welfare and interests of your patient—for I myself go so far as not to tolerate even the slightest indulgence of curiosity or of conceit—I can promise you, Madame, *with certainty,* successes which will amply compensate you for all your trouble, by providing you with the purest and sweetest source of satisfaction" (1807, p. 431).

The magnetists were also faced with the problem of terminating treatment, as is apparent in "Young Hébert's Diary" ("Le Journal du jeune Hébert," in Puységur, 1813, p. 94) : "Somnambulism, inasmuch as it is a crisis of the illness that gives rise to it, must in fact decrease in intensity, become attenuated, and finally cease altogether when the illness comes to an end. To foster it in a patient after his recovery is exactly like wishing to keep up his fever or profuse perspiration, on the grounds that these crises had favorably influenced the restoration of his health. The magnetists of the harmonic societies of Strasbourg, Nancy, the artillery regiments in Metz, and others, obtained so many radical cures only because, following my example, they always brought their somnambulists to a state of magnetic insensitiveness."

We do not know what were the precise criteria, in 1813, of mental health or of cure—an uncertainty which, in actual fact, has to this day not been entirely resolved. However that may be, Puységur and his pupils had felt the necessity of bringing to an end the subject's dependence. In the same way as the analyst decides to "liquidate" the transference towards the end of treatment, every good magnetist accepted as evidence of cure the fact that his patient was able to dispense with his support to the point of stating: "As from such a date, you will no longer be able to magnetize me."

Together with the resolution of the symptoms, so also did the patient's susceptibility to magnetism disappear. In broad outline, the process might be conceived as follows: The first symptoms appear in association with a traumatic experience—for example, in a child who at the time sought help, but failed to find it. His "hypnotizability" could therefore be motivated by this sense of disappointment, which now eventually renders him receptive to help from another person. The discharge of affect during treatment finally leads to the removal of tension and of the need for submission; it is then that the susceptibility to hypnosis disappears.

In other words, the symptom represents a conflict which compels the patient first to a deep regression and submission to an omnipotent being and then, after a certain sadomasochistic interplay (to which further reference will be made), to a curative identification with a powerful personality figure. The help, formerly awaited in vain, having now been provided, the patient no longer feels in need of the doctor's support.

This susceptibility to magnetism is similar to what may be observed in certain traumatic experiences in wartime. For example, a soldier, finding himself in a dangerous situation, wishes to call for help but is unable to do so. It is found that he is then susceptible to hypnotism, but once the distressing episode has been assimilated under hypnosis, he loses this susceptibility.

Some magnetists, although unable to formulate explicitly the analysis of this situation, appear in some degree to have apprehended it intuitively. Thus Puységur stated: "It is through strongly *desiring* that the patients, having become somnambulists, shall cease to be such at the moment of their recovery that this effect will invariably come about, provided, however, that no weakness of the constitutional diathesis shall preclude such an outcome, the attainment of which is always all the more desirable, inasmuch as it is for the magnetized patient the proof of his recovery, and for the magnetist that of his success" (1813, p. 98).

In other words, the patient has "lost his need for dependence." And we may ask ourselves whether the patients who are well motivated for analysis are not in fact those who, as children, were frustrated in their hopes that their call for help would be answered and have suffered from this experience until the day when they agreed to undergo treatment. For the symptom, apart from its various libidinal meanings, may also be seen as an appeal for help.

Puységur, having taken up residence on his estate at Buzancy, near Soissons, practiced his magnetic activities in a spirit of altruism amongst the local rural population. This spirit of charity is encountered in all the reputable magnetists of the period, particularly Deleuze, the best known of Puységur's pupils. Indeed, it may be said to have constituted a kind of protection against the potential erotic temptations to which some practitioners of magnetism had succumbed, and which Bailly had denounced in his Secret Report (Rapport, 1784c). The King's commissioner, defenseless in his struggle against these erotic implications, had decided in favor of the total prohibition of magnetism, without, however, launching a ruthless attack against all magnetists and all their patients. His report indicated in careful terms that the female patients were more or less conscious of the possible erotic reactions on the part of the magnetists, and themselves showed a relatively complaisant attitude in this respect. He specifically noted that D'Eslon, aware of these hazards, never undertook magnetism unless in the presence of a witness.*

---

* Already in 1891 Freud examined his own attitude to this practice—or precaution (1891b, p. 107). It is certain that it presented a problem to the practitioners of his time. For his own part, however, he was more inclined to see disadvantages in the presence of a third party. This provision is still "the custom" in some countries—and is sometimes even required by law. But Freud preferred to carry out such treatment without a witness, a fact which, as will later appear, was to have unexpected and providential consequences.

DELEUZE (1753-1835)

However moderate its terms, Bailly's report offended the reputable magnetists who, in putting forward their defense, admitted the possibility of erotic complications but asserted that, as Deleuze observed, these could be obviated: "It cannot be doubted that, inasmuch as magnetism establishes a relationship between the magnetist and his subject, whether through a more frequent association, or through trust, or indeed through the very nature of the agent, its use between persons of opposite sex may give rise to the greatest disadvantages; but it is sufficient to be forewarned of these hazards, to avoid becoming exposed to them. A mother will not allow her daughter to be magnetized by a young man, however high an opinion she might hold as to the young man's moral integrity and the propriety of his conduct. Nor will a young woman wish to be magnetized by a man of thirty, unless it be always in the presence of her husband. On the other hand, a man who is aware that the practice of magnetism is a sacred ministry will always be on his guard against whatever might arouse in him any feeling other than the wish to cure or alleviate a person's suffering, and he will take every possible precaution never to place himself in the position of having to fend off ideas which would give him cause for shame" (Deleuze, 1819a, I, pp. 216-217).*

Deleuze further stated: "I must give warning that magnetism may sometimes give rise to a tender relationship entirely divorced from those feelings which ought to be resisted" (1819a, p. 217). He therefore admitted the possibility that, between the magnetist and his subject, there may arise feelings of affection, which he regarded as entirely distinct from reprehensible erotic feelings, but the idea might here be implicit that such affectionate feelings can contribute to the cure. Deleuze, however, could not express it formally, because for him the moral aspect always prevailed over the psychological.

The two following quotations provide a good illustration of the foregoing comments: "I was staying in the country, in a household who were concerned with magnetism. Having myself been for some

---

* Freud was to state in 1904 that every psychotherapist must be "Irreproachable"— particularly on the moral plane (1905a, p. 267).

time in poor health, a young woman of our company was so kind as to magnetize me within a chain which included her relatives, her friends, and two or three patients. No sooner did she touch me, than I went into a light sleep which lasted throughout the entire session. After ten or twelve days I became aware that she aroused in me a very special affection, and that in spite of myself she preoccupied my mind. Two weeks later I felt well, and our relationship ended. From then on, the impression which she had made on me gradually decreased, and I regarded her as formerly, with a feeling of respectful attachment, but devoid of all emotion. In relating this, I can affirm that, during the time that her image was constantly before my mind, I never had one single thought that I could not have admitted without giving her cause to blush. This, whether because the feeling of affection induced by magnetism is in some way independent of the senses,* or because the confidence and friendship with which I was favored by the family excluded from my mind any unworthy thought" (1819a, I, pp. 217-218). One can clearly perceive here Deleuze's need to defend himself against a feeling of attraction towards the young woman.

Here is a second example of this "tender attachment": "I cured a patient whom I put to sleep on the very first day, and who within a week had regained the strength and health which he had lost six months before. I continued to magnetize him for fifteen days or three weeks. He was a foreman who supervised the other laborers in the grounds and in the fields. Just as soon as he was able to leave his work, he would come to me; he was happy to see me; should I happen to be taking a walk, he would come to join me and would follow me as a dog his master. It will be said that this was through gratitude; I cannot prove the contrary, but for my part, having well observed the circumstances, I am convinced that there was something else, and that it was a consequence of the relationship that the magnetism had established between us. Fifteen days after my having ceased to magnetize him he continued to give me signs of his grati-

---

* As we shall see, Freud was to refer to love in hypnosis as a state "with the directly sexual trends excluded." And Janet, in this same connection, was to speak of a "very special kind of love."

tude, but he no longer had the need to see me" (1819a, I, pp. 218-218) (resolution of the transference).

This observation is interesting in more than one respect. Deleuze is seen to be inclined to concede the role of the emotions in the relationship (transference); from another standpoint, he shows greater objectivity when speaking of the emotions experienced by others, rather than his own. His only feeling that is a personal one, and which at times he extols, is associated with the concept of doing good: "I am able to assert," he wrote, "that the satisfaction of doing good surpasses all others" (1819a, I, p. 316).

Deleuze, it should be emphasized, is the most judicious of the fluidists, the most discerning in his opinions. While not a few magnetists were ostentatiously and inordinately pretentious, he for his part frankly recognized the limitations of the treatment which he employed: "Not only do I not believe that magnetism cures all ailments, but I am indeed convinced that it cures but a very small number, that most frequently it alleviates without curing, and that it can sometimes prove harmful" (1819a, I, p. 215).

Three works by Deleuze would seem to be the best ever written by a fluidist magnetist: the *Critical History* (1819a), the *Defense of Animal Magnetism* (1819b), and the *Practical Instruction on Animal Magnetism* (1825). Apart from the theories already mentioned, they provide useful material for a "prehistory" of the object relationship. Let us see in what way this relationship was involved in the procedures used by the magnetists, while they themselves had no clear conception of it—and how they explained its action.

According to them, the therapeutic agent, the fluid, was of a physical order—a concept which, as we have shown, implies a certain depersonalization of the relationship. To describe the latter in purely physical terms is a way of avoiding having to take cognizance of the emotional factors involved in the object relationship. Thus, Deleuze wrote: "When one wishes to magnetize, it is first of all necessary to establish rapport through contact, and this for the following reason. In order that the fluid which emanates from me shall act on that of the man whom I am magnetizing, it is necessary that the two fluids unite, that they have the same tone of motion" (1819a, I, pp. 95-96).

Deleuze was, therefore, above all seeking the somatization of the relationship; this is clearly shown in this further statement: "The magnetist and the magnetized subject must eschew, for the duration of the treatment, all that can give rise to intense emotions and upset the peaceful course of nature; in a word, all that can disturb the peace of mind and cause a commotion in the nervous system" (1819a, I, p. 116).

In his view, the transmission of the fluid was essential: "I lately magnetized a lady who for three months had been in poor health. After four sessions of one hour each, she found that she was cured. She failed to inform me of this fact the same day, and on the morrow I still proceeded on the same lines as hitherto. Seven or eight days later, I learned that her health was causing her anxiety on quite opposite grounds. I suggested that I should magnetize her once again; she answered me, no, because the effect of the treatment had been too great. I assured her that she had nothing to fear. Previously, I had kept my hand a long time on her knees, then passing it right down her legs. This time, I confined myself to placing my hand on her stomach, and the symptoms which had alarmed her were allayed from that very day. I mention this fact to show that a difference in the procedure may bring about a very great one in the action of the magnetism" (1819a, I, p. 113-114).

Deleuze conceded the existence of a fluid, but, like Puységur, he differed from Mesmer in implicating the magnetist's will and his confidence in effecting a cure. He wrote: "When I magnetize. . . . I send the fluid, by my will-power, to the extremity of my hands, I impart to it, by that same will, a direction, and this fluid communicates its motion to that of the patient. Nothing prevents my emitting it; but, in the individual upon whom I am acting, there may happen to be an obstacle to the effects I wish to produce: I then experience a greater or lesser degree of resistance, as when I apply my strength to lifting too heavy a load. This resistance may indeed prove impossible to overcome" (1819a, I, p. 93). And further: "We have stated that the necessary requirements, in order to magnetize, were an active will for good, belief in its power, and confidence in applying it. Let us first explain why the direction of the will towards good is an essential prerequisite. . . . Were my will intent on harming the person upon whom I wish to act, it would be repelled by him just as soon as he became aware of its action. Belief is necessary, because he who does not believe in the possibility of producing an effect would be incapable of naturally and constantly applying his power to its production. The same argument applies to confidence without which one becomes exhausted and acts weakly. An active will also presupposes a sustained attention; for, without attention, it would not be possible to direct one's will, in a constant and uniform way, toward one and the same end" (1819a, I, pp. 94-95).

In this one-to-one relationship, action and decision alike rested entirely with the therapist, while the patient must assume a passive role. This dependence or submissiveness on the patient's part was, however, more subtle than with Mesmer: "Consider the magnetized individual as forming, in a certain sense, a part of his magnetist, and you will no longer be surprised that the latter's will should act upon him and determine [his fluid's] motions" (1819a, I, p. 97).

With regard to this question of "primacy of the magnetist," we would today say that the transference is initiated by the doctor who wishes to cure the patient, and that from the patient the counter-transference may, on occasion, arise. Deleuze put it differently: "For the magnetist faith is required, without which his action will be weak, but it is not necessary for the subject who is being magnetized. Were the latter to experience effects only to such extent as he is convinced beforehand that he is going to experience them, one could attribute these effects to the imagination. However, absolute disbelief on the part of the magnetized person can repel the magnetist's action, frustrate it, delay it, and counteract its effects for a more or less lengthy period" (1819a, I, p. 141).

Deleuze was taken in by his own argument when he sought to attribute every quality to the fluid and almost nothing to the emotions. In his view, the cure owed nothing to confidence—the latter was at best a state of mind favoring the action of the fluid. For the treatment to prove effective, there was according to him but one prerequisite: that the magnetized subject be inactive, that he think of nothing—in short, that he remain passive.

He insisted upon the indispensability of this passivity: "If in touching I apply my will and attention, and the person upon whom I wish to act is in a passive or inactive state, it is my fluid which will determine the motion of his own. There then occurs something similar to that which takes place between a piece of iron that is magnetized, and one that is not; when one is drawn across the other several times and in the same direction, the first of these transmits to the other its motion or its quality. This is not an explanation but a comparison" (1819a, I, p. 96).

It is thus apparent that to refer everything back to the magnetist was for Deleuze a way of (unconsciously) protecting himself from affective involvement—so much easier is it, up to a certain point, to control one's own emotions rather than those of others.

Deleuze regarded the role of the imagination as limited: "You explain several of these facts by the imagination," he wrote, "but those that cannot be so explained are innumerable" (Deleuze, 1819b, p. 263). Insofar as he conceded such a role at all, it was referable to the imagination of the magnetist alone: "It is belief which magnetizes, or which activates magnetism. No doubt. But it is not the belief of the individual who is being magnetized; it is the belief of the magnetist. I can say the same of the imagination. It may be that the magnetist's imagination imparts more energy to his action; but the imagination of the magnetized subject has no need to be excited in order that the action shall be all that it can possibly be" (1819b, p. 101).

Whether we are reading the works of Deleuze or those of his contemporaries, one must here give to the word "imagination" the same value as would later be given by Braid and his followers to the term "suggestion."

DE VILLERS (1765-1815), VIREY (1775-1846)

Deleuze had, therefore, at least sensed, if not discerned, the concept of the object relationship. But his reaction, even though unconscious, was defensive; he protected himself against this idea. Firmly believing in the existence of the fluid and in the traditional methods inherited from Mesmer, often operating on patients linked "in a chain" (with the consequent dispersion amongst several subjects of the interpersonal relationship), he remained at a conceptual level which was superseded by de Villers, to whom we shall now refer.

The latter felt intuitively that the relationship had to be appropriately manipulated.

Starting from the study of mesmerism, we then spoke of Puységur, who dealt with the subject of magnetism as early as 1784, and next to whom we placed his pupil Deleuze whose work was imbued with the same spirit. But we must retrace our steps in order to draw attention to a few minor authors who were not, however, lacking in originality. Charles de Villers was the author of a sort of novel entitled *Le Magnétiseur amoureux* ("The Amorous Magnetist"), with the imprint "Geneva, 1787," but in fact published at Besançon—a town in northeastern France, whose public library possesses the only copy of this work known to us (de Villers, 1787). Deleuze hoped that it would be reprinted, asserting that everything possible had been done (because of the title?) to impede its distribution (Deleuze, 1819a, II, p. 114).* At all events, de Villers' book is the very first to consider an object relationship as a curative factor—a cure which, according to that author, is attributable to the convergence of two strong emotional drives, that of the individual who wishes to be cured, and that of the doctor who wishes to cure. This is a remarkable proposition, in view of the magnetists' aversion to conceding any part to the emotions, their habit of literally "hiding" behind the concept of a fluid, their will or sometimes their desire to do good and, in any case, to exclude the slightest expression of feeling that might be liable to intervene between patient and doctor. The same distrust of the emotions was to be experienced by psychiatrists at a later date.

De Villers attributes no specific function to the fluid, nor any particular efficacy to the methods employed. In his view the cure is conditioned by the object relationship and by the mutual exchange of feelings between magnetist and patient.

The soul, so de Villers states, can of itself "convey its actions to another being. If this other being is organized, the soul will unite with the principle of the motion which will be present therein, and that is how I shall exert a salutary effect on the patient. . . . This

---

* See: Gay-Lemonnyer, *Bibliographie des Ouvrages relatifs à l'Amour*, III, 3: ". . . most of the copies were seized and pulped on the orders of M. de Breteuil" (a minister under Louis XVI).

conveyance can take place only insofar as the soul shall desire it, . . . [It] is brought about by the process of thought" (1787, pp. 95-98).

He proceeds: "Since this man's soul acts within his body and mine acts within it also, they therefore both act in concord, and to that end they needs must unite . . . they will unite so much the better . . . as I shall have more *moral* affections in common with this man. And which then is the moral affection that is most marked in a patient? It is to be cured. Thus I must also assume this will to cure, in order to act upon him with the greatest possible efficacy" (1787, p. 104).

With de Villers we witness the transition, before its time, from magnetism to suggestion: the object relationship is manipulated under the healer's authority, but the author is in fact already describing a "transference-countertransference" relationship when he states that the practitioner's ascendancy depends not only on the latter's disposition (emotional attitude), but also on the inner disposition of the patient towards the practitioner.

De Villers' work precedes by more than a century Freud's first allusions to the transference, and shows that a few magnetists had understood the necessity of manipulating the object relationship— and this in such a way that it does not diverge from the aim, which is to effect a cure. To be sure, they had not yet understood that the magnetic regression tended to revive affective reactions from the past; but they had grasped the fact that the therapeutic involvement must be complete and reciprocal, if one were to avoid the degeneration of magnetism into love. De Villers states, moreover, that the magnetist "is truly the *active* being, whereas the other, who receives the influence, is a purely passive being. It is this superiority that I term *ascendancy* . . . [and which will depend] . . . on the patient's moral condition, . . . on the greater or lesser rapport of our inner dispositions, and above all on the *sincerity* that I impart to my will" (1787, pp. 120-121).

While emphasizing the need for a desire to be cured on the patient's part, de Villers makes no mention of the resistances that may be shown. As to the desire to cure, he disposes of this question in a single sentence, whereas today it is necessary to investigate the patient's various motivations in order to select the most suitable form of treatment.

It is to be regretted that his contemporaries paid far too little attention to the views of de Villers,* who, although he did not subsequently take up psychotherapy as a career, nevertheless at the age of 21 had intuitive ideas which outlined an original theory of the object relationship.

In his *Defense of Animal Magnetism,* Deleuze was replying to a lengthy article by the physician, Julien Joseph Virey, published in the *Dictionnaire des Sciences Médicales* in 1818 (vol. 24) under the title, "Impartial enquiry into magnetic medicine" (Virey, 1818). Received with but scant regard by the magnetists of the period, this article appears to us to be full of interesting comments.

First and foremost is Virey's definition of magnetic procedures; he immediately recognizes the object relationship as the essential feature in treatment: "The name *animal magnetism* is used to describe a reciprocal influence which sometimes acts between individuals, according to a harmony of rapport, either through the will or the imagination, or else through physical sensibility" (Virey, 1818, p. 1).

The word "reciprocal" should be noted, implying as it does bilateral affective relationships (transference and countertransference) —a remarkable concept for the period, and one which suggests that Virey personally undertook experiments in magnetism.

Virey regarded the object relationship as a factor of such importance that he entitled his first chapter: "History of animal magnetism, or, On the influence exerted upon others in Mesmer's day."

From certain passages in his second chapter, it is apparent that Virey had fairly well observed the mutual exchanges of feelings: "It will be seen therefore that the affections can produce equally marvelous effects on all sentient beings, without its being necessary to postulate an agent, the existence of which is not proved" (1818, p. 23). And further on: "It follows that the latter [the magnetism] is none other than the product of the nervous emotions arising nat-

---

* *Le Magnétiseur amoureux* presents not a few original features. One of these at least deserves to be mentioned here: the author's observations on printing, which in the 18th century (and we are on the brink of the French Revolution) has "increased our needs to infinity"; as a direct consequence the "nervous type," as de Villers notes, has become afflicted with a "continual disquietude which troubles the mind" (and which is subject to the competence, among others, of magnetism).

urally, either from the imagination or [from] the affections between various individuals, and particularly from those which emanate from sexual relationships"* (1818, pp. 23-24). In this connection, Deleuze felt obliged to point out that "All magnetists do not exert the same effect on every subject" (1819b, p. 255).

NOIZET (1792-1885)

Endowed with equal discernment, other magnetists, whose works are of later date than those of Puységur and Deleuze, referred to the action of "the soul," using this term in discussing the feelings—especially those of trust—which may develop between the magnetist and his subject. Among these was General Noizet (*Memoir on Somnambulism and Animal Magnetism,* written in 1820 but not published until 1854) who states: "It is thus that in the normal state, the impressions perceived by the senses are but the germ of the ideas and of the diverse combinations which appear to arise from the soul itself" (1854, p. 244).

Here Noizet goes on to criticize Puységur who attributed to a "magnetized" tree the same properties as a magnetic iron rod, on the grounds that the patients in whom he had once induced sleep beneath such a tree would, several years later, in the same place, fall into a similar sleep. In this connection Noizet writes: "To me it is obvious that the effect of the tree was non-existent, and that the crises which occurred in its shade were entirely the result of the confidence that was placed in its magnetic virtues" (1854, p.245).

It should not be inferred from this passage that Noizet regarded magnetism solely as a manifestation of confidence, for he states: "The effects of animal magnetism result from the action which the magnetist's vital fluid, impelled by his will, exerts on that of the magnetized person" (1854, p. 275).

It is difficult for us, after two centuries of evolution of the terminology, to apprehend all the shades of thought of the magnetists. Should someone like Noizet refer, for example, to the soul, he will see it as simultaneously a psychological and a metaphysical concept,

---

* Needless to say, "sexual relationships" in this context does not have the meaning of coitus, but merely of relationships on the affective level (the level of the libido, in the sense that Freud was to give to this term).

which undoubtedly comprises the totality of our emotions—but one
so far removed from our own modes of thought that it is, all in all,
well nigh impossible for us to profit by the magnetists' intuitions
without misrepresenting, or at the very least grossly distorting, their
ideas. At best we might extract from their writings sufficient material
for a historical outline of the object relationship during the pre-
analytic period.

FARIA (1755-1819), BERTRAND (1795-1831)

From 1813, in Paris, the Portuguese Abbé de Faria had adopted a
revolutionary position in regard to fluidism, asserting that no specific force emanated from the therapist, but that everything takes
place in the subject's mind. Introducing a new technical approach,
in order to induce sleep in his patients he made use of visual fixation
on a given object (a procedure which was to be employed by Braid)
and of verbal suggestion (as did Liébeault at a later date). In im-
perative tones he gave the order "Sleep," and then, "Wake up." His
book, *On the Cause of Lucid Sleep* (1819), appeared in the year of
his death.

A friend of Noizet's, Bertrand, a physician and former student at
the *École polytechnique,* had joined the ranks of the fluidists, before
becoming their determined opponent. He is regarded, together with
Abbé Faria, as one of the initiators of the theory of suggestion later
developed by the Nancy School: the main cause of somnambulistic
phenomena is to be sought in the subject's imagination and not in
that of the magnetist. In his *Treatise on Somnambulism,* published
in 1823, Bertrand writes: "The patient submitted to the magnetic
procedure goes to sleep thinking of his magnetist, and it is because,
while going off to sleep, he thinks of the magnetist alone, that he
hears the latter alone in his somnambulism" (1823, pp. 214-242).
Bertrand compares this selective relationship with that which exists
in normal sleep—a comparison subsequently to be taken up time and
again by the theorists, as to a certain similarity between hypnosis and
sleep: "That which is observed in this respect in somnambulists, is
no different from what occurs every day in normal sleep. A mother
who goes off to sleep beside her son's cradle, even during her sleep
does not cease to watch over him; but she watches over him alone;

and insensible to far louder sounds, she hears the slightest cry which issues from the mouth of her child" (1823, p. 242, note). A century later, the same example will be used by the Pavlovian School to illustrate their theory of hypnosis: a partial cortical inhibition, with continuance of "waking points" which allow "rapport," communication between the subject and his hypnotist (Chertok, 1966b, p. 16).

CHARPIGNON (1815-?)

Louis Joseph Jules Charpignon, a physician and magnetist of fluidist persuasion who was well known around 1840, gives an inkling of the role of the interpersonal (doctor-patient) relationship, and especially of the importance of the therapist's mental state, as also its possible repercussions on the patient: "If it is the magnetist who is ill, the sensation is among the most acute, and often persists on awakening. Should one continue for several days to magnetize while in this sickly indisposition, the somnambulist is inoculated with the same illness. One must therefore exercise very great reserve in this respect and extend prudence to the very affections of the soul, for it cannot be conceived how dreadful is the influence on some somnambulists of a mind that is disturbed" (Charpignon, 1841, p. 62). This is a good illustration of the concept of countertransference. (This concern about the possible repercussions on the patient of the therapist's mental state would lead Freud, some 80 years later, to establish the principle that every prospective psychotherapist is under the obligation of undergoing a personal psychoanalysis.)

The classical works on magnetism, as we have seen, are agreed that the susceptibility to hypnosis ends with the cure, but should the magnetist literally "force" the subject in order to succeed in inducing sleep, such a procedure is not without danger: "It should however be noted," as Charpignon also states, "that the frequency of the magnetizations increases it [magnetic lucidity] but also that excessive use exhausts the subject and clouds his faculties" (1841, p. 59).

Here we touch upon another aspect of the object relationship: the subject may on occasion express his opposition by anger or revolt, but also by self-destruction—a contingency that is well known from the masochistic reactions arising during analytic treatment.

DYNAMICS OF THE MAGNETIC TREATMENT

We have attempted to give a faithful account of the ideas of Puységur and Deleuze on the sole basis of their own works. The latter, however, adumbrate what, from the psychoanalytic viewpoint, actually took place in the course of magnetic treatment (see Saussure, 1968).

Why was it that animal magnetism as practiced by Puységur and Deleuze was therapeutically successful in so many cases—far more frequently than in the practice of their predecessors, or of those who later failed to adhere precisely to their instructions?

Before pursuing our inquiry further, it is relevant to mention here a fact which at first sight appears paradoxical. Freud, as we shall see, made use of free association and rejected acting out. The good magnetists, on the contrary, effected their cures by prohibiting free association, while making use of acting out (somatic discharges, as will later be described). They insisted upon a one-to-one relationship, no other persons being present. In this interpersonal situation, they continued hypnosis until such time as the subject could tolerate neither the presence of a third person nor extraneous odors or sounds, thus compelling the patient to regress to a strictly "preverbal" stage —admittedly a questionable term, inasmuch as a dialogue was maintained between the magnetist and his subject. Herein lay precisely the originality of this form of object relationship.

Deleuze emphasized the need to induce in the patient a state of deep sleep, without, however, understanding the reason, which Freud was later to elucidate—namely, the pathogenic traumata having been deeply repressed in the unconscious, only by reaching the latter was it possible to gain access, even in a symbolic way, to the causes of the illness and so effect a cure.

It may be noted, incidentally, that Freud arrived empirically at a similar procedure, albeit with less extreme inferences. For him, the state of regression is produced and maintained by reason of the analytic situation; the sessions are conducted without witnesses, and the patient is advised not to discuss his analysis with anyone—all conditions that are conducive to the elaboration of phantasies. The interpretation of what was actually taking place during the therapeutic sessions is an aspect that has been all too often neglected by the historians of magnetism in general. They have indeed been content merely to record the accounts given by contemporary authors.

Towards the end of their lives, both Deleuze and Puységur tended to assign a secondary place to the action of the fluid. In their view, kindness and the care extended to the patient played no less important a part in effecting a cure. They nevertheless continued to make use of magnetic passes, principally in response to the patients' demands, and, even when faced with unreasonable patients, held this rule of compliance to be essential.

Around 1850, it was possible to distinguish three categories of magnetist. The first of these attributed to their subjects mediumistic faculties and made use of them for purely experimental purposes; this group included many a charlatan capable of inducing crises, without, however, seeking the slightest therapeutic gain. The second group, comprising such men as Faria, Bertrand, Noizet and Liébeault, relied above all on the suggestibility of those whom they magnetized (suggesting to them that they would get better), but gave no great weight to the patients' own "prescriptions." Here it was indeed the therapist and not the patient who played the major role—and this apparently more rational theory based upon suggestion was to remain predominant until the advent of Freud's contributions. Finally, a third group, under the leadership of Puységur (towards the end of his life), Deleuze, and their pupils, formulated on a purely empirical basis a certain number of principles, which together constituted what they termed the "magnetic treatment" (*"la cure magnétique"*). We may here consider briefly the nature of these principles and the therapeutic procedure which they required:

1) *Isolation*—"The first distinctive characteristic of somnambulism, which I consider to be the best and the most complete, is *isolation*; which is to say that a patient in this state mantains communication and rapport with his magnetist alone, hears none but him, and retains no relationship whatever with external objects" (Puységur, 1811, p. 43).

This principle recurs, in various forms, in many works by Deleuze and his pupils. It may be noted that these practitioners, and in particular Résimont (1843), encountered more than one setback when they failed to observe this rule in the course of magnetic treatment.

2) *Commitment* — The magnetist required of the patient, as also of his relatives and those in his immediate circle, an undertaking that, even were alarming symptoms to arise, the treatment should be continued until a cure was achieved. The commitment had to be for a period of not less than six months; in practice, the treatment was far more protracted (see Deleuze, 1825, p. 213; Puységur, 1811, p. 53).

Magnetism is thus seen to emerge from the empirical stage and the period where it was thought that a few sessions which brought about an improvement and sometimes a cure were all that was required. It is to the credit of Puységur and Deleuze that they realized that a cure could be effected only after a lengthy course of treatment, interspersed with both successes and setbacks—a process in which the physician fulfilled the indispensable role of "catalyst."

"If you are not firmly resolved beforehand to withstand the first pains which you may experience from magnetic treatment, and if your magnetist has not sufficient confidence and strength of character not to be alarmed thereby, it were better that you did not embark upon it. That which was set in motion, were it no longer supported or regulated, would become harmful" (Deleuze, 1825, p. 178).

Deleuze did not explicitly formulate a theory of regression, but a perusal of his work clearly reveals the following conceptual outline. In the presence of the physician's neutrality, a series of symptoms arise; the patient thus purges away his conflicts, experiencing as he does the need for these successive somatic discharges until such time as it eventually disappears—an event which heralds the conclusion of the treatment. The patient no longer feels under the necessity of being magnetized. This he intimates by giving notice, sometimes several weeks in advance, that on a given date he will be subject to an exceptionally violent attack (crisis), after which he will no longer require magnetic treatment. He then makes a complete recovery without convalescence. On the other hand, should the magnetic treatment be prolonged beyond this stage, he enters into a half-somnambulistic, half-normal, confusional state. In such a case, magnetization is reduced to the level of a simple experiment in suggestion resulting in dissolution of the object relationship which had arisen spontaneously from the patient's need for affective discharge.

If we have here reviewed this mode of treatment in some detail, it is because it clearly owes its effectiveness to a congeries of transference reactions; and although no theoretical explanation of the latter was proffered by them, the magnetists already sensed their value and practical usefulness. At all events it will be seen that the magnetists had recourse in their therapeutic practice to procedures far more complex than those employed by the adherents of suggestion.

Puységur in particular, without going so far as to elaborate a theory of the transference, was well aware that animal magnetism found expression in a series of cathartic discharges which made it possible to go back to the prime cause of the illness—but also that these discharges could occur only at the cost of an affective (and prior) cathexis by the subject on to the magnetist. Although he failed to record it, he had therefore perceived the value of the transference, understood that it was not sufficient merely to put the patient to sleep from time to time, as was the custom of so many practitioners, and realized the need to undertake a really adequate treatment which had a beginning and an end.

"Any magnetist," he wrote, "who has neither the possibility nor the will to take sufficient time to bring to a successful conclusion a magnetic treatment, ought never to undertake it. For, once a patient has experienced good and salutary effects from the magnetic action, too sudden a termination of this action will invariably prove detrimental to him" (Puységur, 1811, pp. 375-376).

Yet another indication may be recorded of the importance that was attached to the transference: the magnetists witnessed its disappearance after recovery—a proof that it was necessary during the treatment. In this connection, we may quote Olivier (1849, p. 66) : "The patient's being drawn to his Magnetist ends with the illness from which it has arisen. . . . So long as the patient feels that the Magnetist is necessary to him and is doing him good, an intense feeling impels him towards the latter. As soon as he is cured he leaves him, and *this kind of attraction* ceases, giving way to a feeling of gratitude, or more often one of indifference, and sometimes of ungratefulness" (italics ours) .

"This kind of attraction"—here indeed we apprehend the actual intuition of the concept of transference, identified as a feeling of a very special nature and one that relates to the illness.

It may however be noted, incidentally, that the magnetists hardly ever had an intuition of the concept of the negative transference. To account for this fact, which at first sight may seem surprising, we would proffer the following explanation: the negative transference found expression mainly in acting out, which assumed the form of symptoms. Such manifestations, literally purging the patients of their aggressiveness, were already regarded as salutary crises by Mesmer, who considered it indispensable that the physician be present on each occasion. This procedure was subsequently followed by all responsible magnetists; indeed, one cannot hope to bring to a successful conclusion a treatment which proceeds under the sole influence of the positive transference.

The symptom, invariably of a psychosomatic nature, often obliged the magnetist to call at night in order to carry out on the patient protracted passes. Kindness and the wish to alleviate suffering, so widely advocated by Puységur and Deleuze, then found an application which, on the face of it, appears prosaic—namely, not to become angry with the subject and to show patience when confronted with his symptoms. And, in fact, the magnetists had well understood the need to accept these manifestations with benevolent neutrality, just as the analyst accepts his patient's phantasies. The ability to witness the symptoms as they unfold, with attention, equanimity, and the will to cure, implies in psychoanalytic terms the absence of counter-transference reactions.

In the "magnetic" relationship, the patient regresses to the stage of his conflicts in infancy. The feelings which he experiences (e.g., "You make me sick," "You give me the shits," "I want out," etc.) are expressed not as verbal discharges, but as equivalent symptoms: vomiting, diarrhea, fainting fits, or other psychosomatic manifestations. It should be noted that these symptoms were already present prior to treatment, and could not but grow worse as long as they were not "addressed" to someone who accepted them, and who simply made use of magnetic passes (symbolic of fondling) to cause them to vanish.

The magnetic treatment was, in fact, a catharsis experienced through a sadomasochistic relationship with the magnetist (object of the transference). The deep regression imposed by Puységur and Deleuze simultaneously with a strictly dual relationship (such as the preoedipal relation between mother and child) excluded all acute erotic manifestation (transference-love). This latter risk arose, however, in the event of imperfect isolation. Thus, for example, Résimont (1843), who was satisfied with the induction of a light sleep, allowed amorous outbursts or fits of anger to break through, while being incapable of controlling them.

In sum, it is apparent that the magnetic treatment constituted a far more complex and varied method than that provided by mesmeric magnetism, which acted mainly through suggestion. Unfortunately, the treatment did not get beyond the empirical stage and, having failed to produce a theorist of its own, fell into disuse. It is only in the light of Freud's discoveries that we are today able to demonstrate its mechanisms—the essential factor being that acting out, like phantasies, can have a cathartic value capable of "discharging" an emotion which lies at the root of a symptom.

It is relevant to ask ourselves whether certain principles of the magnetic treatment might not, in our own time, still prove of some worth in the treatment of psychosomatic disorders.*

---

* Is it not possible to rediscover one of the principles of the magnetic treatment, namely, deep regression, in "anaclitic" treatment where the therapist assumes the role of a mother in relation to her infant? As we know, this approach has been advocated in the treatment of patients suffering from ulcerative colitis (Margolin, 1954).

II

The Object Relationship in the Era of Hypnotism

AN IMPORTANT TURNING POINT in the history of psychotherapy in the mid-19th century was marked by both a change in technique and the emergence of a new theoretical concept. The term "animal magnetism" was abandoned in favor of "hypnotism" (from the Greek *hypnos,* meaning sleep), introduced by the Scotsman James Braid.

This new term may perhaps at first have had a reassuring effect. Ernest Jones (1923, p. 363) has drawn attention to the latent sexual connotation of the word "magnetism." According to him, the Greek term for magnet, *magnés,* is in fact derived from two Phoenician words, *mag* (a big powerful man) and *naz* (that which flows out and influences something else); the sexual symbolism is clear. Jones further observes that "the word 'coition' was formerly used in English to denote the coming together of magnetized substances," e.g., by Sir Thomas Browne (1646) in his famous treatise on "Vulgar Errors" (Book II, chap. 2). "Magnetism" was thus first applied to human attitudes, then to inanimate substances, and finally was used to designate, as "animal magnetism," the hypnotic process.

We have seen how widespread among the general public was the belief—and among some magnetists, the conviction—that the curative action of animal magnetism was attributable to the transmission of a vital fluid, a nervous fluid of a special kind, a "concrete force" emanating from an omnipotent operator. In this connection, Jones quotes the following passage from Du Prel (1899): "In every magnetic cure the magnetist transfers his vital force, that is, his very essence, on to the magnetized subject." Jones (1923, p. 363) refers moreover to the special significance attached by popular belief, from time immemorial, to the power of the human eye. In his opinion, "this takes its origin in the eye and its glance being symbolically regarded as the expression of the male organ and its function."* Some magnetists believed that the magnetic fluid emanated from their eyes; we know what importance in the hypnotic process was soon to be assumed by the fixation ("fascination") of the subject by a steady gaze.

Notwithstanding the change in name, the general public came to regard the hypnotist as invested with the same powers as the magnetist. It was above all to doctors that the reassuring effect already mentioned would prove beneficial.**

Several decades were yet to elapse before the general adoption of the term "hypnotism," and, later, "hypnosis." Although it was published as late as 1887, the classical work by Binet and Féré on the history of hypnosis still bore the title "Animal Magnetism." As we shall see later, hypnotism was to arouse resistances similar to those which had been encountered by animal magnetism. The term "imagination" would be replaced by the concept of suggestion, whose sexual connotation would be sensed—with consequent antagonistic reactions.

With the adoption of the new terminology and the theoretical revival to which we shall presently refer, hypnotism was to become more closely related to the sphere of medicine, and the majority of investigators would be medical men. This was, of course, not the case of the magnetists, Puységur, Deleuze, and others, who were succeeded

---

* This would explain why Deleuze (1825, p. 32) advised his pupils to seat themselves beside a female patient, rather than facing her. On the symbolism of the eye, and its "sexual significance" which can be traced even in popular sayings, see Held's (1952) colorful and brilliant exposition.

** In a comparable way, some medical men have in recent years proposed that the term "hypnosis" be replaced by "sophrosis," hoping thereby to eliminate all possibility of a "magical connotation." (See the criticism of this proposal by Chertok, 1966b, p. 12).

by the physicians, Braid, Liébeault, Bernheim and Charcot. Already in Mesmer's day, medical and non-medical men fought over the exclusive right to practice the "psychological" treatment. The same rivalry subsequently characterized the era of hypnotism and, even more so, that of psychoanalysis. It will be recalled that the conflict between Mesmer and the proponents of somnambulism (disciples of Puységur) came near to dividing the ranks of the magnetists. The advocates of somnambulism were prepared to establish a school of their own. Mesmer regarded somnambulism as dangerous and feared that its propagation would so attenuate animal magnetism as to encourage quackery. The proponents of somnambulism then put forward the proposal that they should practice under medical supervision, but this was opposed by Mesmer. The dispute was brought to an end by the outbreak of the French Revolution (Chertok, 1966a).

In the era of hypnotism (late 19th century), a heated controversy brought the medical profession into conflict with Delboeuf (1890), who upheld the cause of the non-medical magnetists. Freud, it is true, called upon laymen to train as analysts. The debate still continues to this day in the psychoanalytic world. The American Psychoanalytic Association, for example, admits only physicians to its membership. In Great Britain, on the other hand, one out of three analysts is not medically trained. Jones (1957, pp. 309-323) devotes an entire chapter of his biography of Freud to the question of lay analysis.

BRAID (1795-1860)

In France, by 1840, the major scientific bodies had discouraged the pursuit of studies on animal magnetism. It was in Great Britain, with James Braid, that investigations in this field reached a new turning point. Braid, then a general practitioner and surgeon in Manchester—who had hitherto considered magnetism to be nothing but "a system of collusion or delusion"—in 1841 became convinced of the reality of the phenomena which he witnessed when attending several public demonstrations by the celebrated Genevan magnetist, Lafontaine. (Charcot and Freud were both to obtain similar confirmation of the reality of hypnotic phenomena while attending public performances of this kind.)

Thereupon, Braid undertook a series of experiments which led him to conclude that magnetic passes were useless. These he replaced by a technique consisting in fixing the subject's gaze on a bright object. The essential process (as Faria and Bertrand had already suspected) took place "within the subject himself," independently of any external force. Thus, in his *Neurypnology*, Braid (1843) rejected the fluidist theory, and in its place advanced a "psycho-neuro-physiological" theory pertaining to the "brain mythology" then in fashion:* a "physico-psychical" stimulation of the retina acted on the subject's nervous system and induced a "nervous sleep," which Braid called "hypnotism."

Braid at first believed that this state differed from those induced by Faria and Bertrand; the latter were, in his opinion, attributable to imagination, while he regarded the state he described as the result of physical stimuli. He opposed his "subjective" theory to the "objective" theory of the fluidists, and considered his own procedure more effective than those of the magnetists. Stating that "great prejudice has been raised against mesmerism, from the idea that it might be turned to immoral purposes," he felt quite certain that hypnotism deserved "no such censure" (1843, p. 10). It was not until some years later that he came to recognize that the two states were identical and that it was possible to elicit various hypnotic phenomena through verbal suggestion: "The phenomena in question are as much psychological as physiological in their nature" (1860, p. 231).**

---

* The term "brain mythology" (*Hirnmythologie*) was introduced by H. W. Gruhle (1932), Professor of Psychiatry at the University of Heidelberg, to designate the more extreme "organic" trends in 19th century psychiatry, as typified by Griesinger, Meynert, etc.

** The reference "Braid, 1860" relates to Braid's last paper, a manuscript on hypnotism written in January, 1860, shortly before his death, in which he summarized the development of his work and researches since 1843. He sent a copy to Dr. E. E. Azam (1822-1899) of Bordeaux, a dedicated and eminent follower, with a view to a report to the Académie des Sciences in Paris. The manuscript was passed to Dr. G. M. Beard of New York who, in turn, lent it to W. Preyer, Professor of Physiology at the University of Jena. It was first published (in German translation) in 1881 in Preyer's book on hypnosis and later (1883) translated from German into French as an appendix to Dr. Jules Simon's translation of the *Neurypnology*. (The page references in the text are to the French version from which quotations are retranslated into English.) The original English manuscript appears subsequently to have been lost; at all events, it was never published.

"Subjective," in Braid's sense, meant that everything occurs in the subject's brain, without the involvement of an external force such as was conceived by the magnetists. For him there was no question either of object relation or of feeling, although he did refer to confidence in the operator. He stated: "The remarkable tendency of these patients to sympathy and imitation, leads them to observe and copy the operator's every gesture" (1860, p. 255). The patients "are subject to an extraneous will" (1860, p. 250). They "are convinced that this other person [the hypnotist] possesses some mysterious and omnipotent power" (1860, pp. 243-244). "In this state, [the patient's] imagination becomes so alive that every pleasing idea, whether spontaneously acquired or suggested by someone to whom he gives very special attention and confidence, assumes for him the full force of actuality and reality" (1860, p. 235).

In Braid's opinion, "the operator acts like a *mechanic* who would set in motion the forces in the patient's own organism" (1860, p. 236). But in the absence of a fluid between doctor and patient, there is nothing to link them together. The subject is isolated and the operator is himself surrounded, as it were, by a sanitary cordon. This manner of studying patients was, in fact, prevalent among the physicians of the time—in the same way as a naturalist might examine an insect.

Braid carried his theories, strictly confined as they were to the physical plane, to such limits as to incur the criticism of Binet and Féré (1887). These authors, while asserting that it was thanks to Braid that "hypnotism emerged from animal magnetism, just as the physicochemical sciences emerged from the occult sciences of the Middle Ages" (p. 46), considered that "Braid's conclusion was too absolute. . . . It would be a mistake to believe that the operator's personality never plays any part in the phenomena which unfold before him. . . . The patient shows a kind of affinity to the person who put him to sleep and who touched his bare hands" (p. 49). We shall see later how these same authors, who belonged to the Salpêtrière School, would in their own way depersonalize this "affinity."

So great was the importance which Braid systematically ascribed in psychology to purely mechanical factors that he came to accept the views of the phrenologist Gall* who visualized the brain as an assemblage of numerous distinct areas, each of which corresponded to a specific emotion, instinct or function. Braid experimented with "phreno-hypnotism," pressing on a given area of the subject's skull, which area he held to be the "seat" of a given feeling. If, for example, he pressed on the "seat of veneration," he induced in the subject an attitude of prayer.

For Braid, on the whole, everything comes down to cerebral mechanisms, whence his complete failure to recognize the affective factors which might exist between the two persons who come into contact. However, the introduction of the concept of suggestion—although conceived in physiological terms—constitutes a definite advance; it definitively rejects fluidism and prepares the way for the study of the psychological action in the hypnotic relationship.

As so often happens, Braid's work met with but little response in his own country. Although presented in scientific terms, it nevertheless aroused some degree of antagonism, albeit less pronounced and less impassioned than that encountered by the magnetists in France. It was French physicians such as Etienne Eugène Azam, Paul Broca, and A. A. Velpeau who gave it the closest attention.

Azam, a surgeon of Bordeaux, as soon as he became acquainted with Braid's work, started to employ hypnotism as a method of anesthesia. He mentioned it to Broca, who then performed an operation at the Hôpital Necker in Paris under hypnotic anesthesia, of which he gave an account to the Académie des Sciences on December 5, 1859. On February 27, 1860, Velpeau presented to the Academy an account of Braid's work, as a new discovery; no one suspected that animal magnetism was thus making its reappearance before the same learned body that had condemned it 80 years earlier. At all events, the increasing use of chloroform (introduced by Simpson in 1847),

---

* Franz Joseph Gall (1758-1828), the founder of phrenology, like Mesmer studied medicine in Vienna before coming to Paris. A distinguished anatomist and pathologist, he elaborated a theory of the relationship between cerebral and cranial topography and intellectual and emotional functions. This theory proved as controversial as it was sensational (it was highly esteemed by the physiognomist Lavater—as also by Balzac), but very soon collapsed. Nonetheless, just as Mesmer has been considered the father of hypnosis and thus the precursor of psychoanalysis, there are those who regard Gall as a forerunner of the theory of cerebral localization, if not indeed of modern neurology. A book has been devoted to him (Lanteri-Laura, 1970).

which was regarded as a more reliable anesthetic, put an end to the vogue of hypnotic anesthesia and the Academy did not pursue further the investigation of Braid's methods.

THE NANCY SCHOOL—LIÉBEAULT AND BERNHEIM

Velpeau's paper had, however, aroused the interest of Ambroise Liébeault (1823-1905), whose studies in hypnotism began in 1860 (Chertok, 1968a). Already as a student, Liébeault had shown an interest in animal magnetism, but his teachers had dissuaded him from engaging upon this course which they considered harmful to his career. In 1850 he had established himself as a country doctor, practicing conventional medicine, at Pont-Saint-Vincent near Nancy, where his patients thought very highly of him. Ten years later, when he began to practice hypnosis, he incurred the ridicule of his colleagues. It was then that he abandoned classical medicine. Living simply on his modest savings, he started to provide his patients (for the most part poor) with free treatment by hypnotic procedures. And the better to propagate his method, he set up his practice in Nancy in a house with a plate bearing simply the name "A. Liébeault," and no longer "Dr. Liébeault." He wished to be a healer.

He first employed Braid's hypnotizing technique; however, he did not find it entirely satisfactory. He therefore added some of Faria's procedures and thus arrived at a composite method. While asking the subject to fix his own gaze, as the Portuguese abbé had done, he gave him the order to sleep. But, as he was later to record, "in addition to Faria, I went on to state the principal symptoms of the induction of sleep: the need to sleep, the heaviness of the eyelids, the feeling of sleepiness, a decreased sensory acuity, etc. And these symptoms I repeated to them several times in a soft voice. Thus, through multiple suggestions, but all directed to the same end, the idea of sleep gradually infiltrated their mind, and there it eventually became fixed" (Liébeault, 1886, p. 107).

Liébeault came to the conclusion that it was not the physical action which constituted the hypnotizing factor, but instead a psychological process, an idea, verbal suggestion. Hence his conclusion that suggestion was "the key to Braidism," and thus it became the primary object of his investigations. In his view, hypnotic sleep is related to normal sleep: it is a partial sleep which has been introduced into his brain (a concept subsequently adopted by the Pavlovian School). During this "sleep," the subject remains in contact with the operator.

The published account of his work, entitled *On Sleep and Related States, with special consideration of the action of the mental on the physical* (Liébeault, 1866), not only failed to arouse the slightest interest on the part of medical men, but indeed incurred the contempt of orthodox medical circles. Foville, reviewing this work in the *Annales médico-psychologiques* for March, 1867 (pp. 340-342), described it quite plainly as a retrograde step: "The kind of physiology expounded by M. Liébeault diverges in every respect from that which today guides medical practice along the road to progress. . . . We could not possibly place our confidence in the method of treatment which he advocates."

Liébeault did not, however, lose courage, despite the contempt of his colleagues. In 1882, Bernheim, who had for ten years been a professor in the Faculty of Medicine at Nancy (where the University of Strasbourg had reestablished itself after the war of 1870), went to see his experiments. Convinced of the value of Liébeault's work, he himself started to practice hypnosis, and his first book, published in 1884, was entitled *On Suggestion in the Hypnotic State and in the Waking State* (Bernheim, 1884). From this point on, Liébeault's ideas began to spread more widely and the number of his followers increased. Among these were Beaunis (1886), professor of physiology at Nancy, who wrote a book on *Induced Sleep: Physiological and Psychological Studies*; and Liégeois (1889), professor of law at the same university, whose first published work was *On Suggestion and Somnambulism in Relation to Jurisprudence and Forensic Medicine*. Thus was born the Nancy School, whose research work was to have a worldwide impact.

The adherents of this School undoubtedly regarded verbal suggestion as a psychological concept, although they described it— purely metaphorically, of course—in terms of cerebral physiology. Practicing suggestion, they were not yet aware of the importance of the latent interpersonal factor involved. Liébeault (1866, p. 7) refers to "attention, impressions, perceptions, memory, imaginary ideas, pure ideas, recall, sensations, thoughts, organism, free attention, accumulated attention," but there is no mention of the word "feeling." Unaware of the role of the interpersonal relationship in the mechanism of his cures, he even believed for a while in a possible coexistence, in hypnotism, of a psychological factor and a fluid. This followed cures which he effected in young children, not as yet susceptible to verbal suggestion, who were suffering from symptoms such as anorexia, diarrhea, and vomiting. He even went so far as to employ for therapeutic purposes "magnetized water" and the laying on of hands. However, an experiment carried out at Bernheim's instigation, using the "placebo effect" (administration of pseudo-magnetized water) with equal success, caused him to abandon the fluidist hypothesis.

He then attributed the success of the treatment to the indirect suggestion induced by the magnetized water and the laying on of hands—and to the fact that the child himself, as well as those close to him, felt that the practitioner's aim was to help him get well.

In an article referring to this period of Liébeault's life, one of the authors (Chertok, 1968a) showed how a psychoanalytical approach enables us to understand the mode of action of these cures. It was through his kindness and his prestige that the doctor allayed the mother's anxiety, thereby curing the child's psychosomatic disorders. Liébeault sensed the curative value of psychological means, and even of the mother's role; but he failed to grasp the fact that everything took place within the framework of the emotional relationships established between the therapist and the mother on one hand, and the mother and her child on the other.

Liébeault belongs to the tradition of the reputable magnetists whose conscious motivation was one of charity and a genuine wish to help their patients; we have seen how he treated his patients without charge.* As Freud (1925a, p. 17) was later to record: "I

---

* Did Liébeault's philanthropic vocation conceal an unconscious sense of guilt? Did he seek to "clear" himself of an activity which he suspected was charged with "erotic hazards"? Whatever the answer, Freud for his part showed less detachment. It is true that, before engaging in psychotherapy, Liébeault, in ten years of general practice, had put aside a sufficient sum to provide him with a modest living. For the most part, with the exception of Mesmer, the magnetists who preceded him were not medical men; their psychotherapeutic activities were to them of secondary importance and they did not expect to derive therefrom any material gain. Freud, on the other hand, needed his patients' fees to insure his own livelihood. Convinced, moreover, of the

witnessed the moving spectacle of old Liébeault working among the poor women and children of the labouring classes."

Beside Liébeault, a simple country practitioner, philosopher by inclination and philanthropist by vocation, Bernheim the university professor appears as a clinician endowed with a strict scientific mind. His line of thought, starting from Liébeault's ideas on suggestion and hypnosis, was to evolve to the point where the two concepts became confused, to the advantage of suggestion.

This inclination was already reflected in the title of the second edition of Bernheim's first book. The first edition (Bernheim, 1884) was entitled *De la Suggestion dans l'État Hypnotique et dans l'État de Veille* ("On Suggestion in the Hypnotic State and in the Waking State"), whereas the subsequent edition, revised and enlarged (Bernheim, 1886), bore the title *De la Suggestion et de ses Applications à la Thérapeutique* ("On Suggestion and its Therapeutic Indications").* In the foreword to this second edition, he clearly stated: "It is *suggestion* which dominates most of the manifestations of hypnosis; the allegedly physical phenomena are, in my opinion, none other than psychical phenomena. It is the idea conceived by the operator which, grasped by the hypnotized subject and accepted by his brain, gives rise to the symptom, by means of a heightened sugges-

---

symbolic sexual significance of money, he expressed the view that money matters be discussed with the patient as frankly as sexual problems (Freud, 1913, p. 131). He also considered the financial sacrifice accepted by the patient to be an important factor in the successful outcome of treatment. Nevertheless, Freud sometimes provided needy patients with free treatment.

In 1897, he wrote to Fliess: "I have decided to take on two cases without fee. That, including my own, makes three analyses which bring in nothing" (Freud, 1954, p. 227). Such generosity, as Eissler (1971, p. 95) remarks, is almost unknown among analysts in our day. On occasion, Freud even gave money to one or another of his patients (Eissler, 1971, p. 10). He had a phantasy, to which we shall return, which he in fact described in a humorous way: detecting, at a distance, a neurosis in the Czar Nicholas II, he set out to treat him, to cure him, and thus to make his fortune—which subsequently enabled him to treat his own patients without charge (Freud, 1954, p. 263).

This question of fees has been widely discussed in the psychoanalytic literature. Indeed, the psychological role of money concerns doctors in all branches of the profession; socialized medicine gives rise to new problems in this same area. At the Symposium of the Société de Psychologie Médicale in 1970, there was a discussion on the subject of "The Physician and Money" (Colloque Psychologie Médicale, 1971).

* It was this edition that Freud translated into German and to which he contributed a preface (Bernheim, 1888b).

tibility resulting from the special concentration of mind in the hypnotic state" (Bernheim, 1886, p. i).

Thus he still referred here both to suggestibility and to the hypnotic state. But within a very few years, contrary to the views of his teacher Liébeault, he would assert that there is no such thing as hypnotism; there is only suggestion. It should be recalled that this was to lead to the complete "dilution" of the concept of hypnosis and its replacement by that of suggestion in the waking state, and then by autosuggestion (the method of Coué, 1913). For Bernheim as for Liébeault, suggestion always remains a nervous mechanism: "Every brain cell, activated by an idea, activates the nerve fibres which arise from it and transmit the impression to the effector organs. This is what I call the law of ideodynamism" (Bernheim, 1907, p. 47).

The precedence given to suggestion, its "dominance" in hypnotic phenomena, was to lead Bernheim into ambiguity, to a theoretical impasse, and even to the near negation of hypnosis which was destined, as it were, to lose its specificity; it would become nothing more than suggestibility (see Chertok, 1966b, pp. 26-28).

The fact must be clearly recognized that we are today still faced with the problem of hypnosis as a specific state, in the absence of reliable physical and psychological criteria which would enable us to define its precise nature.* It would, however, seem to be widely accepted that suggestibility is a consequence, an epiphenomenon, and not the cause, of the hypnotic state. Some researchers maintain that the specificity of hypnosis depends upon factors which are neither purely physical, nor purely psychological; rather it is situated in a psychophysiological setting which has yet to be defined (Kubie, 1961). At all events, hypnosis has not as yet been "deciphered," and considerable methodological difficulties are encountered as soon as it is attempted to evaluate the part played by the several factors involved. It is a complex in which nature and nurture, the inborn and the acquired, psychology and physiology, are intricately combined.

However vague his theories, Bernheim's great merit is that, to-

---

* Barber (1969) denies the existence of hypnosis as a specific state. His numerous opponents include Ernest R. Hilgard (1970) and Orne (Orne *et al.*, 1968).

gether with Liébeault and the entire Nancy School, he gave a predominant place to psychology, thus clearing the way for the advent of affective psychology. The latter was to demonstrate the purely interpersonal relationships that lay concealed in the process of suggestion. We shall see later how much Freud's discovery of the unconscious owes to the work of the Nancy School.

It is, however, relevant here to put forward a few hypotheses in explanation of the evolution of Bernheim's ideas, taking into consideration both rational and irrational factors—the latter indicating a resistance to the therapist's involvement in interpersonal relations.

Bernheim, who must quite soon have become aware of the limited number of deep hypnoses obtainable, did not wish his psychotherapeutic activities to be restricted in this way.* In his report to the Congress of Hypnotism in 1889, he estimated the proportion of cases in which deep hypnosis could be induced as one-fifth, or even one-sixth, of his private patients, as compared with four-fifths of his hospital patients (Bernheim, 1889, p. 79). The differences then noted between the two socioeconomic groups have not been observed in recent research, whether clinical (Gill and Brenman, 1959) or experimental (Hilgard, 1965). These investigators consider the degree of hypnotizability to be a constant, affected neither by the subject's social situation nor by the technique employed, nor indeed by the hypnotist's personality.

Researchers in experimental psychology—who nowadays "quantify" (so far as it is possible in this field) the degree of hypnotizability by means of "hypnotic susceptibility scales" (Weitzenhoffer and Hilgard, 1959, 1962; Shor and Orne, 1962) —have adduced further evidence in support of this view. Replacing the hypnotist by a tape recorder, which can hardly be suspected of "personalized action," they obtained similar results. Their statistics on deep trances vary, but on the whole the figures are lower than those relating to Bernheim's private patients.**

---

* As we shall see, the limited number of subjects capable of entering into a deep trance was also one of the reasons which led Freud to abandon hypnosis.

** These data would thus appear to be clearly contradictory to the views expressed by Ferenczi (1909), who considers that the "percentage for successful hypnosis" may vary from 10 to 96 percent according to the hypnotist. In actual fact, even if the "absolute degree" of hypnotizability seems fixed for a given "normal" individual,

The majority of researchers are agreed that at the present time it is possible to induce a deep hypnotic state in at most some 3 to 5 percent of those subject to experimentation, whose hypnotization is the result of a "prepared" induction (probably a still lower percentage, if we consider only the "man in the street," susceptible to being "put to sleep" in a matter of seconds by the simplest form of induction and who, on awakening, shows complete amnesia). And even in this 3 to 5 percent, it is difficult to distinguish what, in their somnambulism, is the "essential nucleus" and what has been "learned." It may be surmised that in a large number of patients in Bernheim's hospital practice the "learned" element predominated. He, too, would thus seem to have been dealing, as it were, with "trained" subjects, acting by imitation, in the same way—as we shall see—as those to whom the doctors of the Salpêtrière were accused of applying "training" methods.

But apart from the practical consideration of the restricted number of deep hypnoses, Bernheim's attitude may have been otherwise motivated. Unlike his teacher Liébeault, he had no system of defense available against the dangers of personal involvement—the magnetists' tradition of charitable idealism. However unconsciously, he preferred to avoid the hypnotic relationship and to act upon the patient by suggestion in the waking state.

Another possible reason might explain the evolution of Bernheim's theories. Basing everything on suggestion, denying in practice the possibility of the existence, or of a strict definition, of the hypnotic state, he may have wished to demystify hypnosis, and at the same time demonstrate his independence of his teacher's views. At all events, he was to state: "I tried to complete M. Liébeault's work, and

---

hypnotized by a practitioner of "standard" ability, in practice the results obtained in that individual may be subject to modification by the most diverse factors: atmosphere, practitioner's attitude, etc. In a patient, however, in the course of a therapeutic dialogue under hypnosis, these modifications of the "level" of the trance may vary for motives which, in the framework of the relationship, clearly pertain to the "affective-circumstantial" sphere: e.g., a special situation arising from the recall of an anxiety-inducing theme (Brenman *et al.*, 1952). In this connection, it is interesting to recall here the thesis propounded by the magnetists concerning the "end of treatment"; this was indicated by the disappearance of hypnotizability. We may also mention the case of soldiers who were easily hypnotizable during the period of their involvement in combat—but who were no longer necessarily so subsequently.

following him to free the doctrine of hypnotism and suggestion of all the errors and all the aura of mystery by which it is obscured, in order to bring it back to the laws of biology and psychology" (Bernheim, 1907, p. 40).

The Nancy School, while ignorant of the true nature of the object relationship, did in fact admit the existence of certain psychological factors and replaced the earlier term "imagination" by that of "suggestion." But in defining the latter in psycho-neuro-physiological terms, it failed to recognize the affective elements concealed behind suggestion. In this way the Nancy School depersonalized the relationship.

THE SALPÊTRIÈRE SCHOOL—CHARCOT

The Salpêtrière School, for its part, carried even further this depersonalization in ascribing prime importance, in hypnosis, to physical factors. Indeed, this preeminence of the physical aspect was to assume caricatural proportions when Charcot's pupils sought to explain by the action at a distance of metals, magnets or medicines, those phenomena which Bernheim attributed to suggestion. To eliminate in this way the personal factor was a regression to concepts not far removed from the first period of "mineral magnetism." (Before elaborating the fluidist theory, Mesmer believed in the curative virtues of the application of metals.)

It is relevant here to recall the Salpêtrière theory as it was clearly expounded in four propositions by Babinski (1889, pp. 131-132) at the First International Congress of Physiological Psychology, held in Paris, August 6-10, 1889:

1. "The somatic characteristics which are encountered in some subjects under hypnosis are of fundamental importance, since they alone provide a legitimate basis for asserting the absence of simulation."

2. "Hypnotic phenomena may assume a special grouping, in three distinct stages. This constitutes the purest form of hypnotism, which should be regarded as the type, and which it is proposed to call '*grand hypnotisme.*' "

3. "Associated with the two foregoing propositions is a third one,

namely, that the somatic characters of hypnotism, and *'grand hypno-tisme,'* can develop independently of any suggestion whatsoever."

4. "Hypnotism in its purest forms must be regarded as a pathological state."

For the present, let us bear in mind that, according to the Salpêtrière School, hypnosis is a somatic state induced by "physical excitation without the intervention of suggestion" (Babinski, 1889, p. 133). Thus is it defined by Babinski, whose attitude towards suggestion is, however, somewhat ambiguous, for he later states that "the Paris School, which itself emphasizes the importance of suggestion, does not question its reality, but takes the view that suggestion is not the only source of the phenomena observed in hypnotism" (1889, p. 136). To Babinski, suggestion remains a phenomenon which is not only suspect, but opens the way to simulation* as also to imagination—to which, of course, he concedes no scientific value.

It was by presenting hypnosis as a somatic manifestation that it was possible for Charcot, in 1882, to overcome the opposition of the academic authorities who, for almost a century, had rejected something they regarded as no more than a result of imagination. In this way he reinstated hypnosis, which then became an acceptable subject for scientific investigation.

Charcot's School sought to apply to the study of hypnosis the anatomo-clinical approach which prevailed at the time, and was indeed productive in many areas. The actual existence of the hypnotic state was objectively established by physical signs—and factors of an equally physical nature were instrumental in the induction. Dumontpallier maintained that, in hypnosis, light, temperature, atmospheric vibrations, electricity, and magnets brought about "modifications in the nervous system." In his view, "Expectant attention and suggestion play no part in certain determining conditions of hypnotism" (Dumontpallier, 1889, p. 23).

The alleged presence of physical "signs" of hypnosis led henceforth

---

* Simulation is today, albeit on a very different plane, at the center of studies on experimental psychology applied to hypnosis. The training of subjects to simulate hypnosis does, of course, provide suitable "material" for experiments on comparative behavior, one of the present lines of research attempting to define the specific nature of hypnosis (Orne, 1971).

to the acceptance of metallotherapy, the transfer of symptoms by magnets, etc. It is surprising that such famous scientists as Babinski and Luys could have believed in such unscientific ideas. It would seem that an affective factor can alone explain their hostile attitude to suggestion and to all personal involvement entailing a risk of eroticization, a danger which Bailly had denounced a century earlier. Their teacher Charcot had sensed—and, as we shall see, would appear to have told Freud—that *"la chose génitale"* played a part in the etiology of hysteria. Hypnosis, which he regarded as artificial hysteria, should logically have comprised, in his view, elements of the same order. It is, however, a question which he never attempted to investigate more deeply, consolidating his position on the "physical" ground.*

It is noteworthy that Charcot came to know hypnosis through metallotherapy (based on a physical theory), and starting from the experiments carried out by Burq. The latter had observed, in 1850, the case of a female somnambulist who, if she touched a brass doorknob, would fall into a cataleptic state; however, if the doorknob were covered by a glove or other piece of leather, there was no such effect. This, according to Burq, was proof of the direct action of a metal on the hypnotic state. After 25 years of experimentation, Burq succeeded, in 1876, in obtaining a commission of inquiry—appointed by Claude Bernard, then president of the Société de Biologie—to verify his statements. Charcot, Luys and Dumontpallier, members of this commission, confirmed the discovery announced by Burq. After a year of experiments at the Salpêtrière, they claimed to have observed the action of metals on pathological symptoms, which varied according to the particular metal, as well as the possibility of transferring symptoms from one subject to another by means of magnets. These experiments led Charcot to study hypnosis from 1878 on-

---

* A certain "nostalgia for the physical aspect" has never disappeared. It persists today amongst experimental psychologists investigating hypnosis. Thus O'Connell and Orne (1968) have studied certain correlations between the psychogalvanic reflex and the depth of the trance. Other researchers, employing the electronic analysis of EEG records, purport to have detected differences in electrical activity corresponding to the hypnotic state. They also believe that they can modify hypnotizability with psychotropic drugs and reach the conclusion that a "neurophysiological" basis underlies the hypnotic state (Ulett *et al.*, 1972). It would seem that the Charcot-Bernheim controversy is still far from settled.

wards and marked the beginning of the craze in Paris hospitals for metallotherapy, henceforth the subject of a vast number of publications. We may mention here the evocative title of a communication by Luys and Encausse to the Société de Biologie, in 1890: "On the transference at a distance, by means of a crown of magnetic iron, of various neuropathic states from a subject in the waking state on to a subject in the hypnotic state." Burq published a work on metallotherapy in 1882. Bourru and Burot (1887) devoted a whole book to the "action at a distance" of medicines. These same authors are, however, best known for their work on "The Variations of Personality," which is still of undoubted interest (Bourru and Burot, 1888). We shall have occasion to refer again to this work in Chapter IV of this book. They here described their investigations on the hallucinatory reliving of past experiences, which were carried further by Janet, leading him to his discovery of the disappearance of symptoms through the reliving under hypnosis of a past traumatic situation.

Some of the pupils of the Salpêtrière became aware of the reality, in the hypnotic relationship, of personal interaction and "affinities" between hypnotist and hypnotized, such as those, already cited, which were noted by Binet and Féré. And it is indeed, once again, remarkable to see how, at the Salpêtrière, these relations were depersonalized by describing the patients' reactions as purely bodily, mechanical, and independent of all emotion or passion. Referring to hypnosis, Binet and Féré mention subjective symptoms, among which they describe the phenomenon of selective sensibility. In consequence of this sensibility, "patients in a state of somnambulism often show a kind of attraction to the operator who put them to sleep." They go on to say that a person has only to touch a part of the somnambulist's body, to induce in him these selective manifestations: "All these operative procedures have in common the characteristic of bringing into play the operator's personality, a role which was perhaps exaggerated in the past, but which, since Braid, has been far too greatly undervalued" (Binet and Féré, 1887, p. 109).

One could hardly acknowledge more clearly the role of the personality. Yet Binet and Féré did, in fact, consistently disregard it. Even obvious erotic manifestations, to the point of orgasm, were according to them induced, so to speak, mechanically and independently of the personal involvement of the operator. The female somnambulist thus reaches this state through manual stimulation of an erogenous zone (transferable, moreover, by the magnet) which is not necessarily an area that is commonly regarded as such. One of their female patients "presented at the level of the upper end of the sternum a zone of this kind, upon which mere pressure induced all the signs of the paraxysm of genital excitation. These manifestations were induced on several occasions, unrecognized by the *observer*,* who might have found himself charged with a most serious offense, had he not taken the essential precaution in such circumstances of never being alone with the subject" (Binet and Féré, 1887, p. 112). In representing himself as "observer" rather than actor, the hypnotist clearly intends to contract out of the relationship. Speaking of female patients, Binet and Féré went so far as to note personally, without its arousing in their mind the slightest question, that "the excitation of the erogenous plaque is effective only if it is produced by pressure exerted by a person of the opposite sex; if the pressure is exerted by another woman, or by an inert object, it merely gives rise to an unpleasant sensation" (1887, p. 112).

Assuredly, Binet and Féré were not unaware of the importance of suggestion; on examination, their views are seen to be closer than might at first appear to those of Bernheim: "The realm of suggestion is immense. There is not a single aspect of our mental life that cannot be artificially reproduced and exaggerated by this means. One can understand the wonderful advantage that the psychologist can derive from this method, which introduces experimentation into psychology" (1887, p. 127). In fact, Binet was to become a pioneer of experimental psychology.

To Binet and Féré, suggestion was "an operation which exerts on a subject a certain effect by passing through his intellect" (1887, p. 128). All in all, in exactly the same way as Bernheim, they concluded that suggestion is based on a psychological process, which in turn produces a physical effect. According to them, when one tells the patient, with a view to inducing a contracture without touching him, that his arm is becoming bent and stiff and that he is now unable

* Italics added.

to straighten it, the idea of contracture has been instilled in his mind. They do not, however, follow Bernheim when they assert that the contracture of the arm of a female hysteric may be induced by a physical excitation—the percussion of tendons or the massage of a group of muscles. This process, which in no way involves the subject's "intellect," was called by Bernheim "indirect suggestion." Be that as it may, all three authors were unaware of the underlying affective or relational factors.

To Binet and Féré, hypnotic phenomena were of two orders, those giving rise, respectively, to physical excitation and to ideas. "These represent two parallel modes of experimentation. It would be difficult to say which of the two has the widest scope" (1887, p. 129). We shall see later that the modern theories—of psychoanalytic inspiration—of hypnosis (and in particular that of ego psychology) in some degree tie up with the concept that it is possible to induce the hypnotic state by external physical stimuli through a "reduction of sensorimotor activity" (Gill and Brenman, 1959).

The inability to recognize the personal factor is very evident in Paul Richer, a pupil of Charcot, whose book on major hysteria ("*la grande hystérie*") comprises no less than 975 pages in its second edition (1885). Part of this work is concerned with hypnotism. Richer notes in hypnotized subjects "a special state of attraction on the subject's part to certain persons" (Richer, 1885, p. 663). The female somnambulist, attracted to the "observer" who hypnotized her by pressing his finger on the top of her head, becomes anxious and starts to whimper as soon as he leaves her, and only calms down if he returns. This state, which according to Richer is the result of physical excitation—pressure on the vertex—and is to be explained by a "tactile hyperaesthesia," is encountered in attacks of spontaneous hysterical somnambulism. Of this he gives an example, taken from one of Billet's observations: an attack assuming aspects of "libidinous" hysteria, with "generalized tremors throughout the body, and violent movements of projection of the pelvis which then gradually decreased, and finally became timed to the rhythm of sonorous ronchi" (1885, p. 472).

According to Richer, manifestations of this kind occur regardless of the particular person who touched the subject's "magnetic point."

But if, on the other hand, somnambulism is induced by tactile stimulation with an object, this does not give rise to the special state of attraction. The latter requires the intervention of a person, who is not, however, necessarily involved, nor necessarily the person who hypnotized the subject, inasmuch as this state is directed "towards whomsoever first touches the patient, and especially the bared parts of her body, such as the hands" (1885, p. 663). For Richer, there is nothing mysterious about this influence, for "it consists entirely in a special modification of touch which acts separately from the patient's consciousness" (1885, p. 663).

There was, it is clear, a complete failure to recognize the object relationship and the role of feelings. The mechanical nature of all the processes involved was purportedly demonstrated by such absurd experiments as the following, which we owe to Richer: "While the patient is placed in a state of somnambulism, induced by rubbing the vertex with a given object, two observers come forward, each of whom, without the least resistance on her part, takes hold of one of her hands. What is going to happen? Before long the patient with each hand squeezes that of each of the observers, and does not want to leave them. The special state of attraction exists toward both simultaneously; but the patient finds herself as it were divided in two. Each observer acquires the sympathy of only one-half of the patient, and she offers the same resistance to the observer on her left when he wishes to grasp her right hand, as to the observer on her right when he wishes to grasp her left hand. I shall not seek to explain this singular influence of a strange contact" (1885, p. 663).

Pierre Janet, a pupil of Charcot, first supported the theories of the Salpêtrière, but eventually came to concede the validity of those of Nancy—that is, the preeminence of the psychological factor in hypnosis. He observed the kind of feelings which the subject entertains for the operator not only during hypnosis, but also after the sessions. He speaks of "somnambular passions" and states explicitly: "It would seem therefore that, during somnambulism, the subject is particularly concerned with his hypnotist, and that he shows him a preference, docility and attention, in a word, special feelings which he does not have for other people" (Janet, 1898, I, p. 424).

The selective sensibility to which Binet and Féré referred, so impersonal to Richer, appears to have been more personalized for Janet. He compares the hypnotized patient to a lover who enjoys his happiness only in the immediate presence of the loved one, and with whom no one else can communicate. Some subjects, at first apprehensive of hypnosis, come to feel a passionate desire to continue the sessions, and develop an interest in their physician which is manifestly inordinate. It happens likewise that a subject, "while loving his hypnotist, becomes aware of his submission which he accepts more or less readily. He feels affection mingled with fear for a being far more powerful than he" (1898, I, p. 447). Janet notes that the attitude of his female patients towards him was similar to that of children towards their parents: "Most frequently the subjects feel humble and small, and compare themselves to children in the presence of their elders" (1898, I, p. 447).

Janet does not appear to have been embarrassed by these signs of affection, and in fact refused to give them a sexual interpretation: "In all these cases, what is involved is a kind of love, but it must be emphasized that it is a very special kind which is involved" (1898, I, pp. 465-466). This love he defines (1898, I, p. 210) by a "constant need for moral guidance," a "need to love," and a "need to be loved." All this, he believes, is due to a lowering of the subject's psychological tension. This psychoneurological (and therefore physiological) interpretation shows the imprint left on Janet by the teaching of the Salpêtrière, as also a certain tendency to avoid interpersonal involvement.

However keen the rivalry between the Nancy and Salpêtrière Schools, the somatic theory finally failed to compel recognition. The victory of the Nancy School was, however, short-lived with regard to research on hypnosis, which started to decline on Charcot's death in 1893. Indeed, in a wave of denigration, hypnotic therapy was indicted as an assault on the patient's dignity and a dangerous treatment. Even suggestion was accused of being directed towards that which is automatic, and therefore inferior, in the patient's personality. The attack was led by a former pupil of Bernheim, Paul Dubois, who held that suggestion was immoral and dangerous, and wished to replace it by persuasion therapy, which was in his view a rational procedure calling upon the patient's willpower (Dubois, 1904, pp. 103-119).

In opposition to Dubois' ideas were those of Dejerine, a French neurologist of international fame, but a psychotherapist unrecognized in his own country. According to him, no psychotherapy is possible without an atmosphere of confidence created by "feeling," and unless accompanied by an "emotional appeal" which helps to bring about conviction on the patient's part (Dejerine and Gauckler, 1911, pp. vii-viii). Dejerine's name has always been widely mentioned, and quotations from his works translated, in Russian textbooks of psychotherapy. Russian practitioners do, in fact, sometimes combine his methods with those of Dubois (see the textbooks by Konstorum, 1959, and Lebedinskij, 1959. As for Svjadoshch, 1971, he mentions Dubois, but not Dejerine).

In the United States, some historians of psychiatry regard Dejerine as a forerunner. Alexander and Selesnick (1966, pp. 174-176) contrast Dubois and his theory of persuasion by reasoning with Dejerine who propounded the importance of "feeling." In this controversy they recognize a continuation of the age-old argument about the respective claims of reason and emotion, of Aristotle and Plato, as well as, in more recent times, in the controversy between the psychoanalysts who emphasize the prime significance of intellectual insight, or alternatively, of emotional experience. These same authors also note (p. 176) the importance which Dejerine ascribed to the part played by emotional trauma in the etiology of hysterical symptoms (e.g., the case of a woman who suddenly developed a contracture of the right arm when she wanted to strike her husband; and another of a young girl whose leg became paralyzed after an attempted rape).

Was Dejerine acquainted with Breuer and Freud's *Studies on Hysteria?* Alexander and Selesnick do not think so; they point out that his writings contain no reference whatever to the question of dreams.

Let us leave here the "persuasive" theories of Dubois. Referring to the latter, Janet trenchantly observes: "He is inclined to blush because he has himself had recourse to suggestion in the case of a child given to bed-wetting" (1919, I, p. 202).

Discussing the reasons for the decline of hypnotism, Janet (1919, I, pp. 203-207) implicates among others the undue confidence which the general public placed in this form of treatment. Often applied indiscriminately and without regard for the subject's hypnotizability, it inevitably produced some disappointing results. He adds that, in the absence of a coherent scientific psychology which could, moreover, be used by medical practitioners, the victory of the psychological School could not but have been short-lived.

According to Jones (1923, p. 383), the entire evolution which led from hypnosis to suggestion in the waking state, and thence to autosuggestion, can be explained by the physician's reluctance to impose on his patient an affective (and indeed erotic) dependence upon himself.

Be that as it may, and regardless of whether hypnosis or suggestion was concerned, the period under consideration was marked by a resurgence of the "resistantial" current already noted as a feature of the late eighteenth century, and the moralizing language of the opponents of hypnosis is not without similarity to that used in Bailly's famous Secret Report. Charcot, with all his authority and his prestige, would seem to have created a reassuring atmosphere for hypnotism; he imparted to it a moral sanction and, with his physiological theory, endowed it with a scientific rationale. His death may well have brought about a recurrence of the old anxieties.

Viewed in analogous perspective, one can understand why, in Russia, the decline of hypnosis was far less evident than elsewhere. For in that country it was never the object of moral reprobation. It would appear that Pavlov, backed by his high reputation, fulfilled here the same role as Charcot, and that, similarly, hypnosis was sanctioned by his work and that of his School. The Pavlovian theory of a physiological interpretation of hypnosis has prevailed in the U.S.S.R. to this day. However, since the "rehabilitation" of psychology about 1956, there is some indication that, here and there, the explanation of hypnosis by physiology alone is being called in question. The Russian translation of a French book on hypnosis (the first work with a psychoanalytic orientation to have appeared in the U.S.S.R. for more than 40 years) has recently been published in Moscow. It is worth reproducing here the following excerpts from the Russian preface, relating to the explanation of the mechanism of the hypnotic relationship:

". . . Here L. Chertok gives preference to psychoanalysis with the theory of transference and countertransference. . . . Such a position, frequent among foreign exponents of psychosomatic medicine, is one to which the Soviet reader is unaccustomed, but we believe that it is not without interest to know about it. There is no doubt at all that the reader will be critical of this position, but he will be able to discern its rational core which, in our view, consists in its giving a warning against an excessive simplification of the queston of relationships [*rappórt'*]" (Traugott, 1972, p. 6).

It is a simplification, indeed, to disregard the unconscious motivations which are the rule in every psychotherapeutic relationship. All the more so, in a hypnotic relationship, the "fact" of the unconscious becomes clearly apparent (and we shall see later what an essential role posthypnotic suggestion played in Freud's discoveries).

Perhaps in the long run, impelled by the wish to determine at least the relational component (transference) of hypnosis, and unable to penetrate what must still be called its enigma, it might be possible for the Soviet psychiatrists, passing beyond the stage of "excessive simplifications" and overcoming their resistances, to come one day to recognize the complexity, and indeed the reality, of a dynamic unconscious.

In spite of the rivalry which marked the decade 1880-1890, and while it had not been possible to achieve any satisfactory analysis of hypnotic phenomena, the two French Schools played an essential part, going beyond the framework of hypnosis and preparing the way for the advent of psychoanalysis. During this period, the profusion of ideas, and the new lines of research which speeded up and completed the accumulation of experimental data patiently assembled over a century had reached a quantitative saturation-point, thus creating the prerequisite conditions for the "qualitative leap" which, with Freud, was to bring about a revolution in the understanding of the human mind.

Apart from Liébeault, Bernheim and Janet, the hypnotists of the late nineteenth century were principally interested in the "physiology" and experimental investigation of hypnosis. Freud, for his part, sought to cure*—and his very failures in the use of hypnosis and suggestion led him to new hypotheses which proved fruitful in the field of psychotherapy.

It was inevitable that Freud should pass through hypnosis before arriving at his discoveries. As he subsequently stated, in 1923: "It is not easy to overestimate the importance of the part played by hypnotism in the history of the origin of psychoanalysis. From a theoretical as well as from a therapeutic point of view, psychoanalysis has at its command a legacy which it has inherited from hypnotism" (Freud, 1923, p. 192). In fact, psychoanalysis, arising as it were from the study and criticism of the hypnotic relationship, shed new light on the latter, whose mechanisms were not understood. We may ask ourselves whether hypnosis (a rather old-fashioned, not to say disreputable, ancestor) will not be able likewise to throw light on certain areas of psychoanalytic research. No less an authority than Kubie (1961) did not hesitate to describe hypnotism as "a focus for psychophysiological and psychoanalytic investigations."

---

* Undoubtedly, he wished to cure. But, as we shall see in the section of Chapter III dealing with Freud's stay in Paris, this statement requires some qualifications.

III

The Birth of Psychoanalysis

FROM MESMER to the Salpêtrière and Nancy Schools, the history of psychotherapy provides evidence enough that the object relationship, although clearly recognized and frequently described, had, because of its affective and even erotic implications, encountered such a degree of mistrust that therapists were reluctant to become involved in it. At the period when Freud embarked on his career, this resistance was particularly strong in medical circles. The "magnetists," of naturalistic tendency, had been succeeded in the second half of the nineteenth century by the "hypnotists" who, imbued with positivism, were consequently little disposed to concede the slightest importance to emotional factors.

Suggestion was held to be a mechanistic process, formulated in psycho-neuro-physiological terms which purported to be scientific. For Liébeault's pupil, Bernheim (1884, p. 73), it was "the influence exerted by a suggested idea that is accepted by the brain." The hypno-suggestive relation became in this way "depersonalized," which may be interpreted as a trend to increased resistance on the physician's part to assuming a role in this relationship. This attitude was still very much in evidence during the First International Congress of Hypnotism (Congr. Int. Hypnot., 1889), convened in Paris, whose participants included the world's foremost authorities on the subject of hypnosis. Not one of the participants, however, raised the question as to what might actually lie behind the suggestion (Chertok, 1967).

61

The psychological aspects of the doctor-patient relationship were, therefore, expressed in psychological terms. Freud's teachers—Breuer, Charcot and Bernheim—who opened the way to his future discoveries did not provide him with any data that might have been helpful in elucidating the true nature of this relationship. Still less were these forthcoming from the Helmholtz School, whose alleged influence on Freud has been so greatly emphasized, and has in recent years once again become a subject of investigation in the United States (Holt, 1965; Pribram, 1965).

The young Freud could not fail to experience, likewise, the resistances which prevailed throughout the entire medical profession of his time. He did, indeed, feel them most acutely, as much in consequence of his own personality, as of the Victorian atmosphere of the Viennese middle-class environment to which he belonged. He succeeded, however, in overcoming them by entering gradually into this relationship which psychotherapists had hitherto evaded. This personal involvement constituted the foundation stone of psychoanalysis. Needless to say, Freud did not discover this solution right away. In the following pages, we shall attempt to retrace briefly those paths which he was to follow.

It is in practicing hypnosis that Freud was faced for the first time with the problems of the object relationship and its erotic connotations. He had, however, already come up against the problem of sexuality, in connection with hysteria.

FREUD AND HYSTERIA—THE CASE OF ANNA O.

The year 1882 was of paramount importance for Freud. On June 17, at the age of 26, he became engaged to Martha Bernays. In the following November, he heard of the case of Anna O., a patient in the care of his great friend, Josef Breuer, and this marked an important turning point in his medical career.* Although he had until

* The generally accepted identification of "Anna O." with Fräulein Bertha Pappenheim was questioned by Ellenberger (1970, p. 481). We shall have occasion to observe throughout the present work, as did so many others before us, that for the historian truth would seem to be remarkably elusive. In fact, Ellenberger (1972) was subsequently able to prove, to his own satisfaction, the reverse of his earlier proposition: he discovered that, after all, Anna O. and Bertha Pappenheim were indeed one and the same person.

then devoted himself to work on cerebral histology in a physiological laboratory, he henceforth turned his interest to the study of psychology.

Breuer had started to treat Anna O. in December 1880, but less than two years later, in June 1882, he brought the treatment to an end. This decision was largely influenced by the jealousy of his wife, to whom he had mentioned the case. It is also possible that he was disturbed by his own feelings towards his patient. In any event, so great was this patient's attachment to Breuer, that she was unable to bear the severance of the relationship; the very same day that she was informed of it, she developed an acute hysterical attack, symbolizing childbirth at the term of an imaginary pregnancy which had escaped the notice of her physician. The latter managed to calm his patient by hypnotizing her. He was, however, so profoundly upset by this incident that the very next day he and his wife left for Venice. Breuer was all the more disconcerted by this misadventure in that he had always regarded Anna O., in spite of her considerable charm, as an asexual being.

This story came to Freud's notice on November 18, 1882, and he passed it on to his fiancée in a letter written on the following day. One year later (letter dated October 31, 1883), he reverted to this subject, no doubt having in the meantime learnt further details from Breuer himself. It was after receiving this second letter that Martha identified herself with Breuer's wife, while expressing the hope that she would never find herself in a similar predicament. Freud replied (on November 11) that she had nothing to fear, because "for that to happen one has to be a Breuer."*

Freud seems to have been deeply impressed by the history of Anna O. and he may have already sensed its appreciable interest from the scientific point of view. It is also possible that, because of his "sexual temperament," her case held some special "attraction" for him. We know that Freud was of an austere disposition. Apart from a passing, and certainly "platonic," infatuation for Gisela Fluss

---

* The letters here referred to are mentioned by Jones in his biography of Freud (1953, pp. 247-248). They do not appear in any of Freud's correspondence that has so far been published. Those letters between Freud and his wife that are still unpublished will not become generally available until the year 2000.

at the age of sixteen, he does not appear to have had any further love affair until his engagement and marriage. In a letter to Dr. James Putnam, dated July 8, 1915 (Freud, 1960, p. 314), he wrote: "Sexual morality as defined by society, in its most extreme form that of America, strikes me as very contemptible. I stand for an infinitely freer sexual life, although I myself have made very little use of such freedom."* Jones (1953, p. 110) believes that, prior to Freud's marriage, "even physical experiences were probably few and far between," and that during this period he was the subject of "considerable repression." We know, however, that repression implies an ambivalent attitude, comprising both attraction and rejection. Thus, by stating that he was not "a Breuer," Freud was seeking not only to reassure his fiancée, but just as much to reassure himself.

In the case history of Anna O., Freud discovered two major and closely related problems: that of hysteria and that of hypnosis. He was hardly inclined by temperament to face these problems, whose mere mention frequently aroused the suspicion, or indeed incurred the opprobrium, of most medical circles of the time, including those of Vienna. Hysteria even came to be considered as a form of malingering unworthy of scientific study—a matter to which we shall return later. As for hypnosis, we have seen with what mistrust and antagonism it had been regarded during a whole century. Freud's great merit lies in the fact that he allowed his scientific interest in these questions to prevail by overcoming the double obstacle of both internal and external resistances. The latter, paradoxically, even helped to provide him with answers, as will later be seen, through their integration in the development of his discoveries.

On June 11, 1882, Freud, then a medical graduate of only fifteen months' standing, informed his teacher Brücke of his decision to leave the physiological laboratory, where he had been working for six years, in order to enter general medical practice. Yet he liked this research work and did not conceal his distaste for general practice. But Brücke himself had encouraged Freud to make this change,

---

* We may perhaps wonder what Freud's attitude would have been towards the "sexual liberation" of our own times, as it is manifested in America and elsewhere. Does this liberation affect the prevalence of neuroses? It would be difficult at present to give a definite answer to this question.

in view of his precarious financial circumstances. As for Freud, due to become engaged in a few days' time, he was no doubt already thinking of his eventual family responsibilities. Were he to remain in the laboratory, his future could not but be extremely uncertain, since the position of full professor must, in due course, necessarily devolve to one of Brücke's two chief assistants, Fleischl or Exner, both of whom were some ten years his senior.

Before settling down in general practice, Freud wished to acquire clinical experience as a resident in Vienna's General Hospital. He first worked in the departments of surgery and general medicine. Then, on May 1, 1883, he was appointed to Meynert's psychiatric section, and soon afterwards to his laboratory, where he worked on the histology of the nervous system. He was to spend two years in this work, carrying out research of prime importance. However, after only five months, he left the psychiatric department. He had by then given up the idea of general practice and had decided to become a neurologist. After spending three months in dermatology, he entered the neurological department where he remained from January 1, 1884, until February, 1885. In fact, this department dealt only with organic disorders and, many years later, Freud asserted that, at the time, he understood nothing about neuroses (Freud, 1925a, p. 16).

In January, 1885, Freud started to take steps towards attaining the position of *Privatdozent*. He had long aspired to this title, which provided confirmation that a young doctor had reached a certain level of scientific competence; at the same time, it assured him of a successful practice. The title was conferred on Freud in September of that year. One month later he was on his way to Paris, where he arrived on October 13.

FREUD'S STAY IN PARIS

In March, 1885, Freud had expressed his intention to apply for a postgraduate traveling scholarship offered by the Faculty of Medicine. To this end he engaged in actively seeking support and remained highly anxious until the day of the official decision. On the preceding night he even dreamed that his application had been rejected. As it turned out, he was successful (June 20) , and immediately sent his fiancée a most enthusiastic letter saying he would "go on to Paris and become a great scholar and then come back to Vienna with a huge, enormous halo, and then we will soon get married, and I will cure all the incurable nervous cases . . ." (Freud, 1960, p. 166).*

For what reason did Freud select Paris? In his application for the scholarship (Gicklhorn and Gicklhorn, 1960, p. 77), he expressed the wish to spend three or four months in the department of nervous diseases at the Salpêtrière, with a view to studying a wide range of clinical material to which he could find nothing comparable in Vienna. The report which he compiled on his return (Freud, 1886a) is even more explicit; he there states that he had felt attracted by the

---

* Here Freud's phantasy made its appearance (and it would appear again when Freud started to practice hypnosis), in which he saw himself already as a famous therapist. But what in actual fact was the situation regarding his therapeutic vocation?

It may be noted, first of all, that, allowing his medical studies to "drag" somewhat, he continued, years on end, to work in Brücke's laboratory of cerebral histology.

In 1896, he wrote quite plainly to Fliess: "When I was young, the only thing I longed for was philosophical knowledge, and now that I am going over from medicine to psychology I am in the process of attaining it. I have become a therapist against my will" (Freud, 1954, p. 162). (Fliess, a Berlinese physician and Freud's confidant, exchanged with the latter for fifteen years correspondence of which we only know Freud's contribution; but this does throw light on the evolution of Freud's discoveries.)

More than once did Freud (albeit with many a hesitation or reticence) allow his predilection for philosophical speculation to break through—provided that it did not conflict with his psychological researches, which he wished to maintain on a scientifically rigorous plane. At all events, having become a therapist, he expressed a remarkable optimism and faith in a "cure." It is in this same letter, which has been cited above, that he boasted that, "granted certain conditions in the person and the case, I can definitely cure hysteria and obsessional neurosis" (Freud, 1954, p. 162). He even amused himself (as earlier mentioned) by diagnosing at a distance a particular neurosis in the Czar Nicholas II and jokingly assured Fliess that he could cure the Czar within a year (Freud, 1954, p. 263).

Did Freud actually provide a radical cure for more cases of severe obsessional neurosis and hysteria than are cured today? We simply do not know, for the very good reason that no exhaustive catamnestic study exists on the subject.

All things considered, we believe that the wish to cure was as sincerely held by Freud as by every therapist—but that he was urged on by an additional motivation: to cure a patient was, for him, to prove the validity of his etiological hypotheses and of his technical innovations.

It should moreover be noted that, at this time, Freud thought that the patient's "acquisition of insight" was sufficient and decisive in ensuring a complete recovery. It was not until later that he realized that this "intellectual factor" was not the sole determining factor—indeed, the "emotional experience" constitutes, in the analytical relationship, an essential factor in the cure. The question of the curative elements in analysis still remains very largely a controversial one.

French school of neuropathology, directed by "the great Charcot." He goes on to say that, "In consequence of the scarcity of any lively personal contact between French and German physicians, the findings of the French school—some of them (upon hypnotism) highly surprising and some of them (upon hysteria) of practical importance —had been met in our countries with more doubt than recognition and belief" (Freud, 1886a, pp. 5-6; cf. Gicklhorn & Gicklhorn, 1960, p. 82). His curiosity about these two problems had been aroused by the case of Anna O.; but it was hardly likely to find satisfaction in the neurological department where he had by then been working for 13 months.

At the Salpêtrière, Freud first devoted himself to research on cerebral anatomy, while simultaneously attending Charcot's lectures. Then, early in December 1885, he abandoned the laboratory on the pretext that it did not provide satisfactory working conditions. In actual fact, he was already on the "road to Damascus," which was leading him to psychopathology. In this connection it is necessary to consider Charcot's influence on Freud, which was of paramount importance.

CHARCOT AND FREUD

As Freud wrote (letter of November 26, 1885), "Charcot . . . is simply wrecking all my aims and opinions. I sometimes come out of his lectures as from out of Notre-Dame, with an entirely new idea about perfection. . . . My brain is sated as after an evening in the theater . . . no other human being has ever affected me in the same way" (Freud, 1960, p. 185). Freud was later to acknowledge openly his debt to Charcot; witness the obituary notice (published September, 1893) in which he ascribes to his teacher the merit of a discovery which "assured him for all time . . . the fame of having been the first to explain hysteria" (Freud, 1893b, p. 22). Some authors, including Jones (1953, p. 240), have considered this to be somewhat excessive praise. However, in 1925, on the occasion of the centenary of Charcot's birth, Freud reaffirmed his earlier views in this respect (Codet and Laforgue, 1925).

Psychoanalysts in general have subsequently recognized Charcot's influence on Freud. In their *History of Medical Psychology,* Zilboorg and Henry (1941, p. 485) speak of a new era of psychology beginning with Freud, but linked to a chain of predecessors comprising Mesmer, Charcot, Liébeault, and Bernheim. When, in 1956, the centenary of Freud's birth was commemorated at the Salpêtrière, S. Nacht (1957, p. 319) particularly stated in his address: "I have sometimes wondered whether, without Charcot's teaching, Freud would ever have engaged upon the path which he followed." And Freud's personal physician and biographer, Schur, reverted to this question in 1972 (pp. 38-39), regarding Charcot as one of the three teachers (together with Breuer and Bernheim) who exerted a decisive influence on Freud.

Charcot's influence was on two levels, intellectual and affective.

Intellectual Influence

In the first place, Freud received from Charcot confirmation that hysteria, an illness which although known for several millennia was often still regarded as a form of malingering, deserved to be studied scientifically and was susceptible of psychological interpretation. Its symptoms were the result of a psychical, and not a physical, trauma. Dealing with the post-traumatic hysterical paralyses (to which subject we shall return), Charcot demonstrated in his lectures (1887), which are famous to this day, that these conditions were attributable not to physical causes, but quite definitely to a traumatic psychological experience. In other words, the neurotic symptoms were induced by *ideas.* In order to prove this, he induced experimentally, by means of suggestion under hypnosis or in the waking state, "artificial" paralyses which he could subsequently cause to disappear. On the other hand, Charcot conceded that neuroses generally tended to develop on a hereditary substratum. We know how faithfully Freud adhered for some years to these theoretical views before eventually proceeding to develop his own concepts.

The stages of this development until 1896 have been painstakingly retraced in Ola Andersson's *Studies in the Prehistory of Psychoanalysis* (1962). This author shows very clearly how Freud arrived at his own conceptualization of hysteria by placing considerable emphasis on the importance of psychical factors and allotting a lesser role to

heredity,* while giving a predominant place to the acquired con-
flictual factor, in the "neuropathic" predisposition. It is unnecessary
here to recall the sequence of Freud's researches which led him to
his great discoveries. He recognized, however, that all had not yet
been explained in the matter of hysteria, since in 1909, referring to
hysterical conversion, he still spoke of "the leap from a mental
process to a somatic innervation . . . which can never be fully comprehensible to us" (Freud, 1909, p. 157). It may be added that existing psychosomatic theories have so far failed to provide a satisfactory
explanation of this condition.

As to hypnosis, it was used by Charcot to induce hysterical symptoms. It is for this reason that he regarded it as an artificial hysteria—
a point of view strenuously contested by the Nancy School. Toward
this controversy Freud always retained a hesitant attitude (Chertok,
1968a). The particular part which hypnosis played in his discoveries
will be discussed later. Freud did, indeed, attempt to find an explanation in depth of hypnotic phenomena without, however, pursuing
these investigations as far as he had done in studying hysteria. He
was obliged to admit in the end that hypnosis remained for the most
part "unexplained and mysterious" (Freud, 1921, p. 115). It is
hardly less so today, and no researcher has yet succeeded in penetrating its mystery.**

* In any event, Freud never excluded the part played by heredity in the neuroses.
For further details on this question, see the summary by Jones (1957, p. 351). It may
be noted that in 1904 Freud was still using the expression "neuropathic degeneracy"
(we shall have more to say on this concept later), in connection with the contra-
indications to analysis (Freud, 1905a, p. 263). It may also be mentioned that, at the
same period, he indicated as suitable for analysis cases of severe chronic psycho-
neurosis, in particular obsessional neurosis and all forms of chronic hysteria (hystero-
phobia, conversion hysteria) (Freud, 1904, p. 253; 1905a, p. 264).
The situation has altered since that time, and far more prudent discrimination is
exercised today in evaluating the indications and contra-indications for analysis.

** There is thus a "psychosomatic mystery"—and a "hypnotic mystery." Will the
solution of the latter provide the key to the former? We may perhaps mention here
a commonplace example. One of the authors (Chertok, 1966b, p. 83) has recalled the
well-known influence of hypnotherapy on common warts (a condition of true virus
origin). The "psychosomatic fact" is a matter of record, but the mechanism involved
is completely unknown. Schneider (1968, p. 657) has reexamined this dermatological
problem: ". . . we do not know what takes place when by suggestion a virus disease is
made to disappear, as in the common wart which is caused by a polyoma virus.
Virologists know the precise structure of the RNA molecules of this polyoma virus,
their replication, and their anomalies. The psychologists believe that they have a

The net result of Freud's stay at the Salpêtrière was to bring about a profound alteration in his attitudes to nervous ailments. He had hitherto been influenced by teachers of the German school, such as Meynert who, from the start and systematically, sought to ascribe to every psychiatric disorder an anatomo-physiological explanation. Under Charcot, Freud had witnessed the practice of an anatomo-clinical approach which was far more flexible and less dependent on physiology. Charcot applied himself to the precise definition and classification of any given clinical phenomenon, but, in Freud's words, "he can sleep quite soundly, without having arrived at the physiological explanation of that phenomenon" (Freud, 1886a, p. 13; cf. Gicklhorn and Gicklhorn, 1960, p. 88). Freud further recorded a remark made by Charcot: "I practice pathological morphology, I even practice a little pathological anatomy; but I do not practice pathological physiology—I expect someone else to do it" (Freud, 1892, p. 135).

On hypnosis as a pathological state, Meynert (1888) certainly agreed with Charcot, as also on the description of "hysterical hypnotism" or "major hypnotism" and its classification in various stages (lethargy, catalepsy and somnambulism; these three stages could occur either severally or concurrently). On the whole, like Charcot, he regarded hypnosis as a neurosis, an artificial hysteria, and he spoke of spontaneous hysteria in referring to certain hysterical manifestations.

As we shall see, however, Charcot postulated the existence in every neurosis of an anatomo-physiological substratum which had yet to be defined ("dynamic and functional lesions"). Meynert, on the other hand, envisaged clear-cut physiological connections with the hypnotic neurosis, e.g., variations in the cerebrovascular circulation according to the particular stage reached: functional anemia or hyperemia, and so on.

---

better knowledge of suggestion. But, of the inmost mechanism of the disappearance of the wart, in spite of the researches that have been undertaken by psychosomaticians in dermatological units in the United States, we know nothing." It may be noted, incidentally, that a laboratory for research on hypnosis in the United States recently received from the National Institute of Mental Health a very substantial grant for a four-year project specifically concerned with investigating the psychocutaneous effects of hypnosis and suggestion—including their use in the removal of warts and the treatment of skin inflammations!

Meynert is certainly open to criticism for his obdurately rigid ana-tomo-physiological theory, as compared with the cautious flexibility of Charcot's anatomo-clinical concepts. But, through its extreme nature, this rigidity may have done some good. For example, in the matter of metalloscopy, and the "transfer of symptoms at a distance" by magnets, Meynert was able to detect at once the snare of the illusion (indeed, on the vasomotor level, these "transfers" were contrary to the most elementary physiological principles).

Meynert was thus undoubtedly beyond the reach of the "psycho-logical risk"; he guarded against "falling into the inexplicable." To Charcot, on the other hand, the situation presented no problem. Knowing how to exercise discretion in the realm of psychology, he took care to leave open every available way of access to that realm.

It was in Paris, therefore, that, "liberated from the physiological obsession," Freud was able, under Charcot's influence, to approach the study of psychology in the strict sense. As we know, after having made his fundamental discoveries in this field, he was to return, very much later, to his earliest interests.

In addition to these brief comments on Charcot's intellectual influence on Freud, it would seem desirable to consider at greater length two aspects which in our opinion are of paramount importance: the question of experimental paralyses and that of major hysteria.

Experimental Paralyses

In March, 1885, Charcot published an account* of the controversy that was current at the time, concerning the psychical disorders consequent upon railway accidents ("railway spine"). Some doctors (of the German school) took the view that such disorders were the result of organic nervous changes and constituted a "traumatic neurosis" distinct from hysteria. Others (of the Anglo-American school) regarded them not as a lesion of the central nervous system, but quite definitely as hysteria. Charcot lent support to this latter view by observing the presence in such cases of hysterical stigmata (hemi-

---

* Lecture 18, originally published in *Progrès Médical* (Paris), May 2, 1885. English translation in Charcot, 1889, pp. 220-243.

anesthesia, constriction of the visual field, hysterogenic zones, etc.),
and especially by showing that the symptoms of these traumatic
paralyses following accidents could be reproduced by suggestion.

In dealing with the psychical paralyses in general, Charcot mentions the work of the British physician, Russell Reynolds (1869)
who had previously investigated them.* Charcot adduces experimental proof of their existence,** and we believe that it will be useful in this connection to give a summary of the case of his patient,
Pin—, which may justifiably be regarded as historically significant.***

In his "Paris Report," Freud referred to post-traumatic hysteria
and mentioned briefly "the case of a patient who for nearly three
months formed the center-point of all Charcot's studies" (Freud,
1886a, p. 12; cf. Gicklhorn & Gicklhorn, 1960, p. 87). He was to
describe this case in greater detail in the lecture which he delivered

* Charcot's Lecture 21, originally published in *Progrès Médical* (Paris), September
12, 1885, English translation in Charcot, 1889, pp. 274-295 (reference to Reynolds,
p. 289). In the German translation, the passage concerning Reynolds' work has been
placed in Lecture 22 (Charcot, 1886, p. 274). Freud completed his translation of the
Leçons sur les Maladies du Système nerveux, Tome 3, on July 18, 1886 (date of preface), and it appeared in August of that year, whereas the original French edition
was not published until December (and bears the date 1887). The German version
differs from the original in some respects (in addition to the instance already mentioned): thus it comprises 28 lectures, whereas the French edition has 26 lectures,
followed by an Appendix containing further clinical cases. After Lecture 25, the
German translation differs in its arrangement from the French text. (The English
translation closely adheres to the first French edition.)
** With regard to local hysterical symptoms which are not solely confined to
paralyses, Charcot makes frequent laudatory mention of the work of another British
author, the famous surgeon Sir Benjamin Brodie. In his Lecture 23 entitled, "On
a case of hysterical hip disease in a man, resulting from injury," first published in
Progrès Médical (Paris), January 30, 1886 (English translation in Charcot, 1889, pp.
317-329), he deals at some length with the investigations undertaken by Brodie. The
latter was the first to describe "hysterical affections of the joints" which, together with
other local hysterical manifestations, were the subject of a small treatise, *Lectures
illustrative of certain Local Nervous Affections* (Brodie, 1837). This work is worthy
of serious attention even today, particularly by rheumatologists who would find in it
much food for thought.
*** This is Case VI (Charcot, 1889, pp. 252-259) of Lecture 19 which, together with
Lecture 18, comprises an account "Concerning six cases of hysteria in the male"
(1889, pp. 220-260). (Lecture 19, delivered in April, was published in *Progrès Médical*
(Paris), August 8, 1885.) Charcot (1889, pp. 286-288) again referred to this case in
his Lecture 21 (delivered on May 15, 1885) which, together with his Lecture 20 (May
1st) and Lecture 22 (May 29), constituted an account "On two cases of hysterical
brachial monoplegia in the male, of traumatic origin.—Hystero-traumatic monoplegia"
(1889, pp. 261-316). The patient Pin— was one of these two cases.

on October 15, 1886, before the Society of Medicine in Vienna, about which we shall have more to say. It can, however, be confidently asserted that the patient in question was indeed Pin—.

On May 24, 1884, Pin—, a mason's apprentice aged 17, fell from a height of about two meters (6½feet) and remained unconscious for some minutes. Although he had sustained only slight contusions, a few days later he first noticed a weakness of the left arm and was admitted to the Hôtel-Dieu Hospital. The paresis increased, and twenty-two days after the accident the patient had developed a complete paralysis of the left arm. This was his condition on leaving the hospital. On March 11, 1885, he was admitted to Charcot's wards at the Salpêtrière. He then presented the stigmata of hemianesthesia and constriction of the visual field. After a very comprehensive examination, a diagnosis of hysterotraumatic monoplegia was established. Amongst the stigmata, the convulsive seizure was lacking in the clinical picture (a fact which, however, in no way excludes such a diagnosis). Four days later, another thorough investigation revealed the presence of hysterogenic zones, one situated beneath the left breast, another in each of the iliac areas, and a fourth over the right testicle. Stimulation of the hysterogenic zones induced a fully developed hysteroepileptic attack—the first ever to have occurred in this patient. As Charcot described it, "This attack was in fact absolutely classical; the epileptoid phase was soon succeeded by that of the *'grands mouvements'* [clonic contractions].* These were extremely violent, even to the extent of causing the patient, in his gestures of salutation, to strike his face against his knees. Shortly afterwards, he tore his sheets and the curtains of his bed, and turning his rage against himself, bit his left arm. The phase of *'attitudes passionnelles'* [hallucinatory phase] then followed. Pin— seemed to be prey to a frenzied delirium; he insulted and provoked imaginary persons, inciting them to murder: 'Here! Take your knife. . . . Go on. . . . Go ahead and strike!' At last he regained his senses and, on recovering consciousness, asserted that he had no recollection of what had recently occurred" (Charcot, 1889, pp. 257-258—translation revised).

---

* For a description of the "classical" attack, see the following section on "Major hysteria."

After one of these attacks, he began to regain movement in his paralyzed arm.* Charcot was in a way disappointed at losing, through this patient's cure, an experimental subject for purposes of demonstration. "The idea, therefore, occurred to me," as he stated, "that, perhaps by acting on the mind of the patient, by *means of suggestion,* even in the waking state—we had learned previously that the subject was not hypnotizable—we might reproduce the paralysis, for a time at least" (1889, p. 258—Charcot's italics). He did, in fact, reproduce it, without any feeling of anxiety about the outcome of this artificial paralysis, for he knew "from long experience, that *what one has done, one can undo,*" in the matter of suggestion (1889, p. 259—Charcot's italics). Thus began a series of experiments in which Charcot induced artificial paralyses or other hysterical symptoms by suggestion, either in the waking state or under hypnosis. Freud attended demonstrations of this kind, in particular Lectures 23 and 24, "On a case of hysterical hip-disease in a man, resulting from injury" (Charcot, 1889, pp. 317-340). As for the patient Pin—, he was still in Charcot's unit while Freud was studying there. It is in fact from Freud that we learn (translation of Lecture 22, footnote) that this patient was cured of his monoplegia, although the hemianesthesia and the convulsive attacks persisted, when he was discharged from the hospital in January, 1886, for . . . insubordination! (Charcot, 1886, p. 300).

It would seem that the question of the psychical paralyses and the experiments concerning them made a great impression on Freud and, in our view, implanted in his mind one of those seeds of which he wrote to his fiancée. As we know, while acknowledging the psychical causality of the neuroses (especially the post-traumatic neuroses), Charcot nevertheless postulated the existence of a physiological substratum which he called "dynamic functional" lesions (as

---

* It may well be asked whether the description of this patient's attack, with which Freud was of course acquainted, and such similar attacks as he no doubt witnessed personally, did not give rise in his mind to the concept of therapeutic abreaction. He may perhaps also have been led thereby to speak to Charcot of Breuer's cathartic method. Needless to say, it is possible that the patient was imitating other patients at the Salpêtrière, but even were this so, his behavior comprised a distinctly personal element: it is indeed conceivable that he was projecting his own aggressive impulses, which lay at the root of his paralysis, on to some imaginary person.

opposed to "structural" lesions). He considered that the latter even had an anatomical localization which, however, could not be detected by existing methods of investigation. Thus, his explanation remained two-sided: a psychical causality, together with an anatomo-physiological substratum, as yet undiscovered. As Andersson has noted (1962, p. 60), Charcot did not attempt to investigate more deeply the relationship between these two explanations of the etiology of the hysterical paralyses.

Charcot did not fail to observe the difference between the clinical pictures of hysterical and organic paralyses, respectively. To give an example which Freud was to cite later: in hysterical hemiplegia, "the paralyzed leg is not moved in a circular wheeling motion at the hip," as is the case in organic hemiplegia, "but is dragged along like a lifeless appendage" (Freud, 1888, p. 46).* It seems truly remarkable that, his observations notwithstanding, Charcot could have spoken of a similar anatomical localization in both types of paralysis. Freud appears to have begun to question this postulate already during his stay in Paris. Indeed, when on February 22, 1886, Freud called at Charcot's private residence to take leave of his teacher, the possibility was discussed of undertaking a comparative study of organic and hysterical paralyses. If we confine ourselves to the references to this episode in Freud's works, it is by no means easy to arrive with any certainty at the truth. Jones takes into account two (unpublished) letters dated February 21 and 25, 1886. In the first of these Freud mentions his decision to go and see Charcot next day and place before him two ideas, "of which at least one seems to me to be very important" (Jones, 1953, p. 257). The idea in question, according to Jones, was the comparative study of hysterical and organic paralyses. In the second letter (Jones does not give the exact words, merely a summary) Freud "told of his great pleasure when Charcot said they [the ideas] were not so bad, that although he could not accept the ideas himself he would not contradict them, and that it would be worthwhile to work them out" (Jones, 1953, p. 257).

It is hardly necessary to emphasize the ambiguity of such a state-

---

* Freud again referred to this clinical description in his "Comparative study" (1893a), where he acknowledged his indebtedness to Charcot for having drawn his attention to this fact.

ment on Charcot's part, at least if we accept Jones's summary. The latter refers (p. 256) to the "somewhat different account" which Freud gave of this episode, some forty years later, in his *Autobiographical Study,* where he stated that Charcot "agreed with this view, but it was as easy to see that in reality he took no special interest in penetrating more deeply into the psychology of the neuroses" (Freud, 1925, p. 14).

The difference between the two versions may, on the whole, seem rather tenuous. One is left with the impression that Charcot was, in fact, divided between two contrary tendencies: on the one hand, he had no wish to discourage the investigations of his pupil and translator; but on the other, he showed little inclination to get to the bottom of these matters, or to revive the controversial question of the correspondence of hysterical symptoms with an anatomical localization. Be that as it may, he promised to publish the report that Freud would write on the results of his comparative study, and the paper did indeed appear (in French) in 1893, in the *Archives de Neurologie* (Freud, 1893a).

The fact therefore remains that we do not know in what terms Freud presented his theory to Charcot. At all events, in 1888 he was to state it in the clearest terms: "A further and extremely important characteristic of hysterical disorders is that they do not in any way present a copy of the anatomical conditions of the nervous system. It may be said that hysteria is as ignorant of the science of the structure of the nervous system as we ourselves before we have learnt it" (Freud, 1888, pp. 48-49). This idea is reaffirmed in the "Comparative Study": ". . . *in its paralyses and other manifestations hysteria behaves as though anatomy did not exist or as though it had no knowledge of it"* (Freud, 1893a, p. 169—Freud's italics).

We know that in 1888 this study was almost completed, but, for reasons so far unknown, Charcot did not receive it until five years later. Strachey (editorial note in Freud, 1893a, S.E. 1, pp. 157-159) supposes that the first three sections, which are concerned with neurological aspects, were written in or before 1888; whereas the fourth section, introducing entirely new ideas in the psychological field, must date from 1893. For it is in this past section we find, implied if not fully named explicitly, the concepts in which Freud had become increasingly absorbed during these five years: repression, abreaction, and the principle of constancy. In Strachey's opinion, it is not impossible that Freud may have held back the publication of his paper until these new ideas had really taken shape, feeling that they might provide some tentative explanation of the clinical data which had been dealt with in the preceding sections.

All things considered, it must be recognized that, while Freud was able to formulate his postulate in exceptionally clear terms, the fact remains that its fundamental concept had already appeared in various forms in the multitude of investigations undertaken at a definitely earlier date. In fact, in 1893 Freud acknowledged a predecessor when he expressed his full agreement "with the views advanced by M. Janet in recent numbers of the *Archives de Neurologie*" (Freud, 1893a, p. 169). He was no doubt referring to Janet's study of hysterical anesthesia; here the author stated that, in localized anesthesia, "the ideas which we form of our own organs play an important part" (Janet, 1892, p. 329). Freud thus appears to concede Janet's prior claim to this postulate—while purely and simply forgetting that it was he himself who, already in 1888, had in all essential points expounded this hypothesis! It is, however, only fair to add that, one year earlier, Janet came close to grasping the problem when he declared that "anesthesia, whether systemic or even general, induced by suggestion or resulting from hysteria, is not a true anesthesia" (Janet, 1887, p. 462). But we can go back yet another year, for Janet refers to Bernheim (1886, p. 45) who, while treating "negative hallucinations," clearly had an inkling of the principle of non-correspondence in respect of experimental paralysis and anesthesia.

It would certainly be possible to trace back further still those long, complex lines of "filiation of influences" to which we referred in our introduction. At all events, it is undoubtedly Freud alone who had the vision to draw from a known clinical and experimental phenomenon conclusions which are now famous. It was in Paris that a process was set in motion which would eventually enable him to explain, by a psychical mechanism that gave them a meaning, the paralyses and other symptoms of hysteria. In the light of this explanation, the hysterical symptom is seen to be the symbolic expression of an unconscious phantasy.*

Major Hysteria ("La Grande Hystérie")

Together with the experimental paralyses, major hysteria was one of the first ferments to activate Freud's discoveries. The manifestations of the "major neurosis" or hystero-epilepsy that he witnessed at the Salpêtrière had made a great impression on his mind, for reasons which we are inclined to believe were as much intellectual as affective.

It should, in the first place, be recalled that Charcot recognized two forms of hystero-epilepsy: one "with distinct attacks" (*"à crises distinctes"*), where hysterical attacks (which he called *"attaques"*) alternate with true epileptic fits (which he called *"accès"*), and the other "with mixed attacks" (*"à crises mixtes"*), where hysterical attacks alone occur, but which may comprise one phase resembling epilepsy (Charcot, 1889, pp. 33-34). He subsequently discarded the term "hystero-epilepsy" in favor of *"grande hystérie"* ("major hysteria") in order to obviate any possibility of confusion with purely epileptic manifestations. Major hysteria was typically held to comprise four phases, of which the most precise description is given by Paul Richer, in his vast work, *Études cliniques sur la Grande Hystérie ou Hystéro-Epilepsie* (1885).

We may here confine ourselves to the concise account given by Freud (1888, pp. 42-43) according to Charcot, in which the first three phases are described as follows: the "epileptoid" phase, resembling an epileptic fit; that of the *"grands mouvements,"* i.e., with

---

* Referring to the treatment of hysteria, Charcot stated: "Certainly our therapeutic activity would prove more effective if, instead of relying solely on empirical concepts, it could be founded on a physiological basis; if, for example, we were able to recognize, at least in part, the mechanism of the production of these traumatic hysterical paralyses" (Charcot, 1889, p. 288—translation revised).

It may be said that Freud discovered, if not the physiological mechanism, at least the psychical mechanism of these symptoms. He thus continued, along a different path, the work that his teacher wished to accomplish, and more than realized his own phantasy, as he expressed it in a letter which he wrote to Martha from Paris (February 2, 1886): ". . . I could achieve more than Nothnagel, to whom I consider myself superior, and might possibly reach the level of Charcot" (Freud, 1960, p. 214).

movements of wide compass, such as the so-called "salaam" gestures, arching of the body (*"attitudes en arc de cercle"*), contortions, etc.; and the "hallucinatory" phase (of *"attitudes passionnelles"*), where the subject acts out scenes that he is reliving in a hallucinatory form, often accompanied with corresponding words. (As stated by Richer, 1885, p. 89, "the patient participates in scenes in which she often plays the principal role.") The fourth phase, that of "terminal delirium," does not always occur and is sometimes omitted in Charcot's writings. It is noteworthy that Charcot characterized the *grands mouvements* as "contradictory, illogical," and the *attitudes passionnelles as* "logical" (the English translation uses the terms "purposeless" and "purposive," respectively—Charcot, 1889, p. 13). No doubt he saw in the latter a certain expressive coherence, or, as we would say, a "meaning."

Like all those who were interested at the time in the "major neurosis," Charcot based himself, as we know, on the work of Briquet (1859), to whose monumental treatise he often paid tribute. As he stated, "much credit is due to Briquet for having established in his excellent book, in a manner beyond dispute, that hysteria too is governed, in the same way as other morbid conditions, by rules and laws, which attentive and sufficiently numerous observations will always enable us to elucidate" (Charcot, 1889, p. 13—translation revised). In fact, Briquet had already recorded all the manifestations of major hysteria as it was described by Charcot. The latter, however, thought to make things clearer by placing hysteria in a more precise nosological framework. This urge to classify phenomena was indeed characteristic of the period; it showed itself not only in respect of hysterical neurosis, but also in psychiatry—in the study of the psychoses—where determined efforts were being made to find rigorous definitions for nosological entities.*

Charcot wished to apply to the neuroses the same physiological and anatomical laws as to neurological conditions. Otherwise, there

---

* It is hardly necessary to recall that hysteria (the hysterical neurosis) was at that time principally the concern of neurologists, then known in Central Europe and in Russia as "neuropathologists," a term which is used to this day in the USSR. A "hysterical psychosis" was, however, also recognized, which came, on the other hand, within the realm of psychiatry. It should be remembered, in this connection, that neither Briquet, nor Bernheim, nor Charcot was a psychiatrist.

loomed the specter of "the imagination" which, a century earlier, had already haunted the King's commissioners. Yet he was very well aware that neurosis was an affection *sine materia* (without substance), one that, in contradistinction to neurological disorders, revealed no detectable anatomo-pathological substratum on postmortem examination. Whereupon, as we have seen, he postulated the existence in the neuroses of "dynamic functional lesions" which remained to be discovered. This urge to find an anatomical correspondence between the neuroses and neurological disorders prevented his realizing that his postulate was in direct contradiction to his own clinical observations. Charcot had, admittedly, been able to observe that a given hysterical symptom might assume the same form as a neurological symptom; but he had also seen other cases (for example, the hysterical paralyses) where there were differences in the clinical picture. What is more, he was aware that hysterical symptoms were the result of a psychical trauma, but was nonetheless unable to conceive that they arise independently of the effects of a lesion of the nervous system.

Much has been written about major hysteria, which is a rarity today—at least in the so-called "developed" countries. Charcot's classification is, in effect, obsolete. In speaking of the Salpêtrière, such opprobious terms were used as "dressage" (as applied to the schooling of horses), "products of cultivation," "simulation" and "fraud" —and the myth persists that Charcot was often taken in by his patients. To be sure, psychical contagion and imitation may well have played some part amongst the hysterical patients at the Salpêtrière, as elsewhere. The borderline between imitation and unconscious simulation is well-nigh impossible to define, and it is well known that these two behavior patterns are inherent in hysteria. As for conscious simulation, or fraud, it would seem that its importance in Charcot's experiments has been exaggerated through a failure to distinguish between malingering and the imitation by one illness of another—admittedly no easy task. We therefore agree with Guillain (1955, p. 137) that the myth of Charcot's being deceived by his patients is without foundation, for he was very well aware of the existence of "intentional simulation" (Charcot, 1889, p. 14).

On consideration, the recognition of four distinct phases in major hysteria seems artificial. Nonetheless, if one has occasion to witness a major attack, such as one of the authors was able to film,* it is possible to identify more than one characteristic feature described by Charcot (the epileptoid and hallucinatory phases in particular).

Charcot's concepts of major hysteria have today, for the most part, been superseded. Their role was nonetheless historically important, by the very fact that this illness became the subject of investigation at the Salpêtrière, a research center of worldwide repute at the time. In the contemporary context, Charcot could not but approach the question at the cost of extreme systematization. So far as psychoanalysis is concerned, Charcot's artificial classification, however erroneous, was certainly providential since it was the hallucinatory phase which seemingly impressed Freud most forcibly and allowed him to obtain a glimpse of the phantasy world of the unconscious.**

Freud undoubtedly witnessed attacks of this kind at the Salpêtrière. We also know that he was acquainted with Paul Richer's book. In the preface to his translation of the third volume of Charcot's *Leçons sur les Maladies du Système nerveux* (July 18, 1886), he wrote: "Anyone who is encouraged by these lectures to enter further into the French school's researches on hysteria may be referred to P. Richer's *Études Cliniques sur la Grande Hystérie*, of which a second edition appeared in 1885 and which is in more than one respect a noteworthy volume" (Charcot, 1886, p. iv—English transl. in Freud, S.E. 1, pp. 21-22). Richer's book, which contains a vast number of revealing case histories, is a mine of information which deserves to be more thoroughly exploited than hitherto by historians of psychoanalysis. From its thousand odd pages, let us at least cite two significant passages:

> The patient is in the grip of hallucinations which entrance her and transport her to an imaginary world. . . . She acts as if her dream were reality (Richer, 1885, p. 89).

---

* L. Chertok: "Hysteria—Body Language" (Sciencefilm, Paris, 1967).

** Another providential error, typically of heuristic value to science, was Charcot's belief in the presence of physical signs in hypnosis (which have so far entirely eluded detection). If Charcot "the physiologist" had not thus been mistaken, he would not have devoted himself to the study of hypnosis, nor would he consequently have undertaken his famous and far-reaching experiments.

> The content of these hallucinations is more often than not derived from the patient's past. The scenes . . . are reproduced with a vividness that time cannot dim, and especially those which have influenced the evolution of the illness (1885, p. 90).

Scenes relived in this way frequently assume an erotic character.

Freud's interest in this hallucinatory phase appears in 1892 in his footnotes to his translation of Charcot's *Tuesday Lectures,* where he emphasizes the importance, in every hysterical attack, of the reliving of a scene that had played an important part in the inception of the illness. "The core of a hysterical attack," as he wrote, "in whatever form it may appear, is a *memory,* the hallucinatory reliving of a scene which is significant for the onset of the illness. It is this event which manifests itself in a perceptible manner in the phase of *'attitudes passionnelles' "* (Freud, 1892-94, p. 137). These concepts were further elaborated in the sketch entitled "On the theory of hysterical attacks" (Freud, 1892)—the forerunner of the "Preliminary Communication" of 1893 which appeared under the joint signature of Breuer and Freud (1895).

In the "Theory of hysterical attacks," some important ideas are already expressed: "The constant and essential content of a (recurrent) hysterical attack is the return of a psychical state which the patient has already experienced earlier—in other words, *the return of a memory. . . . The memory which forms the content of a hysterical attack is not any chance one; it is the return of the event which caused the outbreak of hysteria—the psychical trauma. . . . If a hysterical subject seeks intentionally to forget an experience or forcibly repudiates, inhibits and suppresses an intention or an idea, these psychical acts, as a consequence, enter the second state of consciousness; from there they produce their permanent effects and the memory of them returns as a hysterical attack"* (Freud, 1892, pp. 152-153 —Freud's italics). All these ideas were integrated in the "Preliminary Communication" of 1893. In his formulation of the concept of hysteria, Freud therefore incorporated elements of the major attack: the reliving of past experiences,* the return to the particular trau-

---

* Was it not this that suggested the concept of "repetition compulsion"? The patient *relives* traumatic situations: *"Hysterics suffer mainly from reminiscences"* (Breuer and Freud, 1895, p. 7—their italics).

matic event which induced the illness,* and the possibility that this event was of a sexual nature. To mere description Freud was subsequently to add a dynamic interpretation by introducing the concepts of repression, conflict, phantasy, and the unconscious.**

In summary, it is necessary to lay stress on the period which Freud spent at the Salpêtrière, for it was for him an experience of fundamental importance; it was in Paris that Freud found the first germ of his theories. He seems to have sensed this already in his letter of November 24, 1885, in which, having expressed his enthusiasm about Charcot's lectures, he asked himself "whether the seed will ever bear any fruit" (Freud, 1960, p. 185). And eight years later, in concluding his "Preliminary Communication" entitled, "On the psychical mechanism of hysterical phenomena," he asserted that by uncovering this mechanism "we have taken a step forward along the path first traced so successfully by Charcot" (Breuer and Freud, 1895, p. 17).

It should be added that other "impacts" of Charcot on Freud have been recorded: researchers of the Chicago Institute for Psychoanalysis have noted that Charcot, as an experienced clinician, without having formulated any coherent psychopathological theory, understood intuitively the role of certain psychological factors in the etiology of neurosis, notably the effect of traumatic episodes in adult life as well as in childhood. They further noted that Charcot also had an inkling of the problem of "secondary gain" which reinforces the illness, as well as of the problem of a possible harmful parental influence which may call for the removal of the child from his family with a view to appropriate treatment. The American researchers emphasize, moreover, an aspect of Charcot's personality that is not widely recognized: as a psychotherapist, in addition to hypnosis and suggestion he in fact employed "environmental and transference

---

* We know that Freud was to pass beyond the theory of trauma, while not discarding it entirely, and that he eventually integrated it into a far more intricate etiological complex (phantasy life, history of infancy, predisposition, etc.). In the historical context, the theory of trauma retains its importance as a decisive landmark.

** We have already mentioned the rarity today of major hysterical attacks of the "Charcot type"; and also that one of the authors fortunately had the opportunity to film such a case. This audiovisual record clearly reveals the dramatic struggle between the onslaught of impulses and the defenses mobilized for their repression. The patient is at grips with phantasies from the depths of another world, that of the unconscious. It is thus easy to understand that so striking a spectacle could not have failed to stimulate Freud's creative genius.

manipulations in ways which were apparently effective and which are quite similar to their current use" (Miller *et al.*, 1969, p. 612). They also point out that Charcot's formulation is strikingly similar to Breuer's "hypnoid hypothesis" elaborated in the *Studies on Hysteria* (Breuer and Freud, 1895).

Affective Influence

Having assessed the significance of these several aspects as they affected Freud during his stay at the Salpêtrière, we have yet to consider—it might be said, paradoxically—the most important aspect of all. With regard to Charcot's "contribution" to Freud, we must leave the intellectual plane and turn to what can only be called a veritable "affective conversion." Breuer had provided Freud with the typical example of the physician who flees before a case of hysteria, and especially from its sexual implications. There is every reason to believe that, had Freud remained in Vienna, he would hardly have ventured upon such hazardous ground. But at the Salpêtrière he witnessed the fact that a teacher of such great renown as Charcot was studying hysteria scientifically and with equanimity, without any fear of its erotic manifestations. This example was gradually to dispel Freud's resistances and involve him in the study of the "major neurosis." An examination of the prevailing sociocultural climate which he encountered in Paris will make it easier to understand how this conversion came about.

The sources that are available to us in this respect are limited. They are all derived from Freud's correspondence which, it will be recalled, has never been published in its entirety. Jones has made use of several previously unpublished letters in his biography. Nevertheless, it can hardly be doubted that there still remains—to mention only the particular period which concerns us here—material that has not so far been made available for study.

Freud's earliest experiences in Paris must certainly have been trying. On October 19, that is six days after his arrival, he wrote to Martha: "I have no one to talk to" (Freud, 1960, p. 184). He felt very isolated, speaking French badly with a strong German accent, and the physicians at the Salpêtrière, while courteous enough, were not very sociable. In addition, in the chauvinistic "Boulangiste" atmosphere prevalent in France at the time, his Teutonic accent was not helpful. It is noteworthy that, to a French doctor who one day addressed him in somewhat jingoist terms, he immediately made it clear that he was Jewish, and not German or Austrian. He eventually made friends with other foreigners: a Russian, Darkshevich, and a Viennese physician, Richetti, who practiced in Venice and was accompanied by his wife.

He found the French people "arrogant" and "inaccessible," and all Parisian women ugly. The "elegant ladies" whom he saw strolling down the Champs-Élysées struck him as most disdainful (Freud, 1960, p. 184). Apart from these distressing impressions, Freud had more immediate grounds for finding life difficult in the French capital: his grant was meager and he struggled against financial difficulties.*

However, the despondency which at first afflicted him would seem to have lifted shortly; on November 24 he wrote: "Am I under the influence of this magically attractive and repulsive city?" (Freud, 1960, p. 197). For, in spite of all its disappointments, Paris was still able to offer him certain compensations. First of all there were the theaters which he started to frequent. He saw Sarah Bernhardt in *Théodora* by Victorien Sardou; although he considered it a poor play, he was completely captivated by the actress. But he stated that he "again had to pay for this pleasure with an attack of migraine" (Freud, 1960, p. 193). He suffered, in fact, from frequent attacks of migraine and occasional fits of depression—in short, he was in that state which he was later to describe as neurasthenia, a subject of which he was to make a special study. At certain times, in order to provide himself with stamina, he resorted to small doses of cocaine. Freud was, moreover, deeply interested in the museums and monuments. He visited the Louvre and the Cluny Museums, but it was above all the Cathedral of Notre-Dame which filled him with enthusiasm.

However, of all that Freud discovered in Paris, nothing impressed him as deeply as Charcot's personality. He was immediately won over

---

* Gicklhorn and Gicklhorn (1960, p. 10) have attempted to assess Freud's financial resources at the time.

by his brilliant mind and his manner, and saw in him "one of the greatest physicians and a man whose common sense borders on genius" (Freud, 1960, p. 196). Eight years later, in the obituary notice which he wrote on Charcot, he was to express an equally great admiration: "As a teacher," said Freud, "Charcot was positively fascinating. Each of his lectures was a little work of art in construction and composition; it was perfect in form and made such an impression that for the rest of the day one could not get the sound of what he had said out of one's ears or the thought of what he had demonstrated out of one's mind" (Freud, 1893b, p. 17). In the same article, Freud did not hesitate to compare his teacher's achievements with those of Pinel.

THE CRISIS

Was it possible for Freud to overcome the difficulties encountered during his stay in Paris, through the compensations that we have mentioned? In actual fact he appears to have hesitated for some time between the wish to leave and the desire to stay. On October 19, he wrote: "I expect so little from my stay here," but two days later (after his first interview with Charcot) he stated: ". . . my stay here is going to be well worth it, this I can see clearly" (Freud, 1960, pp. 183, 188).

Freud does, however, seem to have passed through an acute crisis in early December, 1885. Basing his account on the letters of this period, Jones (1953, p. 228) concludes that Freud was not happy in Paris and was on the point of returning to Vienna. On December 3, he had declared his intention to give up his work in the Salpêtrière laboratory.* Then, on December 9, he told Martha of his decision to ask Charcot's permission to translate the third volume of his *Leçons* (Jones, 1953, p. 229). On December 12, he was able to convey to Martha the good news that he had obtained his teacher's consent (Freud, 1960, p. 201). Henceforth, there was no further question of his leaving the Salpêtrière, and while mentioning his

---

* He did not, however, withdraw from the laboratory forthwith. From his letter to Martha on January 27, 1886 (Freud, 1960, p. 212), we may gather that he was still working there, albeit with the intention of abandoning his studies on cerebral anatomy.

proposed visit in the near future to his fiancée, at Wandsbeck (near Hamburg), he added that he would be returning to Paris right away. Thus, Freud's attitude underwent a complete reversal, the reasons for which we must attempt to ascertain.

There are very few indications as to the motives which might have induced Freud to leave Paris at the beginning of December. This intention coincided with his decision to abandon the Salpêtrière laboratory. On this last point we have slightly more information. Having already on December 3 mentioned the unsatisfactory working conditions, Freud in his next letter advanced "seven convincing reasons" for his decision, according to Jones (1953, p. 231) who does not, however, reproduce them. Freud's biographer believes, moreover, that a personal factor, of an emotional as well as a practical nature, may also have been involved. Freud may indeed have feared that he would become far too deeply engrossed in laboratory work, at the risk of causing him to neglect his bride-to-be. Also, with his impending marriage in view, he may well have considered that clinical work would offer him greater financial security (Jones, 1953, pp. 231-232).

In any event, in Jones's opinion these were not the essential motives. He is inclined to regard the "seven convincing reasons" as a simple rationalization concealing the fundamental reason, namely, the fascination for psychopathology that Charcot had implanted in Freud. It can be said that in this respect Freud had found a great deal more than he expected. As we have seen, he was himself to state in his "Paris Report" that he had been moved to go to Paris above all by "the certainty of finding collected together in the Salpêtrière a large assemblage of clinical material" (Freud, 1886a, p. 5). And indeed, during his stay in Paris, not only did he have the opportunity to study a large number of neurological cases, but also, and especially, neuroses which, in the light of Charcot's completely new interpretations, were leading him toward psychopathology.

One cannot, therefore, at first sight perceive any causal relationship whatsoever between his decision to abandon the Salpêtrière laboratory and his intention to leave Paris. His obvious interest in psychology might well have been expected, on the contrary, to induce him to stay. This is in fact what he eventually did, but, in our opinion, only at the cost of an internal struggle which we would here attempt to investigate further.

What had Freud actually witnessed during these famous sessions where hysterical cases were demonstrated? We have already described what he was able to see at the Salpêtrière, and in particular the benefit which he derived from observing the major attacks in formulating his etiological theory of hysteria. If, however, the sessions at the Salpêtrière were so conducive to Freud's intellectual enrichment, the question arises: what led him to consider evading them? In the absence of any indication in this respect, whether on his part or that of his biographers, we would put forward the following hypothesis: while these sessions provided Freud with full satisfaction on the intellectual plane, they aroused in him, on the emotional plane, a combination of attraction and repulsion, for the hysterical attacks which he had witnessed presented an obviously erotic character.* As we have mentioned earlier, in some of the experiments at the Salpêtrière female patients showed, as a result of stimulation of "hysterogenic zones," sexual responses which sometimes reached a state of orgasm.

To be sure, this was not the first occasion on which Freud sensed the existence of a relationship between hysteria and sexuality. The idea had already been suggested to him by the history of Anna O., which he had learned of only at second hand; now he was actually an eyewitness. Merely hearing of the case of Anna O. had filled him with anxiety and apprehension, but the situation in which he now found himself was more trying by far. The erotic scenes at present enacted before his eyes could not fail to induce in him at the same time both a wish and a repression.

No doubt he experienced very similar reactions in the face of what he regarded as the erotic atmosphere prevailing in Paris. On December 3, he wrote to his fiancée's sister (Minna Bernays): "Suffice it to say that the city and its inhabitants strike me as uncanny; the people seem to me of a different species from ourselves; I feel they are all possessed of a thousand demons. . . . I don't think they know the meaning of shame or fear; the women no less than the

---

* This can be readily observed in the previously mentioned film.

men crowd round nudities as much as they do round corpses in the morgue or the ghastly posters in the streets announcing a new novel in this or that newspaper and simultaneously showing a sample of its content" (Freud, 1960, p. 199).

At all events, he was not taken in, as were so many foreigners, by the "erotic myth" of the French capital. For example, there is no indication that he ever went to see the French Cancan at the Moulin Rouge. On one occasion, it is true, he found himself in a "place of ill repute," albeit quite by accident. His friends, the Richettis, took him out to dinner one evening, to what they believed to be a restaurant, only to discover that it was a high-class brothel (Jones, 1953, p. 206).

From all available information, Freud was at that time leading a life of sexual continence. When his nephew John, visiting him in Paris, "tried to sound him out" as to whether he kept a mistress, he took this as a joke (letter to Martha, November 26, 1885—Freud, 1960, p. 198). One cannot, therefore, rule out the hypothesis that such abstinence in the midst of the temptations of Parisian life may conceivably have given rise to solitary and guilt-producing practices, which could have caused depression and induced in him that state of neurasthenia, of which he was later to note (in February, 1893) that it is but a sexual neurosis, occurring in men between the ages of 20 and 30 and resulting from masturbation. He observed that "those who have been seduced by women at an early age have escaped neurasthenia" (Freud, 1950, p. 180).

Freud's preoccupation with neurasthenia calls for a fairly lengthy discussion here, because, together with the study of hysteria, it played an important part in the evolution of his thought.

In 1886, referring to his own case, Freud ascribed to neurasthenia the following etiology: ". . . my tiredness is a sort of minor illness; neurasthenia it is called; produced by the toils, the worries and excitements of these last years . . ." (letter to Martha, February 2—Freud, 1960, p. 213).

It may here be recalled that, chronologically, the concept and the term "neurasthenia" were introduced by Beard in 1869 and, very soon popularized, came to comprise a number of disorders such as physical and psychical asthenia, insomnia, various "neuralgic" pains, dyspepsia, and a host of other symptoms which are today referable to the psychosomatic or psychofunctional sphere. The concept of sexual neurasthenia (supposedly the result of sexual excesses) seems to have appeared about 1880,* and another work on this subject, also by Beard, was published in a German edition in 1885 (original, posthumous American edition, 1884). The third edition of Krafft-Ebing's *Lehrbuch der Psychiatrie* (Textbook of Psychiatry) (1888), deals with the subject in detail (but even more rigidly than Beard).

In February, 1893, however, Freud sent Fliess (with the admonition to keep it away from his young wife) a manuscript draft for a study of the etiology of the neuroses. In this document he employed terms that were meaningful at the time and frequently used by Krafft-Ebing in his writings: *"sexuelle Neurasthenie," "Spinalneurasthenie."* Moreover, while accepting "as a recognized fact that *neurasthenia* is a frequent consequence of an abnormal sexual life," he put forward the hypothesis that it is "always *only* a sexual neurosis" (Freud, 1950, pp. 179-184).

This postulate—the sexual etiology of neurasthenia—was in fact to constitute the first link in the chain of Freudian theory of the sexual etiology of *all* neuroses.

Thus Freud was to distinguish the *"actual"* neuroses, whose purely "somatic" and, as it were, contemporary causation was, in his view, to be sought in some *"actual"* (i.e., present) disorder of the patient's sexual life (e.g., coitus interruptus, but equally masturbation).

In contradistinction to the *"actual"* neuroses, namely neurasthenia and anxiety neurosis (which in his view were not accessible to analysis), he recognized the *psychoneuroses*, of "early" etiology (no longer somatic, but psychical—which must be sought in long past conflicts of the patient's childhood). These comprised hysteria and obsessional neurosis, which were regarded as amenable to analysis.

The differences and contrasts between these two categories (the first of which has today been superseded by psychosomatic concepts) were therefore clearly apparent. As we have seen, their common causation, that kind of "sexual bond" which is to be found in one and the other, had already been noticed long before Freud.

---

* In fact, as early as 1869 Beard mentioned sexual excesses as one of the causes of neurasthenia (Beard, 1869, p. 218).

But it is he who paradoxically, while definitely lagging behind his contemporaries, nevertheless discovered this "sexual bond" linked with every neurosis. Here one can plainly see the emergence in Freud of that attitude of unconscious rejection of sexual problems, that blind spot which he would retain for many years to come.

The task therefore remained of elucidating this "sexual causation" and dismantling its mechanism. To be sure, Benedikt had sensed the possible etiological significance of sexual trauma in early life; but it was Freud who, causing thereby a real public scandal, was to develop his theory of infantile sexuality and incorporate it as an integral element in his general theory of the neuroses.

Let us, however, return to Freud's earliest ideas on "neurasthenia-due-to-masturbation." It should be remembered that, at the end of the nineteenth century, masturbation was held to be a vice, at the extreme limit of sexual deviation and invariably pathogenic. People did not, in fact, know (or did not wish to know?) how widespread, not to say commonplace, is its occurrence, nor that its alleged pathological implications are in no way fatal. It is true that investigations on the sexual behavior of "normal" individuals were unknown at the time (more than half a century would elapse before such studies as the Kinsey report were undertaken).

Paradoxically, it was in fact Freud's investigations which brought about a radical change in the narrow outlook then prevalent on the subject of masturbation, of which a most revealing bibliographical illustration is provided in the *Catalogue des Sciences médicales* of the Bibliothèque Nationale in Paris (Tome II, 1873, section "Onanisme," pp. 164-175). From the mid-eighteenth century the most influential work on the "disorders produced by masturbation" was that written by Tissot (1758), of which some forty different editions or reprints were published between then and 1905.* Moreover, throughout the nineteenth century a number of authors wrote various other admonitory works on the subject, with such titles as *Les Souffrances du jeune Hubert* (1805) ("The Trials of Young Hu-

---

* Tissot's treatise on masturbation was first published in Latin, together with a dissertation on fevers, in Lausanne, 1758. A French translation, with considerable additions, was published in Lausanne, 1760. The first English translation (from the most recent French edition) appeared in London in 1766.

bert") ; *Avis aux jeunes Gens des deux Sexes* (1810) ("Advice to Young People of both Sexes") ; *Le Tissot moderne* (1815) ("The Modern Tissot") ; *Mémento du Père de Famille* (1860) ("The Father's Memorandum") , and so forth.

Side by side with the production of these popular works, whose content showed very little change up to the First World War, leading psychiatrists were propounding countless theories on the pernicious effects of masturbation. Among others, Krafft-Ebing (who in 1888, in the third edition of his above-mentioned *Lehrbuch,* expanded the views already expressed in the first edition of 1879-1880) regarded masturbation as a sexual aberration which could result in insanity *("Irresein")* , including the most severe psychoses—*"onanistische Psychosen"* (this, of course, in subjects with a so-called neuropathic predisposition—*"neuropathische Constitution"*). In those not so predisposed, the consequences were confined to neurasthenia* *("Neurasthenia sexualis"*—Krafft-Ebing, 1888, pp. 514-515) . Spontaneous (involuntary) "pollutions," in Krafft-Ebing's opinion, already constituted a pathological sign insofar as they caused severe damage to the ejaculatory center (the lumbar spinal cord) and led to disorders of erection, lumbo-sacral pain, and generalized asthenia *("Neurasthenia spinalis")* . It should, however, be noted that Krafft-Ebing (1879, p. 184) warned against the reading—which he held to be frankly pathogenic—of popular books of antimasturbation propaganda.

There is a complete contrast with current views—today it is only compulsive masturbation (in subjects caught up in obsessional sys-

---

* Krafft-Ebing, like most psychiatrists of the period, was imbued with the theories of predisposition and degeneration which, introduced and developed in France by Morel (1875), were to prevail in France as elsewhere for half a century. The evolution of these theories was the subject of a detailed historical study by Genil-Perrin (1913) and a useful summary by Ackerknecht (1959: "The theory of degeneration," pp. 47-51).

Freud was just as much influenced by these theories when he wrote to Martha from Paris on February 10, 1886 (Freud, 1960, pp. 222-3). He had suddenly recalled, regretfully, that one of his first cousins was a feeble-minded hydrocephalic, another went insane at an early age, and a third died an epileptic. He had, therefore, said he, to acknowledge a considerable "neuropathological taint" in his family. When he told Martha that, as a neurologist, he was "about as worried by such things as a sailor is by the sea," did he see himself on the way to insanity—or else arrested at the stage of mere neurasthenia? Could it not be that these and other such fears were instrumental in orienting him towards the study of psychopathology?

tems) that calls for psychiatric attention—and it is the total absence of masturbation in adolescence which is an early indication of a pathological state. But the evolution was a slow one, before that stage was reached. As late as 1912, the concluding remarks, compiled by Freud, on the lengthy discussions at the Vienna Psychoanalytical Society clearly show that, if at that time masturbation was no longer regarded as a perversion, its harmlessness was, at the very least, still a matter for debate.*

Not only was Freud sexually continent while in Paris, but he almost certainly remained so during the four years of his engagement. In Eissler's view (1971, p. 261), it was no accident that the seeds of a "new psychology," destined to influence the whole of Western culture, took shape during this long period of frustration. Eissler goes on to consider the "sex life of genius," without however being altogether convinced (1971, p. 243) that Freud ceased all sexual relations at the age of forty, as some writers have asserted on the basis of a letter which he wrote to Fliess.** Eissler mentions several famous men of science and letters whose creative genius, so it is said, was concomitant with sexual continence. Newton never had intercourse, never masturbated, and considered nocturnal emissions to be grave sins; Gregor Mendel never once had sexual relations; Goethe first

---

* According to Roazen (1969) who interviewed Oliver Freud, the father-cum-educator Sigmund Freud had not freed himself from the prejudices of his age (*Zeitgeist*) and would seem to have cautioned his son in rather severe terms—to the extent of giving rise to a certain awkwardness in their relations.

** Eissler, who states that he is "reasonably certain" that this was not the case and that Freud had on that occasion succumbed to a passing mood of pessimism, in fact cites but a few words from the letter to Fliess of March 11, 1900, removed from their context: "I have finished with begetting children." Here is the complete sentence (which occurs, it is true, in a letter that is definitely depressive in its tone):

"When my work is over I live like a pleasure-seeking Philistine. You know how limited my pleasures are. I must not smoke heavy cigars, alcohol does not mean anything to me, I have finished with begetting children, and I am cut off from contact with people" (Freud, 1954, p. 312).

Freud, therefore, places the pleasures of smoking and drinking on the same plane with procreative activity. Even allowing that, on this particular day, he had given way to a mere change of mood, it must be admitted that this sentence is open to more than one interpretation. At all events, on October 31, 1897, at the age of 41 years, he wrote to Fliess: "For someone like me, too, sexual excitation is no longer of use" (Freud, 1950, p. 267).

It seems to us impossible to arrive at even the most tentative conclusion since we shall obviously never be in a position to ascertain the true facts.

had intercourse at the age of 35; and as for Balzac, he allegedly deplored the slightest nocturnal emission, believing it to be a loss of grey matter (a not uncommon misconception in psychiatric patients) (see Eissler's references, 1971, pp. 244-5, 261).

These examples are, in our opinion, certainly far too limited to justify such far-reaching conclusions—if we but call to mind the names of so many men of genius whose sexual activity was reputed to be "normal," if not indeed considerably developed. In one particular respect, however, we might find ourselves in agreement with Eissler's theory to the extent that we are prepared to accept that Freud remained "continent" for four years. On the assumption that this continence was associated with masturbation; that the latter was (so he believed) leading him to a state of neurasthenia; and that he thereupon proceeded to study his own neurasthenia—it does in fact then become possible to concede that this "continence" may have oriented his genius towards his well-known discoveries (amongst others).

Let us return to Freud's stay in Paris. His wish to avoid laying himself open to feminine seduction may well have influenced in part the choice of his companions at this time. The language difficulties and his French colleagues' xenophobia, to which we have already referred, were probably not the only reasons for Freud's sense of isolation. The resident physicians at the Salpêtrière had a more unconventional way of life; they were always pursuing women and they had mistresses. Freud happened on occasion to have lunch in the interns' mess, but he is not known ever to have taken part in their corporate "mini-saturnalia," where wine flowed freely and which the interns had christened "tonus." He may have felt unconsciously that such behavior was liable to lead him into "dangerous" byways.

This, in all probability, determined his choice of a friend—a Russian colleague, Darkshevich—whose habits matched his own in their austerity. Freud realized that they were bound to get on together, as he wrote to Martha on November 4, 1885: ". . . it turned out that he is just as much in love as I am and waiting for letters in the very same way, and this brought us that much closer. As he is not looking for any form of social life or pleasure, he is just the right kind of company for me" (Freud, 1960, pp. 189-190).

Nevertheless, however blameless his everyday life in Paris, Freud could certainly not have experienced without affective involvement the erotic stimulation provided by the spectacle of the patients at the Salpêtrière (or indeed by that of the streets). The internal conflict thus maintained must at a certain point have reached sufficient intensity to induce him to leave Paris—in other words, to run away from hysteria, just as Breuer had done. It is, however, important to remember that this situation arose very soon after his decision to abandon the laboratory. So long as he still worked there, Freud may have persuaded himself that he was not yielding to his attraction to erotic manifestations. But as soon as he had given up his laboratory work, and irrespective of the intellectual or emotional reasons for his decision, he may well have felt that his defenses were down and that henceforth he was vulnerable to sexual temptations. Therefore his wish to escape.

THE DECISION

For all that, Freud did not leave. In his letter of December 12, in which he told Martha of Charcot's consent to his translating the book and informed her that there was no more question of his leaving Paris, he was full of optimism and overjoyed (Freud, 1960, p. 201). This translation did not, however, really compel him to prolong his stay, and it may be assumed that, from the moment when he first requested this work, he had already decided to remain in Paris. He had, therefore, resolved his personal crisis in his own way by seeking to identify with his teacher as a person (and the latter's consent to the translation confirmed him in this intent). How then was Freud able to resolve his conflicts through identification with Charcot?

As we see it, the answer must be sought on two different planes. On one hand, in depth, Freud felt that he had received his teacher's permission to concern himself with sexuality, just as a son, on reaching maturity, would likewise receive his father's consent. On the other hand, Charcot provided him with the model for a rationalization tending to "de-carnalize" sexuality, for he had, as it were, severed the connection—confirmed though this had been since Hippocrates by etymology alone—between the uterus (and thus the genital system) and hysteria, and had transformed the latter into a highly "respectable" disorder of the nervous system.

We have seen how Charcot's pupils contrived to mechanize the sexual manifestations in hysterical patients by reducing them to strictly physiological and impersonal processes. For a long time, Freud adhered to this point of view. In his "Paris Report," he already emphasized that Charcot "began by reducing the connection of the neurosis with the genital system to its correct proportions by demonstrating the unsuspected frequency of cases of male hysteria" (Freud, 1886a, p. 11). He subsequently elaborated this view in his lecture of October, 1886, delivered before the Viennese Medical Society. It recurred unchanged in his article on hysteria which appeared in 1888 in Villaret's *Handwörterbuch*. The significance of sexual factors in the etiology of hysteria was, in his view, "as a rule overestimated," and in support of this contention he pointed out that this illness occurs in girls and boys who have not yet reached sexual maturity (Freud, 1888, p. 50).

Almost ten years were to elapse before Freud was able to free himself from this rationalizing and reassuring interpretation of hysteria. It was not until 1894-1895 that he was to propound publicly his theory of the sexual etiology of the neuroses. He particularly emphasized that this was an entirely personal hypothesis. Thus, in 1896, he wrote: ". . . I will only remark that the singling out of the sexual factor in the etiology of hysteria springs at least from no preconceived opinion on my part. The two investigators as whose pupil I began my studies of hysteria, Charcot and Breuer, were far from having any such presupposition; in fact they had a personal disinclination to it which I originally shared" (Freud, 1896b, p. 199).

Freud was, however, later to contradict this statement when in 1914 he affirmed that both of his teachers had in fact spoken to him of the sexual nature of hysteria. So far as Charcot is concerned, there is the well-known episode related in the paper, "On the History of the Psychoanalytic Movement." At one of his receptions, Charcot was talking to Brouardel* about a married couple, where the wife

---

* Paul Brouardel was Professor of Forensic Medicine in Paris at the time, and an outstanding authority in this field.

suffered from hysteria and the husband was impotent, and "suddenly broke out with great animation: '*Mais dans des cas pareils c'est toujours la chose génitale, toujours . . . toujours . . . toujours*' " ("But in such cases it is always the genital question—always, always, always") (Freud, 1914, pp. 13-14). As to Breuer, he had told Freud, around 1881-1883, that in neurotic cases the explanation was always to be found in "*secrets d'alcôve*" ("secrets of the marriage-bed") (Freud, 1914, p. 13). Freud further recorded that, early in his medical career (in 1886), the eminent Viennese gynecologist Chrobak had asked him to take over one of his female patients whose marriage had never been consummated. And taking Freud aside, he told him that the sole prescription for such a case "is familiar enough to us, but we cannot order it": viz., "*penis normalis*" in repeated doses (1914, pp. 14-15).

It is indeed quite possible that Freud may have blotted out the memory of other remarks of the same kind, in view of the fact that, at this time, the concept of a correlation between hysteria and sexual disorders (and as we have seen, similarly between sexual excesses and neurasthenia) was "in the wind." It was even the subject of articles, amongst which may be mentioned a study by Benedikt (1863, p. 713) and a later work by the same author on the significance in hysterical cases of traumatic sexual disturbances, e.g., the rape or masturbation of little girls by adults, etc. (Benedikt, 1889, p. 1613).

In Vienna at the end of the nineteenth century, in spite of, or perhaps because of, the Victorian puritanism that prevailed (or at least, appeared to do so), there was much talk about sexuality. In 1886, Krafft-Ebing first published his *Psychopathia Sexualis* (and it was he who introduced the terms "sadism" and "masochism"), and in the following years there appeared in Austria, Germany and elsewhere numerous works on sexual pathology.

Such being the case, we may well ask ourselves why Freud's works on sexuality aroused such widespread antagonistic and impassioned reactions. One of the reasons was undoubtedly the fact that the authors of the period described sexual disorders in a certain number of people regarded as abnormal and not far short of "immoral," whereas Freud, seemingly in defiance of "bourgeois morality," discerned in every individual, of every social class*—and from earliest infancy—latent tendencies to abnormal behavior. These tendencies were, to be sure, most often unrealized, but he held them to be normal, not to say indispensable, stages of the process of development of the personality.

According to Clavreul (1970), Freud's and Krafft-Ebing's contemporaries would undoubtedly have passed judgment on the two men in the following terms: "Freud says things that are altogether indecent and entirely unconnected with medicine, whereas Krafft-Ebing, quite to the contrary, is a teacher whose concern is the attainment of the greatest possible truth in the description of the psychopathology of mental patients . . ." (Clavreul, 1970, p. 201). And he goes on to say that we are today witnessing "a strange reversal of things, whereby he who was considered obscene now becomes a most serious author, while the grave professor adds his contribution to the library of erotica" (1970, p. 202). Why, asks Clavreul, did Krafft-Ebing employ a complicated vocabulary, crammed with Latin words (*Psychopathia sexualis*, etc.)? Quite certainly to try "to defuse the erotic nature of what he proffered for our information. He himself could not really have been in any doubt as to the licentious character of this scientific work" (1970, p. 202).

In conclusion, it should be emphasized that the works on sexuality of the end of the nineteenth century must have been known to Freud. It is, however, clear that for many years, whether intentionally or not, Freud had forgotten them—as he did his teacher's comments. He had indeed, at the time, been deeply shocked by Charcot's remarks on "the genital question" (*"la chose génitale"*). Having surrounded himself by the system of defenses already mentioned, he could not but be "unreceptive" to the implications of such views. The Charcot whom he had chosen as both teacher and model was the scientist who, in his clinical teaching, dissociated hysteria from sexuality. But, at least on the conscious plane, Freud was unaware of the other Charcot, who in private had such flashes of intuition. Some ten years later he was to discover—or rediscover—this other Charcot, and it was then that he developed his teacher's intuitive

---

* In physicians, too—but no more nor less than in others.

perception on the basis of extensive clinical experience to which he brought exceptional discernment. We shall see that in the meantime his discovery of a concept of prime importance, the transference, had enabled him to "manipulate sexuality" while protecting himself from its effects.

RETURN TO VIENNA

Freud was supposed to read his "Paris Report" before the Society of Medicine in Vienna on June 4, 1886, but, as the program for this meeting was already fully taken up, his paper was postponed until October 15.

We propose here to lay special emphasis on this lecture, "On Male Hysteria," for it throws light on the embryonic development of the ideas which, under the influence of Charcot, had germinated in Freud's mind. It was, moreover, the cause of a rupture between Freud and Viennese medical circles, a lack of understanding between medicine and psychoanalytical concepts which in some respects has persisted to this day. Contemporary medicine has hardly ever admitted the existence of the unconscious and phantasy as factors in numerous disorders—not even in the case of obvious conversion hysteria (whose psychological etiology was so brilliantly demonstrated in Charcot's study on experimental paralyses).

Charcot's "anatomo-physiological substratum" (mentioned in connection with the hysterical paralyses) was at most but a hypothesis on his part. Nowadays, one has at times cause to wonder whether this may not have become a certainty and a "course of action," for to any *local* injury, pain or affection, a precise *local cause* will inevitably be assigned forthwith—entailing at the very start clinical examinations, various kinds of investigation, etc. One can imagine, on a national scale in each country, the economic repercussions of such a "policy of diagnosis."

As to treatment, be it medical or surgical, its financial implications are even worse—and disastrous for the patient's stability. One of the authors has given an account of the caricatural instance of a patient (with conversion symptoms affecting the abdominal muscles) on whom operations, ranging from the abdomen to the brain, were performed on no less than *twenty* consecutive occasions (Chertok, 1972. This case of pathological surgical addiction is also presented in the film "Hysteria, Body Language").

The above-mentioned problems are, in fact, only indices of a deeper and strictly "conceptual" crisis of contemporary medicine, as also of the state of arrest which it has reached. This situation is well described in an article by Bourguignon (1971).

The psychosomatic movement, which originated well over forty years ago, had already attempted, albeit with very limited success, to bridge the gap between traditional medicine and psychoanalysis. At the level of the problems arising from etiopathogenic theories, it is hardly necessary to say that we are still at the stage of hypotheses. On the practical plane, some degree of "integration" of psychiatrists in medical teams has been attempted (psychiatric liaison). For some twenty years a pragmatic solution has been sought in providing the practicing physician, and indeed the medical student, with psychological training (Balint, 1957, whose ideas were developed in France by Sapir, 1972). This trend of providing mental health training for the medical profession at present attracts the interest of only a very small minority of practitioners. It encounters considerable resistance on the part of doctors as well as a certain reserve in psychoanalytic circles (Balint, 1966)—a reserve which is not without recalling the somewhat ambivalent and oscillating attitude adopted by Freud towards the medical world.*

Moreover, the importance in Freud's life of the circumstances surrounding the lecture of 1886 clearly shows the difficulty of attaining complete objectivity in the field of historical research. And here again we may perhaps be allowed a brief digression on the subject

---

* At first Freud hoped to win over the medical profession to the theories of psychoanalysis and it was certainly not without satisfaction that he saw some of his followers taking up the study of medicine (e.g., Sándor Radó, Therese Benedek, and Tausk).

While remaining aloof from the traditional psychiatric circles in Vienna, he was by no means displeased at having recruited pupils from their ranks (Helene Deutsch, Heinz Hartmann, etc.). He even went so far as to state, around 1916, that if psychiatry constituted, as it were, the anatomy of mental life, then psychoanalysis was in fact its histology (Freud, 1917b, p. 255).

From these aims restricted to the medical field, he wished to proceed to a quasi-universal concept of psychoanalysis applied to the human sciences as a whole. To this end he called upon non-medical personnel, as much for therapeutic practice as for pure research.

of works on psychoanalytic history. These, in fact, present a fairly typical cross section of the different "ways of writing history."

Some authors, such as Andersson (1962), from the very outset exclude all mention of Freud's personality. Others (e.g., Sachs, 1944) state quite plainly that they are in no way concerned with objectivity. Stone (1971), a professional writer, does not deny the novelistic nature of his book, *The Passions of the Mind—A Novel of Sigmund Freud.* Martha Robert's penetrating study (1964) also belongs, in a certain sense, to the realm of literature; starting from a series of radio-broadcast talks, she made a significant contribution to our knowledge of Freud in his contemporary setting. As for Wittels, reconsidering in 1933 the biography of Freud which he had written ten years earlier (Wittels, 1924), he felt that it was "defamatory" and proffered it as an "example of his ambivalence." Jones, who ventured to undertake a detailed study (1953-57) of Freud's personality, did not escape most intense criticism. To give but one fairly recent example, he was accused by Cranefield (1970) of an "ambivalent pseudo-franchise."

Not long before, Roazen (1969) —Professor of Sociology at Harvard, and not a psychoanalyst—brought a serious accusation against Freud, whom he held morally responsible for the suicide in 1919 of Tausk, one of Freud's pupils since 1908. While Roazen's contention appears to us contestable, it is not proposed to discuss it in detail here. Suffice it to say that, in terms of traditional psychiatry, there is nothing to show that Roazen is correct in asserting that this was a case of "reactive-exogenous" suicide. It could very well have been a suicide of essentially "endogenous" type.

Eissler (1971), who is Secretary of the Sigmund Freud Archives in New York, took up the challenge most forcefully, denouncing the defamation of which, in his view, Freud would thus be the victim, and regarding it moreover as an all-out attack on psychoanalysis.

Are we then to conclude that, by reason of its imperfections, every psychobiography is worthless? Such an undertaking undoubtedly induces in the historian a sense of humility, for he may be proved wrong in ten or a hundred years' time. It is, above all, manifestly influenced by the biographer's personality and his affective involvement (as also, in this instance, by his personal attitude toward psychoanalysis), however constantly he may strive for objectivity. In the words of Paul Valéry (1928), "Objective is what does not depend upon the *history* of the observer."

Many, therefore, are the hazards and pitfalls thus encountered. Nevertheless, we have been able in the present work to make advantageous use of the psychobiographic approach; but only insofar as it seemed likely to throw light on the mechanism of some of Freud's discoveries in one of the critical periods of his life.

It remains that some will regard our views as consisting in part of questionable interpretation. With the passage of time, strong feelings will become attenuated. In this way it may become possible to attain true objectivity, if indeed the latter is at all conceivable.

The Lecture of October 15, 1886

In his *Autobiographical Study,* written in 1925, Freud described this meeting, held in Vienna in October, 1886: "The duty devolved upon me of giving a report before the 'Gesellschaft der Aerzte' [Society of Medicine] upon what I had seen and learnt with Charcot. But I met with a bad reception. Persons of authority, such as the chairman (Bamberger, the physician), declared that what I said was incredible. Meynert challenged me to find some cases in Vienna similar to those which I described and to present them before the Society. I tried to do so; but the senior physicians in whose departments I found any such cases refused to allow me to observe them or to work at them. One of them, an old surgeon, actually broke out with the exclamation: 'But, my dear Sir, how can you talk such nonsense? *Hysteron* (*sic*) * means the uterus. So how can a man be hysterical?' I objected in vain that what I wanted was not to have my diagnosis approved, but to have the case put at my disposal. At length, outside the hospital, I came upon a case of classical hemianaesthesia in a man, and demonstrated it before the 'Gesellschaft der Aerzte.' This time I was applauded, but no further interest was taken in me. The impression that the high authorities had rejected my innovations remained unshaken; and with my hysteria in men *and my production of hysterical paralyses by suggestion, I found myself forced into the*

---

* The Greek for "womb" is *hystera.*

Opposition. . . . It is a whole generation since I have visited the 'Gesellschaft der Aerzte' " (Freud, 1925a, pp. 15-16—italics added.)

Commenting on this account, Jones (1953, pp. 252-255) considers that Freud may have shown inordinate sensitiveness here, and incidentally draws attention to an inaccurate statement in that Freud did, in fact, subsequently attend several other meetings of the Medical Society. Furthermore, in his anecdote concerning the word *"hysteron,"* Freud gives the impression that his audience denied the existence of male hysteria, whereas Jones points out that, quite to the contrary, this condition was well known to them. The implication that the Viennese doctors were ignoramuses in this respect is thus no more than a legend, kept alive by many a historian of psychoanalysis. To be sure, there were no doubt a few of them, such as the old surgeon whose remarks are recorded by Freud, but it was by no means true of the majority.

Ellenberger, another historian of psychotherapy, has in the last few years reexamined the circumstances of this lecture of Freud's* after undertaking a meticulous study supported by all the relevant documents available: viz., the abridged text of the discussion which appeared in the Medical Society's Bulletin,** and the accounts of the proceedings (five in number) published in the medical press.*** In addition, Ellenberger consulted the "Paris Report" which Freud (1886a) submitted to the *Professoren-Collegium* of the Faculty of Medicine on returning to Vienna. It is indeed generally accepted that the text of the original paper did not, in all probability, differ substantially from that of the "Paris Report." (Neither the original text of the lecture nor the shorthand transcript of the discussion appears to have been preserved.)

---

* In evaluating Ellenberger's views on the lecture of October 15, we had at our disposal an article on the subject which he had published in French (1968). More recently he produced in English an erudite work of truly monumental proportions (900 pages), based on a wealth of historical material and entitled *The Discovery of the Unconscious* (1970). Here we once again encounter the views previously expounded in the above-mentioned article.

** *Anzeiger der K.K. Gesellschaft der Aerzte in Wien,* October 28, 1886, Nr. 25: 149-152.

*** *Allgemeine Wiener med. Zeitung,* 1886, 31, Nr. 4: 506-507. *Münchener med. Wochenschrift,* 1886, Nr. 43: 768. *Wiener med. Blätter,* 1886, Nr. 42: 1292-94. *Wiener med. Presse,* 1886, Nr. 27: 1407-10. *Wiener med. Wochenschrift,* 1886, Nr. 43: 1445-47.

Through this critical, comparative study, Ellenberger has been able to retrace the proceedings of the 1886 meeting more accurately and more fully than had hitherto been possible. He emphasizes that, in order to understand adequately the discussion to which Freud's paper gave rise, it is necessary to place it in the setting of the controversy that was current at the time concerning the psychical disorders consequent upon railway accidents ("railway spine," to which we have already referred). It was the actual existence of this "post-traumatic" hysteria which was contested, and not that of "classical" male hysteria, which was generally recognized. This distinction, clearly established by Ellenberger, dispels such confusion as may have been perpetuated by the above-quoted passage of Freud's, which refers only to male hysteria in general.

In his lecture, Freud expounded Charcot's theories on hysteria, and went on to describe a case observed at the Salpêtrière (certainly that of Pin—, as we have shown), which he designated as post-traumatic hysteria: a young man who, following an accident, presented a paralysis of one arm and hysterical stigmata. But Freud's medical audience refused to accept his interpretation. In their view, "post-traumatic" neurosis could not be equated with hysteria.

Freud retained a deep feeling of bitterness after this somewhat cool reception. Ellenberger has speculated at length on the reasons for the latter. In his opinion, the paper suffered from a lack of originality in that Freud confined himself to reporting one of Charcot's observations instead of presenting the personal, original contribution which tradition demanded. He also asserts that Charcot's ideas were already known in Vienna and thus were not regarded there as anything very new. Referring to the Viennese doctors, he states: "What must have annoyed them most was to hear Freud attribute to Charcot the discovery that hysteria was neither malingering, nor the result of a disease of the genital organs" (Ellenberger, 1968, p. 925). Indeed, as he further remarks, "these two points were known in Vienna, where Benedikt had been teaching them for close on twenty years."

As we have said, to speak of malingering was not out of place, for there still existed at the time, in Vienna and elsewhere, a prejudice linking hysteria to malingering (a view to which, even today, some physicians insistently adhere). At the period with which we are concerned, Krafft-Ebing had felt obliged to state: "I am unable to accept the current view that all hysterical patients show a tendency to deceitfulness and malingering" (1888, p. 4).

With regard to the concept of diseases of the female genital organs as a cause of hysteria, no clear evidence emerges from the available reports to show that Freud ever referred to a "disease of the genital organs." In these reports, the expression used is sometimes *"Reiz-zustände der weiblichen Geschlechtsorgane"** (states of irritability of the female genital organs), and sometimes *"Eigenthümlichkeiten des Geschlechtes"*** (peculiarities of the genital functions). In his "Paris Report," upon which we can rely, Freud employs the term *"Genitalreizungen"* (genital irritation or excitation), a concept upon which, as he states, hysteria was in earlier times supposed to be dependent. He goes on to say that Charcot "began by reducing the connection of the neurosis with the genital system (*"Genitalsystem"*) to its correct proportions by demonstrating the unsuspected frequency of cases of male hysteria and especially of traumatic hysteria" (Freud, 1886a, p. 11).

So far as hysteria in males is concerned, according to one of the reports on his lecture, Freud would appear to have considered that the relationship between this type of hysteria and sexual activities was of no particular interest, because, as he emphasized, the hystero-genic zones (inducing the attack), which in women are often situated in the ovarian region, are similarly encountered in men in a corresponding area of the body.***

From all these facts it is clear that Freud did not refer to "diseases of the genital organs," but to the relation between hysteria and sexuality in general. We have already seen how and for what reasons, during his stay in Paris and even later, Freud developed a selective blindness toward the role of sexual factors in hysteria.

As to the views on hysteria which Benedikt taught, it should be noted that he was not their sole exponent. Thus, Moritz Rosenthal, Professor of Neuropathology in the Faculty of Medicine of Vienna

---

* *Wiener med. Wochenschrift*, ibid.
** *Wiener med. Presse*, ibid.
*** *Münchener med. Wochenschrift*, ibid.

(who opened the discussion which followed Freud's paper), had in 1875 published a work entitled *Klinik der Nervenkrankheiten* ("Clinical Lectures on Nervous Diseases"—Rosenthal, 1875), a revised and enlarged edition of a textbook first published in 1870. The French translation, which appeared in 1878 with a preface by Charcot,* contained some thirty pages on hysteria, in which there was no mention of its being regarded as a disease of the genital organs or as malingering. In actual fact, this last point had already been established at a far earlier date. Certain Egyptian medical papyri (Kahun, Ebers) give a description of "diseases of women" with symptoms resembling those of hysteria—but without referring to malingering. Nor was this mentioned in the works of Hippocrates, to whom we owe the actual term "hysteria." As to the cause of this illness, as early as the seventeenth century such great clinicians as Willis and Sydenham rejected the hypothesis of a uterine etiology.**

---

* In his preface, Charcot draws attention to the curious fact that nervous disorders, and particularly hysterical neurosis, may present a different clinical picture in different (even neighboring) countries. Thus, he notes that in England complete hemianesthesia and the major hystero-epileptic attack are much less frequently encountered than in France, whereas chronic contractures of the limbs ("local hysteria") are more common in that country. On the other hand, on the basis of Rosenthal's book, he draws attention to a similarity between hysterical manifestations occurring in France and in Austria. Charcot thereby raises one of those "cross-cultural" problems which have in recent years come into favor.

** Discredited though it had become, the uterine etiology left some "traces" in its wake. A very special importance was assigned to the ovaries in hysterical symptomatology, even by Charcot, and the work of Briquet (1859) notwithstanding. The latter found that one-half of his hysterical patients suffered from "celialgia," i.e., pains located in the abdominal wall. Pain in the iliac region is a form of celialgia, but has nothing whatsoever to do with the ovaries, as some authors still maintained, including Charcot who spoke of ovarian pain, of an "ovaria," or an "ovarialgia" (Charcot, 1877, p. 269). About 1880, both in France and in other countries, there was widespread debate between "ovarists" and "anti-ovarists"; a summary of the controversy will be found in an article by a Viennese author, M. Ernst, *Über den "Iliacalschmerz"* (On "iliac pain"—1884). The critics of the "ovaria" concept pointed out that the same type of pain is also found in hysterical males and in women who have undergone ovariectomy. From this they concluded that it was not the ovary itself that was responsible for the symptoms, but an important nerve plexus situated in the ovarian region. We had yet to await Freud's discoveries in order to understand that a pain need not necessarily have a local cause, but can be induced by the projection of phantasies on to an area charged with psychological significance.

Even today, it is by no means unusual for this lesson to be disregarded, and for a search to be made at all costs for the local anatomical cause of a pain. It is thus that operations on the ovary are sometimes performed for "ovarian cysts" on patients suffering from iliac pain, without its ever having been established that such cysts are invariably painful.

while already recognizing the existence of male hysteria. For further information, the reader is referred to the detailed history of hysteria by Ilza Veith (1965).

The fact remains that Benedikt was an eminent clinician, the author of many works, who had already in 1863 (p. 713) related hysteria to disturbances in the patient's sexual life. It appears from one of his books that he was a friend, and at one time a confidant, of Charcot, whom he often visited in Paris (Benedikt, 1894, p. 21). Charcot's influence is reflected in Benedikt's conception of hypnosis as an experimentally induced hysteria. In 1891, he gave a "bio-mechanical" definition: "In essence, hysteria consists in a hyper-excitability, whether innate or acquired, of the nervous system" (Benedikt, 1891, p. 94; 1894, p. 71). He also emphasized (1894, p. 72) that this definition had gained Charcot's approval, and even his admiration.

It is apparent, therefore, that Benedikt was able to make known in Vienna some of Charcot's concepts. However, it was Freud, in his lecture of 1886, who was the first in Vienna to expound publicly, and stress the importance of, the work on post-traumatic hysteria under-taken one year earlier by Charcot which demonstrated the *power of idea* in the production of hysteria. And Viennese medical circles failed to grasp (but who could have done so at that time?) the full implication of the theories propounded by Charcot, namely, that the onset of hysteria *follows a psychical trauma* and that the illness is caused by the *mental experiencing* of the accident. This was proved by Charcot's ability to induce paralyses by the purely psychical proce-dure of suggestion. Post-traumatic hysteria is not, therefore, the result of injury to the nervous system through the impact of physical trauma, as was maintained by those who, with the German school, adhered to an exclusively anatomo-physiological orientation.

Did Freud actually refer in his paper to this innovative aspect of Charcot's ideas on the psychical mechanism of post-traumatic hys-teria and on experimental paralyses, respectively? As to the first point, we can answer in the affirmative. In fact, citing one of the five accounts of the lecture, Andersson (1962, p. 34) records the fol-lowing remark attributed to Freud by the reporter: "In men, whether predisposed or not, hysteria is probably produced by a psychical shock.''* Indeed, evidence of this remark is also to be found in an-other of the reports.** Andersson regards as significant the em-phasis placed on psychical shock, not on physical injury to the nervous system.

This point does not appear to have been dealt with during the discussion which followed Freud's lecture. One member of the audi-ence, Rosenthal, did however admit that a psychical shock could in-duce hysteria but hastened to define the anatomo-physiological me-chanism involved: an initial cortical excitation which, by way of the spinal cord,*** would give rise to hysterical spasms. On the whole, physical injury remained to the fore. Did Freud stress the difference between Charcot's thesis, which he had expounded, and that put forward by Rosenthal? It is most unlikely, and we shall presently see why. We know, moreover, that he had been asked to present a case of male hysteria similar to that mentioned in his paper of October 15; this he did in his lecture of November 26, 1886, the text of which has survived (Freud, 1886b). But, on this occasion, he confined himself to a presentation of the case, without discussing the psychical mechanism of the symptom.

As to the second point (experimental paralyses), did Freud bring forward, in support of his theory of the psychical mechanism of hys-terical paralyses, those paralyses induced by suggestion? This is not apparent from the accounts in the medical press, nor is there any mention of the question in his "Paris Report." However, in his *Autobiographical Study*—which, it is true, was written forty years later—referring to his lecture, he cites the experimental paralyses among the innovations through which he was "forced into the Op-position" (Freud, 1925a, p. 16). It is possible that this is no more than a seeming contradiction: we may suppose that at the time of his lecture he had not yet fully appreciated how great would be the impact of these experiments on the concept of psychical causality, although unconsciously sensing their value. He could not suspect the part that they would play one day in the elaboration of his theory of hysteria.

---

* *Wiener med. Presse*, ibid.
** *Allgemeine Wiener med. Zeitung*, ibid.
*** *Anzeiger der K.K. Gesellschaft der Aerzte in Wien*, ibid.

If Freud himself did not, as it would seem, attach any great importance to these new ideas, the lack of interest shown him by his medical audience is hardly sufficient to provide an adequate explanation of his intense bitterness following his lecture. Could it be that other motivating factors were involved?

In Ellenberger's view, the lecture of October 15, 1886, represented for Freud yet another setback in his career, following two earlier ones. Having first launched out into research on cerebral histology in Brücke's laboratory, he had quite soon come to realize how uncertain were the prospects of advancement which the Institute of Physiology in Vienna could offer him. On his teacher's advice, he had, therefore, left the laboratory to take up a resident position in the General Hospital, preparatory to engaging in general practice. But this change of course in his career—due to external circumstances—would seem more likely to have been experienced as a disappointment than as a real setback.

It is perhaps more accurate to speak of a setback where the cocaine episode is concerned. Freud had searched, albeit without success, for practical applications of this alkaloid, while his friend Koller achieved fame by discovering its value as a local anesthetic in ophthalmology. In consequence of his research, Freud had even found himself accused of encouraging cocaine addiction.

Ellenberger considers that these setbacks were all the more painfully felt in that Freud was very ambitious. To be sure, no one could deny the young Freud's ambition. We believe, however, that his sense of bitterness following his lecture is attributable to several factors. The ideas that he had expounded and which had received so cool a reception were those of a revered teacher with whom he identified for many reasons (as we have already seen, when considering Charcot's affective influence). Moreover, inasmuch as *it was at the Salpêtrière that Freud discovered the importance of psychical causality in hysteria, there is good reason to believe that, one year later, when the idea had begun to evolve in his mind, he felt himself the bearer of a significant message.*

Therefore, it is not surprising that, on being misunderstood by the Viennese doctors (who were under the influence of physicochemical determinism as represented by the Helmholtz School), he should have experienced such intense disappointment. To this it may be added that at this time Freud was impecunious, had just started to build up a practice, and hoped that he might count on the goodwill of his teachers, who were present at his lecture, to supply him with patients. Their lack of understanding could well jeopardize his future.

But such was Freud's character that he in no way renounced his ideas, whatever their possible consequences, and so found himself "forced into the Opposition"—a situation which, indeed, was perhaps not without pleasing him. He undoubtedly had the temperament for opposition. In a letter to his fiancée from Paris on February 2, 1886, he wrote: ". . . even at school I was always the bold oppositionist, always on hand when an extreme had to be defended and usually ready to atone for it. . . . I have often felt as though I had inherited all the passions with which our ancestors defended their Temple, and could gladly sacrifice my life for one great moment in history" (Freud, 1960, p. 202). This letter dates from the period when Freud had been won over to Charcot's ideas and when he may have had a premonition of the troubles to which he would expose himself on the path he had chosen to follow.

We must here refer further to Charcot's influence on Freud, as well as to the underlying question of applying objectivity to historical research. For example, Ellenberger (1965) acrimoniously denigrates Charcot's work on hysteria and hypnotism, which in his view constitutes a "regrettable episode" in the history of the Salpêtrière—while, on the other hand, extolling the merits of Charcot the neurologist. "In 1925," he writes of Charcot, "his centennial was celebrated at the Salpêtrière with a strong emphasis on his neurologic achievements and a few rapid apologies about the *légère défaillance* (the slight lapse) which his work on hysteria and hypnotism had been. Psychoanalysts, however, praised him in that regard as a 'precursor of Freud' " (Ellenberger, 1965, p. 265). Barrucand (1965, p. 55), citing Charcot's biographer, Guillain, refers to the same *"légère défaillance"*; he sides with the School of Nancy, which happens to be his own hometown.

Following the golden rule for historical research laid down by Ellenberger (1970, p. v)—"never take anything for granted," "check everything"—we wished, according to his injunction to "replace everything in its context," to ascertain the actual context in which the expression, *"légère défaillance,"* was used. The expression itself was introduced by Pierre Marie, a famous French neurologist and a pupil of Charcot's, who occupied the latter's chair in succession to Raymond and Dejerine. But what Ellenberger has failed to do is to replace it in its context, which leads him to an inaccuracy. In fact, Marie was directing this criticism at Charcot's work on hypnotism and his theory of the major attacks, but not at his research on hysteria as a whole. Here is the original text: "It must not be thought that Charcot's work on hysteria is limited to a few debatable interpretations of the characteristics of the convulsive attacks, or of hypnotic phenomena. These should be regarded as but a very minor facet of the question and as a *légère défaillance.** Where Charcot once again comes into his own, and regains the full extent of his superior clinical genius, is in the truly medical and methodical study of hysteria regarded as an illness. . . . What dominates Charcot's work on hysteria, will not perish and will continue to serve as a guide to medical generations is his demonstration of the existence of *male hysteria,*** and his admirable study of *traumatic hysteria*** with its particular paralyses, its contractures, and at times its painful manifestations: hystero-traumatism and traumatic neurosis!" (Marie, 1925, p. 741).

Another French neurologist, Guillain, who succeeded Pierre Marie, in his biography published in 1955 has fully rehabilitated Charcot's research on hysteria. As to the accusation of a "slight lapse" brought by his predecessor in regard to hypnotism, he finds extenuating circumstances, considering that "these investigations have exerted an influence on later research in psychoanalysis" (Guillain, 1955, p. 173).

From the foregoing data, it will be apparent that, in attempting at all costs to discover sufficient material to support a thesis, even so conscientious an historian as Ellenberger can arrive at erroneous conclusions (Chertok, 1971). He contests not only the originality of Charcot's investigations, but also the importance of the latter's influ-

---

* Italics added.
** Italics in original text.

ence on Freud (Ellenberger, 1968). He even regards this influence as having been in some respects pernicious, although its value is generally acknowledged—as it was indeed by none other than the founder of psychoanalysis himself.

That the conclusions reached by Ellenberger and ourselves should differ on several points, although we started from the same facts, shows how difficult it is to write an objective history of psychotherapy. Some degree of subjectivity is no doubt unavoidable in any attempt at interpretation. While we believe that our views are supported by conclusive evidence, it is of course possible that further research may shed a different light on this question.

Still in the name of scientific objectivity, Ellenberger rallies to the position adopted by Gicklhorn and Gicklhorn who, in their book, *Sigmund Freuds akademische Laufbahn* ("Sigmund Freud's Academic Career"—1960), defend the attitude of the Viennese medical circles. If we are to believe these authors, Freud was the victim neither of injustice nor of anti-semitism. His slow academic advancement would thus be attributable to the fact that he was *Dozent* in neurology only, whereas in conferring chairs preference was given to those holding this title in both neurology and psychiatry, as was the case with Freud's colleague, Wagner von Jauregg. The Gicklhorns provide a series of documents of undoubted value for a knowledge of Freud's career, but they have not succeeded in avoiding a subjective interpretation of the facts. Suffice it here to state, without entering into a detailed analysis of their book, that they place on the same level the respective achievements of Freud and Wagner-Jauregg. There is no question of minimizing the latter's work on the treatment of general paresis by malarial therapy, which constituted a notable milestone in the history of neuropsychiatry—he was indeed, on this account, the only psychiatrist ever to be awarded the Nobel prize. However, in their impact on the whole of our contemporary culture, Freud's ideas have in every respect proved to be of a very different order of importance.

These reservations notwithstanding, the Gicklhorns' book enables us to assess in more measured terms certain extreme pronouncements on the hostility which Freud encountered on the part of his colleagues. In fact, some of them attacked him and some were merely indifferent, but there were others who, while not sharing his opinions, had the fairness to support him in the matter of academic promotion. These latter included such men as Krafft-Ebing and Nothnagel, whose support in this respect Freud himself acknowledged (1954, p. 191).*

FREUD AND HYPNOSIS

We have seen how Freud resolved the crisis which he experienced in Paris. Confronted at the Salpêtrière with the phenomena of hysteria (and hypnosis), he had adopted the method of defense employed by Charcot and his assistants, the depersonalization of the doctor-patient relationship. Would this method prove adequate when, from being a mere observer, Freud was to become a "practitioner" of hypnosis? The question first arose in December, 1887.

Freud was indeed able to feel satisfied, for a few more years, with this defense through depersonalization, and it is only in the long run that its inadequacy became apparent. He then came upon a different, entirely original, solution. This was the discovery of a fundamental concept of psychoanalysis—the transference.

---

* Some time after we had written these lines, Eissler's comments (1971, pp. 343-344) came to our notice. He states that he made "surprising discoveries" when undertaking a careful comparative study of various documents, in particular those published by the Gicklhorns and those preserved in the Archives of the University of Vienna. And on the subject of Freud's academic advancement, as also in the case of other biographical details, Eissler denounces the Gicklhorns' spirit of "falsification" and the "contradictions" in their argumentation.

There would indeed appear to be good reason to despair of ever attaining "historical truth"!

It remains that over the years passions are dulled—and so far as history is concerned, there may on occasion come about a certain change in perspective, if not in "truth." It is thus that a kind of reconciliation between Freud and his hometown was symbolized by the 27th International Psychoanalytical Congress, held in Vienna in 1971, during which the question of the relations between Freud and the Viennese was raised, soberly, in the paper presented by Ticho and Ticho (1972).

The latter consider that such anti-semitism as existed in Vienna at the end of the century was practically confined to the lower middle classes. They observe that it was hardly ever encountered among the aristocracy and the intelligentsia, and very rarely indeed among academics. They conclude that racism is not, therefore, to be regarded as the prime cause of the delay in Freud's academic career; rather this arises quite simply from the shocking and revolutionary character of his theories which led Freud to relative isolation (as would have been the case in any other country). Such solitude was in fact not altogether unwelcome, and must have provided a stimulus to his genius.

It is no longer necessary to establish the importance of this discovery, which introduced a new era in psychotherapy. Its originality consists in having demonstrated the hitherto unrecognized, dynamic forces involved in the doctor-patient relationship and dispelled the resistances which, since the end of the eighteenth century (when psychotherapy was entering the experimental phase), had masked the true role of the two participants in this relationship. Freud was the first to succeed in bringing to light the reciprocal affective currents which unite them. Today it can be quite confidently affirmed that the discovery of the transference was Freud's first major revelation, which opened the way to all those that were to follow.

Among Freud's possible sources of inspiration may be mentioned the concept, which had long since been propounded, that the hypnotized subject's attitude towards the hypnotist is not unlike that of a child towards his parents.* It should also be noted that the idea of reliving an emotional experience was already an integral part of the cathartic method.

How far back can we trace the inception of this discovery and what were the stages of its development? In the absence of direct evidence from Freud, we have very little information on these points. Furthermore, no relevant data in this respect are to be found in the psychoanalytical literature, with the sole exception of an article by T. S. Szasz (1963) who formulates certain hypotheses. We shall return to this subject later. However, several works on the origins of psychoanalysis published in the last twenty-five years, such as the biography of Freud (Jones, 1953), his correspondence between 1873 and 1939 (Freud, 1960), and also editorial comments in Volume I of the *Standard Edition* of Freud's works (Strachey, 1966), have provided new material which sheds further light on the question.

Direct Hypnotic Suggestion

Before considering the actual discovery of the transference, we must ascertain what were Freud's contacts with hypnotism prior to 1887, at which time he himself began to practice it.

---

* Freud himself had referred to this attitude in his article, *Psychische Behandlung* ("Psychical Treatment"—1890, p. 296)—a question which will be discussed later.

While still a student, he had attended a public exhibition by the Danish magnetist, Hansen. It was, in fact, the latter's public performances which had aroused curiosity about hypnosis in Germanic countries.* In 1880 there appeared the first publications on the subject, in particular a work by Heidenhain (1880), a well-known physiologist of Breslau who was influenced by the Salpêtrière School.

Even before this period, however, there was a pioneer of hypnotism in Austria—Benedikt, the neuropathologist, who has already been mentioned and who was to acquire an undoubted reputation.

In 1867, together with Griesinger, the famous Berlin psychiatrist, he had attended a congress in Frankfurt. There they had both met Lasègue, who had told them of his experiments on catalepsy which he induced in women with nervous disorders by closure of the eyes.

On his return to Vienna, Benedikt had successfully reproduced these experiments in Oppolzer's clinic at the General Hospital, where he was working. He was forbidden by an assistant physician to pursue his experiments, on the pretext that the procedure which he employed pertained to animal magnetism. It is interesting to note that the assistant concerned was Josef Breuer. Benedikt had then complied, but some years later had returned to the practice of Lasègue's "transient catalepsies" (*"catalepsies passagères"*) after having become acquainted with Charcot's work on "major hysteria." He was seeking to cure female patients suffering from major hysteria. This method had proved effective in suppressing the symptom. Benedikt had, however, observed the deep psychical influence of hypnosis on the patients, who were seen to be led to what he was later to describe (Benedikt, 1894, p. 19) as "mystical dependence"** upon the therapist. Faced with this danger, he had preferred to resort to metallotherapy which, while obtaining similar results, did not involve the practitioner personally.

In 1878, Benedikt, who had come to Paris to participate in the Congress of Anthropology, had seized the opportunity to meet Charcot. Accompanied by another well-known member of the Con-

---

* Until 1840, there had appeared in Germany a profusion of literature on animal magnetism, albeit imbued with religious concepts.
** A term which was to be employed in turn by Freud.

gress, Virchow, he had attended Charcot's demonstrations on hysterical patients at the Salpêtrière. On his return to Austria, he had, in the course of a lecture, once again spoken in favor of hypnosis, but his medical audience—like Breuer ten years earlier—had proved hostile, asserting that what had been described was mesmerism.

The difficulties encountered by Benedikt can be explained by the fact that the curiosity which hypnosis aroused in Germany and Austria was accompanied by considerable suspicion. The consequent hostility continued to be in evidence for a number of years; for example, when the well-known Berlin neuropathologist, Moll, after a stay at the Salpêtrière and in Nancy, gave an account of the work then being undertaken in France to his colleagues of the Berlin Society of Medicine, at the meeting of October 26, 1887, presided over by Virchow, he was exposed to vehement criticism (Moll, 1888). Meynert for one (1888, p. 498) saw hypnotic therapy as "the dog-like subjugation" (*"hündische Unterjochung"*) of one person by another. Hypnosis—according to him, a pathological state—could lead through repeated induction to a mentally unbalanced condition. Indeed, Benedikt himself contributed to the perpetuation of this mistrust in consequence of his more than ambivalent attitude towards hypnosis. While purporting to be the pioneer in this field in Austria, he was actually opposed to its practice and even to its investigation. In his articles of 1889 on the treatment of hysterical patients, he warned against the general use, as advocated by the Nancy School, of hypnosis and suggestion. As we have seen, he preferred metallotherapy. A fierce opponent of the Nancy theories, he made a violent attack (Benedikt, 1894) on Krafft-Ebing concerning the latter's experiments on somnambulists (Krafft-Ebing, 1893).

All in all, Benedikt's eminence was great enough to induce Freud, who was about to leave for Paris, to ask him for a letter of introduction to Charcot. Not long before his departure, Freud had witnessed the practice of hypnotherapy in Obersteiner's private sanatorium, where he had served as a locum tenens for three weeks. It is possible that, at this time, as Jones believes, he may personally have tried his hand at hypnotization. No sooner had he returned to Vienna than he wished to propagate Charcot's views on hypnotism in two lectures, at the Physiological Club on May 11, 1886, and at the Psychiatric Society on May 25. But he came up against the same antagonism encountered in Vienna by all those who defended hypnosis. His principal opponent was, in fact, Meynert, his former "chief" in the field of cerebral anatomy from 1883 to 1885; from that time onwards, relations between the two men deteriorated.

While he felt enthusiastic about hypnotism, it was not until December, 1887, that Freud introduced it into his regular practice—and then, only in the form of direct suggestion—although he had been in practice since April 25, 1886. What were the reasons for this delay? In the first place, in his concern about his private patients (and it should not be forgotten that he was married in September 1886), Freud might well have hesitated to employ a procedure which was getting such a bad press. At all events he confined himself in the early stages to the use of electrotherapy, a very orthodox procedure at that time. Jones (1953, p. 258) is surprised that Freud should so conform to accepted authority (we have only to recall the distinctly "oppositionist" character of his lecture of October 15) when he was already acquainted with the far more promising cathartic method. In explanation, Jones adduces Charcot's inordinately reserved attitude towards this method when Freud had mentioned it to him in Paris. But this argument is hardly conclusive; instead of electrotherapy, Freud could easily have made use of hypnosis in an elementary form.

Furthermore, it is not inconceivable that unconscious resistances also came into play and that, while championing the cause of hypnotism, Freud was loath to become personally involved in the relationship implict in its practice. The fact remains that when he finally decided to employ hypnotic suggestion in December, 1887, he showed considerable enthusiasm. In his own words, ". . . there was something positively seductive in working with hypnotism. For the first time there was a sense of having overcome one's helplessness; and it was highly flattering to enjoy the reputation of being a miracle-worker" (Freud, 1925a, p. 17).

In actual fact, Freud's expressed judgment on his own attitude towards hypnosis at the period when he practiced it appears to have varied. In 1909, in his *Five Lectures on Psychoanalysis,* he stated: ". . . I soon came to dislike hypnosis, for it was a temperamental and, one might almost say, a mystical ally" (Freud, 1910, p. 22) . It is possible that the trends favored at this time may have influenced his statements; indeed, the year 1909 belongs in the period of the strong opposition to hypnosis which had manifested itself in medical circles from the time of Charcot's death. It is only after the 1914-1918 war that the "rehabilitation" of hypnosis began to take place, in consequence of the services it had rendered in the treatment of combat neuroses. In 1918, Freud, no doubt sensible of contemporary trends, no longer referred to his aversion for hypnosis. He even conceded that it would become possible "to alloy the pure gold of analysis with the copper of direct suggestion," and that a place might also, once again, be found for hypnotic influence (Freud, 1919, p. 168). In 1925, he spoke highly of the therapeutic value of the cathartic method, as used by Ernst Simmel in the German Army during the First World War (Freud, 1925a, p. 22) .

Freud waited eighteen months before passing, in May, 1889, from hypnotic suggestion to Breuer's cathartic method.* This hesitation and reserve are perhaps attributable to Charcot's attitude toward this method, but perhaps also to the persistence of certain resistances on Freud's part. For he may well have feared that verbal communication under hypnosis would involve him so deeply that he would eventually find himself in a predicament similar to that previously experienced by Breuer when confronted with Anna O.

At all events, Freud had serious and rational motives for aban-

---

* Freud stated later that, when embarking on the use of hypnosis, he had from the first employed Breuer's procedure. But this statement contradicts the passage in the *Studies on Hysteria* where he said that the first case in which he employed it was that of Emmy von N., in May, 1889, i.e., eighteen months after he had begun to make use of hypnotism. Jones (1953, pp. 263-264), who notes this discrepancy, believes that in his first use of verbal methods Freud remained essentially on a superficial plane. The editors of the *Standard Edition* of Freud's works question the accuracy of this date, as there are some indications that this form of treatment may already have been employed in May, 1888. But they themselves admit that the question is by no means settled (Strachey, 1955).

Andersson's investigations (1962, p. 74) on the life of Emmy von N. confirm that the treatment did actually take place in the spring of 1889. In fact, he notes that, in an autobiographical manuscript, one of Emmy von N.'s daughters recorded that she and her mother were in Istria when they heard of the Mayerling tragedy (in January, 1889), shortly before leaving for Vienna.

doning direct suggestion. It was not long before he had begun (in 1892) to tire of the monotony of a procedure which, moreover, led eventually to a troublesome situation: "In the long run neither the doctor nor the patient can tolerate the contradiction between the decided denial of the ailment in the suggestion and the necessary recognition of it outside of the suggestion" (Freud, 1892-94, p. 141).

Above all, Freud sensed the importance of what was concealed behind the symptoms and his scientific curiosity was strong enough to overcome such obstacles as might exist within him. The method which he would henceforth employ, as he later stated, "also satisfied the curiosity of the physician, who, after all, had a right to learn something of the origin of the phenomenon which he was striving to remove" (Freud, 1925a, p. 19).

The Cathartic Method

With the change of method, there arose a technical difficulty. So long as he had restricted his therapy to direct suggestion under hypnosis, Freud in all probability had not been much concerned about the depth of the trance. He was, however, faced with this problem in an acute form when using the cathartic method, which requires a deep hypnotic state. He noticed that in practice he did not always succeed in inducing deep trances and that there were certain subjects whom he failed to hypnotize. This he ascribed to the inadequacy of his technique. With a view to perfecting the latter, he decided, in July, 1889, to go to Nancy together with a female patient in whom, as he stated, "her hypnosis had never reached the stage of somnambulism with amnesia" (Freud, 1925a, p. 18). Bernheim, as it happened, did not obtain any better results with this patient. Freud added: "He frankly admitted to me that his great therapeutic successes by means of suggestion were only achieved in his hospital practice and not with his private patients" (1925a, p. 18).

The remarks here attributed to Bernheim do indeed strike one as rather strange* and it seems surprising that the latter should, at

---

* Jones (1953, p. 262) records another "curious" mistake in the same passage of the *Autobiographical Study*. Freud states that, when in Nancy, he undertook to translate into German two of Bernheim's works. In actual fact, he had already published one of these in the preceding year.

this particular period, have depreciated, however slightly, the thera-peutic value of suggestion. All the more so as Bernheim's book, *De la Suggestion et de ses Applications à la Thérapeutique,* which was published in 1886 (and translated by Freud two years later), stressed the value of this method: of a total of 105 cases treated, 81 were completely cured and 22 partially cured. It is more likely that Bern-heim merely questioned the possibility of inducing deep hypnosis at all frequently—an opinion which he was to express before the Con-gress of Hypnotism on August 9, 1889, i.e., only a few weeks after his meeting with Freud. The way in which he thus emphasized the small proportion of subjects susceptible to deep hypnosis is certainly in accordance with the evolution of Bernheim's views, which tended to favor suggestion in the waking state as compared with hypnosis (Bernheim, 1889, p. 79).

It is, therefore, clear that Freud distorted Bernheim's remarks. But when did this occur? Was it thirty-six years later, when he pub-lished his *Autobiographical Study* (Freud, 1925a), in which case it would be attributable to a simple lapse in memory? Or did Freud, at the actual time, interpret Bernheim's words in the way that best agreed with the orientation he had himself adopted? For, having passed from direct suggestion to the cathartic method, Freud showed a tendency to depreciate the former procedure and, with a view to applying the latter, to persuade himself that deep hypnosis was widely and readily practicable. It should be added that Freud, who confined himself to private practice, must have preferred not to hear it said that in such patients deep hypnosis could be achieved only in a limited number of cases. There remains one other possible hypothesis—the distortion of Bernheim's remarks may have occurred *a posteriori,* at a time when any form of suggestion was subject to depreciation in the eyes of Freud.

Let us return to the Congress of Hypnotism, where the world authorities forgathered in Paris from August 8 to 12, 1889—cen-tennial year of the French Revolution which was marked by numer-ous international meetings and the inauguration of the Eiffel Tower. Freud, Bernheim and Liébeault had arrived together in Paris at the beginning of August. All three had been entered as members of this congress, as also of the International Congress of Physiological Psychology (August 6 to 10), of which a major part was to be devoted to the psychological aspects of hypnotism (whereas the Congress of Hypnotism was solely concerned with its "medical" aspects).*

In spite of his undoubted interest in hypnosis, Freud does indeed seem to have neglected the sessions of the congresses, and preferred to revisit the capital in which, three years previously, he had spent four months. Already on the evening of the 9th he was on his way back to Vienna.

The very next day, as one of the authors has elsewhere recorded (Chertok, 1960), Bourru and Burot reported a case in which they had employed a therapeutic procedure very closely related to the cathartic method: recall of a memory and abreaction. Their work served as a starting point for Janet in developing his technique of "reviviscence" (reliving) of past emotional experiences. Had Freud been present, he could have given an account of the cathartic method and thus would the vexed question have been elucidated as to who should be credited with first having conceived this procedure.

The lack of interest evinced by Freud on this occasion is indeed paradoxical, if it is borne in mind that he was, at the time, actively practicing hypnosis, that he had not long since (in 1888) translated and contributed a preface to a book by Bernheim, and that he had written an appreciative review (Freud, 1889) of Forel's recently published work, *Der Hypnotismus* (1889). Inasmuch as Freud himself never proffered any explanation of his sudden departure, we can only fall back on hypotheses. It may be that his lack of interest in the Congresses was linked with the person of Charcot. The latter was to be honorary president of the Congress of Hypnotism, as well as president of the Congress of Physiological Psychology.

But in point of fact Charcot was absent from Paris and attended

---

* Ernest Jones does not mention Freud's registration as a member of this first Congress of Physiological Psychology (Congr. Int. Psychol., 1889). The second, held in 1892, had the title "Congress of Experimental Psychology"; with the third, in 1896, it acquired the title which it has retained ever since: "Congress of Psychology" (the 20th was held in Tokyo, August 1972). The Congresses of Hypnotism proved to be ephemeral—there was but one other, in 1900. Paris had to await 1965 for its successor, and even then hypnosis was only admitted "for conservation." This was the "International Congress of Hypnosis and Psychosomatic Medicine." Also in Paris in 1889 (August 5-10), there was held an "International Congress of Psychological Medicine" (Congrès International de Médecine Mentale).

neither. (It was Ribot who, as vice-president, delivered the inaugural address at the second of these Congresses.) Benedikt, one of the vice-presidents of the International Congress of Psychological Medicine, likewise held aloof from both the Congress of Hypnotism and that of Psychology on the grounds of Charcot's absence which, he said, allowed the Nancy School to get the upper hand (Benedikt, 1889). Freud may perhaps have followed Charcot's example because of the profound admiration which he felt for his teacher; perhaps also the benefit he had derived from his stay at Nancy enabled him already to foresee that he would abandon hypnosis in favor of some other technique.

Abandonment of Hypnosis

Freud practiced hypnosis continuously for a period of some five years (1887-1892). He then decided to restrict its use and from 1896 he no longer employed it therapeutically, although occasionally resorting to it for experimental purposes. Why, then, did he abandon it?

He reproached hypnosis with being unintelligible, with not being widely applicable, and especially with masking the patient's resistances (Freud, 1905a, p. 261), the analysis of which constitutes the essential feature of psychoanalytical therapy. All of these motives of a rational order must certainly have come into play. Lagache (1952) regards the non-applicability of hypnosis on a large scale as the fundamental motive for Freud's decision; as he says, "if all the patients had been hypnotizable, there would have been no psychoanalysis" (p. 7). Jones (1953, p. 267), for his part, believes that Freud's chief motive was that hypnosis concealed the patient's resistances. There is perhaps yet another motive which could derive from Freud's pragmatic attitude: might he have felt that there was little chance, considering the state of research in his day, of penetrating the mystery of hypnosis? On this aspect of Freud's personality, Jones observes: "Freud was primarily a discoverer, and his interest always turned to problems that offered some promising opening for investigation. Where none was visible . . . his interest soon waned; it was a waste of time and thought to speculate about the unknown" (Jones, 1957,

p. 338) .* It should be noted that the first explanations put forward by Freud himself implicate unhypnotizability. In his *Five Lectures on Psychoanalysis,* following the passage already cited on his aversion for hypnosis, he wrote: "When I found that, in spite of all my efforts, I could not succeed in bringing more than a fraction of my patients into a hypnotic state, I determined to give up hypnosis . . ." (Freud, 1910, p. 22) .

In Freud's decision to discard hypnosis these several factors of a rational order undoubtedly played a part; it is difficult to apportion the degree of their respective importance. But we also have in mind a motivating factor of a different order which not only, on his own admission, induced Freud to abandon hypnosis, but whose role was, in our opinion, a decisive one in the discovery of the transference. This was the famous episode in which a female patient flung her arms about Freud. Here is his own description of the scene:

> . . . One day I had an experience which showed me in the crudest light what I had long suspected. It related to one of my most acquiescent patients, with whom hypnotism had enabled me to bring about the most marvellous results, and whom I was engaged in relieving of her suffering by tracing back her attacks

---

* Once again, since it is Freud who is concerned, judgments have to be qualified here. Freud's was an open mind which did not refuse *a priori* to "speculate about the unknown"—witness his interest with regard to telepathy (as Jones himself concedes). He did not, in this respect, go so far as experimentation but, believing that he had here and there observed some such phenomenon, he undoubtedly wondered about these matters. Thus he was moved to write to Carrington, in 1921: "If I were at the beginning rather than the end of a scientific career, as I am today, I might possibly choose just this field of research, in spite of all difficulties" (Freud, 1960, p. 339).

Moreover, he never attributed any mystical quality to telepathy; at all events, he seems not to have feared it. On the other hand, he "disliked hypnosis" and, as we have seen, invested it with a "mystical" character. A paradoxical attitude, indeed, if it is admitted that telepathy may seem at least as mysterious or "mystical" as hypnosis.

We will investigate later whether, in Freud's mind, a certain "fear of the mystical" might not have linked up with a "fear of the erotic."

The question has been raised of the possibility that Freud's interest in telepathy originated in France. It is a fact that Janet dealt with the subject in a lecture (delivered on his behalf by his uncle Paul) in Paris on November 30, 1885 (Janet, 1886b). Freud, who was in the capital at the time, could have been present—but this has never been proved. It remains that Freud himself always asserted that he did not even know Janet's name during his stay in Paris.

of pain to their origins. As she woke up on one occasion, she threw her arms around my neck. The unexpected entrance of a servant relieved us from a painful discussion,* but from that time onwards there was a tacit understanding between us that the hypnotic treatment should be discontinued. I was modest enough not to attribute the event to my own irresistible personal attraction, and I felt that I now grasped the nature of the mysterious element** that was at work behind hynotism. In order to exclude it, or at all events to isolate it, it was necessary to abandon hypnotism (Freud, 1925a, p. 27).

DISCOVERY OF THE TRANSFERENCE

From the moment when Freud refused to admit that his female patient's behavior could be explained by his "irresistible personal attraction," he would seem to have envisaged the existence of a "third figure" interposed between the patient and himself. This may, therefore, logically be regarded as the starting point of the concept of transference.

Unfortunately, it is impossible to assign to any precise date the episode related above, for the *Autobiographical Study* gives no indication on this chronological point. We have, moreover, only one other account of the event, namely, that provided by Jones (1953, p. 275) in his biography of Freud.*** According to Jones, Freud told Breuer the story of his own patient, in order to reassure him of his misadventure with Anna O. Breuer, sensitized by this incident, had indeed long been reluctant to have anything to do with hysteria. "Some ten years later,"† says Jones (p. 248), Breuer called Freud into consultation over an hysterical patient; but, on learning that a phantasy of pregnancy was involved, he was unable to bear the recur-

---

* To be sure; but had the regular presence of a nurse during the sessions made this "famous episode" impossible, would Freud have been led to discover the transference?

** We have seen that Benedikt employed the word "mystical" in connection with hypnosis; we will, however, refer later to the distinction between the meaning of the English words, "mystical" and "mysterious," and that of the German, *"mystisch."*

*** In a personal communication, Anna Freud has assured the authors that there is no mention of the incident in any of her father's letters, published or unpublished.

† "Some ten years later"—It is not clear from which precise event Jones' statement is calculated; it might be the commencement of the treatment of Anna O., considered as a whole, or the terminal incident alone.

rence of the earlier situation, and without saying a word hurriedly left the house.

At this period, still according to Jones (p. 275), Freud kept trying to revive Breuer's interest in hysteria and, in particular, to induce him to publish the case history of Anna O. He was also gradually coming to realize that his friend's reluctance was connected with the incident which had brought the treatment to a premature end. This new evasion on Breuer's part must have confirmed him in this view. It was no doubt subsequently that he gave Breuer the reassuring statement already mentioned, although this must have been before June 28, 1892, since it is on this date—witness Freud's letter to Fliess on the same day (Freud, 1954, p. 62)—that Breuer at last consented to cooperate with Freud in the joint publication of their work on hysteria. Obviously, one can hardly pretend to absolute accuracy in this respect, but it may well be thought that Breuer's agreement was obtained not very long after Freud's reassurance. Freud's misadventure must, needless to say, be placed at an earlier date, albeit not prior to May 1889, at which time he started to practice the cathartic method.

Assuming that the concept of transference took root in Freud's mind on the occasion of his personal misadventure, it must follow that, at the time of his statement to Breuer, this idea had already undergone some degree of elaboration. Indeed, as Jones relates, Freud had then told his friend "of his own experience of a female patient suddenly flinging her arms round his neck in a transport of affection, and he explained to him his reasons for regarding such untoward occurrences as part of the transference phenomena characteristic of certain types of hysteria" (1953, p. 275).

So far as the date of the actual discovery of the transference is concerned, we are now able, in consequence of the disclosure in recent years of two facts, in Volume I of the *Standard Edition* of Freud's works (Strachey, 1966), to place it closer to June 1892 than had hitherto been possible. Strachey informs us that Freud's *Psychische Behandlung (Seelenbehandlung)* ("Psychical (or Mental) Treatment") had been first published not, as it was thought, in

1905 but in 1890.* In addition, this same volume of the *Standard Edition* contains the translation of an article by Freud, "Hypnosis," which had appeared in 1891 in Anton Bum's *Therapeutisches Lexikon* but passed unnoticed until it was rediscovered in 1963 (Freud, 1890, 1891b).

In neither of these works on hypnosis, published respectively in 1890 and 1891, is there any mention of the word "transference." Its discovery must, therefore, be situated between the date when the article of 1891 was written and June 28, 1892.

It is probable that Freud's misadventure also occurred later than the date of publication of this article, which makes no reference whatsoever to the erotic complications of hypnosis. When discussing the question, much debated at the time, of the tête-à-tête between the hypnotist and his subject, Freud on the whole took his stand against the presence of a third person during treatment. All things considered, it would appear that these several events, namely, the incident involving Freud and his female patient, the consultation with Breuer, and the reassurance extended to the latter, all occurred in the above-mentioned interval of time.

We know, moreover, that, following his misadventure, Freud decided to abandon the use of hypnotism. Elisabeth von R. was the first patient whom he treated without hypnosis, in autumn 1892 (Breuer and Freud, 1895, p. 135). This date agrees with our hypotheses.

---

* The *Psychische Behandlung* was known to have appeared in a semi-popular medical handbook, *Die Gesundheit* ("Health") in 1905. It has more recently been discovered that this is actually the date of publication of the third edition of this handbook. The first edition, which included the same text of Freud's contribution, had appeared in 1890 (Freud, 1890). This first edition also contained an article by Erben (1890) devoted to the *"nicht stofflichen Krankheiten des Nervensystems (Neurosen),"* i.e., the "non-physical diseases of the nervous system, or neuroses." Together with hysteria, Erben included under this heading epilepsy, migraine, neurasthenia, Graves' disease, etc. His article illustrates well the conception of the "neuroses" prevalent at the time: they were diseases of the nervous system (Rosenthal, *Klinik der Nervenkrankheiten*, 1875). Psychiatry, on the other hand, was concerned only with psychoses (Krafft-Ebing, *Lehrbuch der Psychiatrie*, 1879). However, nosology was far removed from our present criteria. Conditions that are today classified among the obsessive and phobic neuroses were at one time comprised in the category of psychoses —and there were in common use such terms as *"folie du doute"* or "doubting mania" (i.e. obsessive doubt), *"délire du toucher"* (i.e. touching phobia), and so on.

Transference and the Therapist's Defense

The explanation given to Breuer, that the behavior of some female patients was attributable to the transference, had as its first effect the reassurance of Freud himself. But later, when the two friends were preparing together the *Studies on Hysteria,* Breuer spoke of the transference phenomenon in the following terms: "I believe that this is the most important thing we two have to give the world" (Freud, 1925b, p. 280).

The question of transference was in fact dealt with somewhat briefly in that work, and then by Freud alone. It was there considered only in its libidinal form, and we know how far the original concept was subsequently extended. But, within the limits of the present inquiry, it is the concept of transference at the stage of the *Studies on Hysteria* (1895) which is our principal concern, inasmuch as this was the period of its inception. How, then, was it envisaged at that time?

In Freud's own words: "The wish which was present was then, owing to the compulsion to associate . . . , linked to my person . . . ; and as the result of this *mésalliance*—which I describe as a 'false connection'—the same affect was provoked which had forced the patient long before to repudiate this forbidden wish. Since I have discovered this, I have been able, whenever I have been similarly involved personally, to presume that a transference and a false connection have once more taken place. Strangely enough, the patient is deceived afresh every time this is repeated" (Breuer and Freud, 1895, p. 303). Freud went on to emphasize that "the patients, too, gradually learnt to realize that in these transferences on to the figure of the physician it was a question of a compulsion and an illusion which melted away with the conclusion of the analysis" (p. 304).

The interpersonal relationship was thus seen in a completely new light. It is obviously not intended here to expound the many therapeutic uses of the transference, but rather to draw attention to the way in which it affects the "position" of the physician. The latter no longer feels himself personally involved in consequence of the libidinal demands of any particular female patient. The transference enables him to maintain a certain detachment in his relationship to her, and to view with equanimity the process which unfolds before his eyes.

Until Freud's discovery, psychotherapists had been haunted, whether consciously or not, by the possibility of erotic complications in the relationship. They could henceforth feel reassured, just as Breuer had been, by Freud's words. And as already suggested, Freud himself would seem to have found in the transference a means of defense against possible emotional advances on the part of his female patients—and consequently, against the eventuality of his own personal temptations.

It may here be recalled that, from the theory of a fluid, through the use of the magnet, to the "neurophysiological substratum," long indeed is the series of devices which have been elaborated with the unconscious but perennial aim of depersonalizing the therapeutic relationship.

There is a somewhat ironic paradox in the fact that it should fall to the transference, a substantial reality devoid of all contrivance and a revolutionary innovation in psychotherapeutic technique, to enable us at last to personalize the relationship—while at the same time introducing in its turn a subtle form of depersonalization by the interposition of a third figure between the protagonists. And we may venture the remark—at the risk of further irony—that in this perspective the transference becomes, in its way, reintegrated into the "prophylactic lineage" which had hitherto haunted the unconscious of every practitioner!

Granting all this, there remains a danger of the "transference-panacea." More precisely, on the semantic plane there are those who have come to confuse "transference" and "relationship" in individual as in institutional therapy, and to overemphasize the part played by the transferential component (i.e., the past, the phantasmatic, the "unreal") to the point of ignoring factors in the relationship that are strictly *actual,* original, and non-repetitive. In more recent years, some authors have spoken out, reminding us of all the non-transferential elements that may enter into the framework of classical analytic therapy (Nacht, 1963; Greenson and Wexler, 1969).

The transference and its management undoubtedly opened up vast perspectives. It remains that, on the plane of interpersonal relations, such concepts as "affinity," "sympathy," "harmony," "kindness" or "human warmth" ("love" will be considered later), are far from being explicable by the transference alone. If it is proposed to fathom the problem posed by the interpersonal relationship, "communication" and "exchange," it must first be admitted that, by and large, the unknown quantities balance the certainties.

We have already referred to Freud's attitude toward female hysterical patients, with regard both to Anna O. and to his stay at the Salpêtrière. On the rational plane, he was intensely interested in the scientific problem presented by these patients, while showing an affective ambivalence where fear and attraction were combined. This attitude did not fail to show itself when he himself started to treat such hysterical cases.

He must then have realized even more clearly the importance which these female patients held for his research, and entertained for them a feeling of gratitude. This may be the explanation of his kindly disposition towards them, in contrast to the generally unfavorable, if not indeed aggressive, attitude of physicians of the period. One may mention in particular his excellent opinion of Frau Emmy von N., of whom he wrote: "Dr. Breuer and I knew her pretty well and for a fairly long time, and we used to smile when we compared her character with the picture of the hysterical psyche which can be traced from early times through the writings and the opinions of medical men. . . . Frau Emmy von N. gave us an example of how hysteria is compatible with an unblemished character and a well-governed mode of life.* The woman we came to know was an ad-

* As early as 1859 Briquet had protested against this social prejudice toward hysterical patients. He had reached the conclusion that "hysteria was not the shameful illness whose very name reminds those who are unconnected with medicine, and many medical men, of this verse of our great tragic poet: 'It is Venus tenaciously gripping her prey'; but that, on the contrary, it was due to the existence in woman of the most noble and most admirable sentiments—feelings that she alone is able to experience" (Briquet, 1859, p. vii). This "desexualization" of hysteria, together with Briquet's sympathy for his patients, could not but help him in his work. Such sympathy is somewhat reminiscent of Freud's observations on hysterical cases, in particular those concerning Emmy von N. Freud's attitude differs, however, in some respects from that of Briquet; notwithstanding his kindliness toward these patients, he does not extol their specifically feminine qualities. Indeed, he mentions with approval Emmy von N.'s manly characteristics. Apart from his great love for his wife, who was certainly very feminine, Freud is known to have shown an intellectual partiality for slightly masculine women. On his part it was no doubt a personal tendency, but the "androcentrism" imputed to him was fairly widespread at the time. Benedikt, for example, devotes an entire chapter to women, in which a few praises 1895;, pp. 181-188).

her intelligence and energy, which were no less than a man's, and her high degree of education and love of truth impressed both of us greatly; while her benevolent care for the welfare of all her dependents, her humility of mind and the refinement of her manners revealed her qualities as a true lady as well" (Breuer and Freud, 1895, pp. 103-104). This appears to be a fairly idealized portrait. At all events, returning many years later (in a footnote added in 1924) to the case of Frau von N., Freud mentioned, without comment, the disagreements which had opposed her to her two daughters, noting that she "had broken off relations with both her children and refused to assist them in their financial difficulties" (Breuer and Freud, 1895, p. 105).

Andersson (1965) has undertaken a detailed investigation on Emmy von N., with the help of all available documents (including the unpublished autobiography of one of her daughters, which he very kindly allowed us to examine) and information gathered at first hand from many people who had known her. He ascertained that she was born in Germany in 1848 and died in 1925. Married in 1871 to a wealthy industrialist, a widower 40 years her senior, she bore him two daughters, in 1872 and 1874. On her husband's death shortly after the birth of the second child, she inherited one of the largest fortunes in Europe. It is then that her nervous disorders and her tribulations began. In consequence of rumors accusing her of having poisoned her husband, a judicial inquiry was instituted and a post-mortem examination undertaken with negative results. Suspicions persisted, however, and in European society her name continued to be surrounded by an aura of scandal. She thenceforth confined herself to the role of patron and philanthropist, remaining somewhat aloof from the social life she had known in the past, but gathering about her artists, scientists and writers.

In 1887 she settled in a château in Switzerland. Her love life reveals a partiality to medical men, whether those whom she encountered in spas, or those whom she appointed her "personal physicians" (*Leibärzte!*) * and to whom she gave board and lodging. Her

---

* The German word, *Leibarzt* (plural, *Leibärzte*), signifies "physician in ordinary," i.e. personal physician (originally, to a king, etc.). The literal meaning of the German is, however, "body-physician."

nervous disorders caused her to consult experts throughout Europe, including Auguste Forel in Switzerland, and Freud in Vienna. In the winter of 1893-1894, she underwent a lengthy course of continuous sleep treatment in Stockholm. Forel had referred her to Wetterstrand, a follower of the Nancy School, renowned for his method of treatment by prolonged hypnotic sleep (Wetterstrand, 1888).* Her last years were darkened, as Freud has confirmed, by serious quarrels with her daughters. Moreover, at the age of 70 she became infatuated with a younger man, but gave up the idea of marrying him after discovering that he had swindled her out of a large part of her fortune. Those about her had not until then regarded her as mentally ill, only as an eccentric woman. Following this unfortunate experience, she appears to have become a prey to delusions, believing (mistakenly, so her financial adviser assured Andersson) that she was completely ruined, and bereft of the wherewithal even to maintain a day-to-day subsistence.

The case of Emmy von N., it will be recalled, is one of the five histories presented by Breuer and Freud (1895) as typical of hysteria. In the 1950s, however, the diagnoses of Breuer and Freud were questioned. Thus, Goshen (1952), a nonanalyst and, indeed, an "antianalyst," assigned to these five cases the single diagnosis of schizophrenia. Suzanne Reichard (1956) for her part, writing in the *Psychoanalytic Quarterly,* favored a diagnosis of schizophrenia in the cases of Anna O. and Emmy von N., and of hysteria in the other three cases.

We shall not enter here into a discussion of these opinions which are, to say the least, venturesome. The fact remains that there is at the present time a tendency to call in question the prevalent nosological concepts; there is, moreover, an ever-increasing use of borderline diagnoses. In Schur's view (1972, p. 38), the case of Anna O. would probably be regarded today as a borderline case.

What concerns us from the historical point of view is to retrace the curve of the manifest trend of interest in, or alternatively disaffection toward, hysteria. After having been, with Charcot and

---

* Janet called Wetterstrand's sanatorium the "palace of the Sleeping Beauty." Janet also employed such sleep therapy—and it is still sometimes used in the Soviet Union (Chertok, 1954).

Freud, the subject of undoubtedly fruitful investigations, hysteria came increasingly into disfavor, as is clearly shown (among others) by the title of Babinski's work, *Démembrement de l'hystérie traditionnelle—Pithiatisme** ("Dismemberment of Traditional Hysteria"—1909). Even among psychoanalysts it no longer gave rise to more than a few works.

Already before the Second World War, it was thought that there was evidence of a decrease in the incidence of hysterical phenomena —and an increase in that of certain "obsessional" manifestations, said to be attributable to the sociocultural characteristics of a society industrialized and "automated" in the extreme. An attempt was also made to explain this alleged decrease in hysterical symptoms by the fact that, on the sexual plane, our society is less repressive than in the past (repression supposedly "engendering" hysteria). In her previously mentioned historical survey, Ilza Veith (1965, p. 274) even went so far as to speak of "the near-disappearance" of hysteria.

Actually, this is by no means the case. The form of the illness may have changed (possibly fewer motor disturbances, but an increase in painful symptoms) and it seems to be more frequently encountered in general medicine than in neurology; yet its existence is more than ever an undeniable fact. To mention but one among many examples, it is noteworthy that hysterical conversion, the somatic expression of the emotions (body language), highlights the increasing inability of our physicians, driven even further toward specialization and "technicalization," to establish true interpersonal communication with the patient. In the absence of an available and considerate confidant such as the old "family doctor" in former times, the patient has recourse to physical signals in his attempt to establish some kind of communication. It is now accepted, moreover, that at least one-half of the patients treated by general practitioners are "functional" cases, of which a certain number— (any assessment of the exact proportion would at present involve considerations that are still debatable)—present symptoms due to a conversional process of hysterical type.

We are, at all events, now witnessing a renewal of interest in hys-

* The term *"pithiatisme"* was created by Babinski to signify hysteria as he conceived it. It is derived from the Greek words, *peithō* (I persuade) and *iatos* (curable). hardly balance his sharp comments on "the inferiority of the weaker sex" (Benedikt,

teria. For example, a substantial place was assigned to this subject (together with the transference) at the 28th International Congress of Psychoanalysis, in Paris in 1973. In France it has been the theme of various study groups. And while "Conversion reaction" is listed in both the 1952 and 1961 editions of the American Medical Association's *Standard Nomenclature of Diseases*, "Hysterical personality" on the other hand, of which there is no mention in 1952, reappears in 1961. Notwithstanding this "reinstatement," it is clear that some authors would still wish to abolish the very term "hysteria." Thus Guze (1970) is quite prepared to retain the concept of "Conversion symptom (or reaction) "*—but with regard to what he calls hysteria (which would seem to be equivalent to the "Hysterical personality" of the *Standard Nomenclature*) , he reminds us with what fear, ignominy and ostracism leprosy is still invested. In the same way as the latter is today known as "Hansen's disease," Guze proposes that hysteria be renamed "Briquet's syndrome" (a tribute, perhaps, to a great French clinician who is, however, largely unknown today).

The unpredictable vicissitudes of nomenclature apart, the last words should perhaps be sought amongst the analysts. In May, 1968, the American Psychoanalytic Association, at its 55th Annual Meeting, held a symposium on the "Reconsideration of the concept of hysteria." The chairman of the symposium, in a subsequent letter to one of the authors concerning the film we had shown, expressed a somewhat disillusioned general comment, stating in effect that, when all is said and done in attempting to gain a precise and literal understanding of the nature of hysteria, one realizes in the final analysis that we have hardly advanced at all.

To return to the case of Emmy von N.: Freud seems, therefore, to have made an error of judgment with regard to this patient, which certainly strikes one as surprising. It should, however, be noted that he was more than once mistaken in his assessment of

---

* Guze regards the "Converson symptom" as monosymptomatic: e.g., either aphonia, or retention of urine, or blindness, etc., (all well-known classical symptoms). Hysteria, on the other hand, is in his view polysymptomatic in that it presents a picture (frequently, and dramatically, portrayed by the patient himself) comprising a congeries of pains, anxieties, gastro-intestinal disorders, menstrual dysfunction, sexual and marital maladjustment, medical and medicinal overconsumption, surgical and hospital addiction, etc.

people (including his own pupils) and that, on his own (paradoxical) admission, he was not a *"Menschenkenner,"* i.e., a "judge of men" (Sachs, 1944, p. 56). Eissler (1970, p. 235) for his part, taking up the same point made by Jones (1955, pp. 458, 467), rejects the idea that Freud was not a *"Menschenkenner."* But why not concede that genius does not necessarily preclude a certain naïveté?

When Freud believed that the neuroses of his female patients were the result of their having been sexually assaulted by their father, he was undoubtedly naïve—to the point of not excluding the possibility that his own father* had treated his (Freud's) sisters in this way. It may be recalled that Benedikt recorded similar "observations" concerning the rape of young girls by adults. It is true that this "theory of seduction" which had thus been built up** collapsed in 1897 and that it then caused Freud deep distress. We shall see, however, that this transient "aberration" (of accepting as valid currency confabulations which merely concealed an infantile incestuous phantasy) would set him on the track of certain discoveries of prime importance, in particular that of infantile sexuality (which was to arouse such censure and indignation).

Another instance of Freud's credulity was his adherence for a while to some of Fliess' more farfetched theories (the concept of "periodicity," for example—or indeed that of a nasal reflex neurosis, which induced Freud on several occasions to submit to operations by Fliess himself; the latter, who also underwent several nasal operations, would in fact seem to have been a borderline case of pathological "surgical addiction"). Credulity is, however, but one aspect, among others, of the complex Freud-Fliess relationship. For further information in this connection, the reader is referred to Jones (1953-1957), *The Origins of Psychoanalysis* (Freud, 1954), and the more recent works of Mannoni (1971), and especially Schur (1972) who reproduces several relevant, hitherto unpublished, letters.

Now, no one will deny that Fliess, notwithstanding his "incred-

---

* "... *mein eigener* [*Vater*] *nicht ausgeschlossen*"—"... (in every case the father), not excluding my own ...": this phrase, in a letter to Fliess of September 21, 1897, was, as Strachey has pointed out (Freud, 1950, p. 259), omitted in the German edition of *The Origins of Psychoanalysis,* as it was likewise in the English translation (Freud, 1954, p. 215).

** See, e.g., editor's note to Freud, 1896a, pp. 160-161; and Freud, 1896b, pp. 208-209.

ible" excesses, played for Freud the part of intellectual stimulus on one hand and on the other hand that of "affective catalyst," a kind of "transferencelike figure" at the time of Freud's self-analysis, as Schur has noted.

In the case of Emmy von N., we may ask ourselves whether Freud was not under the influence of his patient's charms. It is possible that on other occasions, too, he was not insensitive to the seductivity frequently displayed by female hysterics. He may perhaps have developed what Jones (1953, p. 246), speaking of Breuer's feelings for Anna O., calls a "strong countertransference."

It remains that Freud was a man of principle, anxious to stay faithful even in mind to his fiancée, later his wife; he could not, therefore, fail to mobilize a system of defenses against the attractions to which he was sensible. We have seen that, in recalling Breuer's experience with Anna O., he had dismissed the possibility of himself becoming the subject of a similar misadventure on the grounds that he in no way possessed his friend's irresistible attraction. It would seem that, all the better to reassure himself and even after he had "invented" the transference, Freud went so far as to develop for a certain time (as previously mentioned) a completely blind spot with regard to the sexual factor in hysteria and in hypnosis, while retaining the physiological explanation of which the Salpêtrière had provided the outline.

This blind spot, if one may so describe it, was an extensive one. For it seems doubtful that so wide a reader as he would not have been acquainted with Bailly's Report (Rapport, 1784c), as indeed with the writings of the magnetists of the nineteenth century, all of whom had clearly drawn attention to the potential existence of an erotic factor in hypnosis. In his *Psychische Behandlung* (1890), Freud did allude, albeit in a summary and incidental fashion, to the element of love in the hypnotic relationship. Referring in this article to hypnotic hallucinations, he wrote: "It may be remarked, by the way, that, outside hypnosis and in real life, credulity such as the subject has in relation to his hypnotist is shown only by a child towards his beloved parents, and that an attitude of similar subjection on the part of one person towards another has only one parallel, though a complete one—namely in certain love-relationships where there is extreme devotion [*mit voller Hingebung*]. A combination of exclusive attachment and credulous obedience is in general among the characteristics of love" (Freud, 1890, p. 296) .

The passage here quoted reveals two concepts which would later give rise to important developments: on one hand, the presence in hypnosis of a parent-child type of relationship, containing in embryonic form the concept of the repetition in the present of a past experience; and on the other hand, the essentially love-like character assumed by the hypnotic relation—a concept which Freud was later to take up again and elaborate in his *Group Psychology* (1921, Chap. VIII) .

In 1890, however, Freud had done no more than put forward these ideas *incidentally;* indeed, he made no further mention of them in his work on hypnosis (1891b) , published one year later. These were not in any case original ideas, for they had already been advanced by other authors. The infantile regression of the hypnotized subject had been described in the era of animal magnetism, and the possible element of love in the hypnotic relationship had, as we have seen, been recognized since the end of the eighteenth century. Closer to Freud's own time, the subject's love for the hypnotist had been described, in analogous terms to those which he used in the *Psychische Behandlung*, in A. Binet's *Études de Psychologie expérimentale* (1888). This author was well known to Freud, since, in the *Studies on Hysteria* (Breuer and Freud, 1895, p. 7) , he referred to another work by Binet, *Les Altérations de la Personnalité* (1892) , which contained an account of a procedure similar to that employed by Breuer and Freud in their cathartic method. Binet, in fact, stated: "The magnetized subject is like a passionate lover for whom there exists nothing else in the world but the loved one" (1888, p. 249) .

Freud appears subsequently to have entirely forgotten the idées-forces to which we have referred. The original text of the article in which these were expressed (Freud, 1890) was not included in his *Gesammelte Schriften* (1924-34), only in the posthumously published *Gesammelte Werke* (Vol. 5, 1942) . Freud must either have overlooked this article or else have considered it of no interest. In fact, as he himself later stated (1925a, p. 18) , he published "scarcely anything" between 1886 and 1891. The first work after 1886 that he mentioned is a monograph on the cerebral paralyses of children, written in conjunction with Oskar Rie (Freud, 1891a). With regard to the love relationship in hypnosis, he did not mention in his work of 1921 the fact that he had previously spoken of it in the *Psychische Behandlung*. As to the parental role of the hypnotist, he credited one of his pupils with its discovery, for he wrote that Ferenczi (1909) "has made the true discovery that when a hypnotist gives the command to sleep, which is often done at the beginning of hypnosis, he is putting himself in the place of the subject's parents" (Freud, 1921, p. 127).

It is curious to note in passing that Freud never personally pointed out the obvious correlation between the "parent-child" relationship in hypnosis (which had been recorded by him in 1890, as also by others), and the origin of the actual concept of transference. Did he refuse to admit the idea that he had "extracted" the transference from hypnosis? It should also be borne in mind that, even more than the actual concept of the transference, it is its *management* which is the cornerstone of all psychoanalytic treatment. Moreover, its theory as well as its mode of application were not fully elaborated until around 1912-1917. And in the case of Dora, Freud (1905c, p. 109) was well aware, after the event, that he had not made use of his discovery to its full extent, and that this had contributed to the failure of the treatment.

Freud's ideas on the love relationship in hypnosis, latent in his mind, remained, therefore, in the "theoretical stage." He did not feel that they concerned him personally. It is following his misadventure that they reemerged from the depths of his unconscious and provided material for his elaboration of the concept of transference and his interpretations of hypnosis. He was to state later (Freud, 1925a, p. 27) that he "had long suspected" the presence of such an element in hypnosis, which would explain his diffidence about practicing it at first. His passion for research was, however, stronger than his resistances, although this situation did not last long. It was, in fact, upset on the day of the famous incident which brought him face-to-face with the erotic potential of the hypnotic relationship. Thereupon his "suspicions" turned into certainties; consequently, the defenses which he had hitherto employed were no longer adequate. In short, in spite of his foreknowledge, he had undergone the very same experience as Breuer, but did not for all that attribute to himself the "irresistible attraction" with which he had credited his friend. From this experiment "in vivo" he now deduced that in this kind of situation the physician, whether "irresistible" or not, was not personally involved. In consequence, the feelings evinced by the female patient must be directed toward some other person. This was indeed the view that he expressed to Breuer somewhat later on when informing him of his own misadventure. Placed in analogous situations, the two men had reacted in very different ways: one had fled, while the other had retained his composure.

It may well be thought that the solution which Freud found was destined to allay his anxieties, inasmuch as, with the concept of transference, the patient's emotional demands come to be diverted from the physician to the person of a substitute. It should be added that, at the moment when it arose in Freud's mind, the concept of the transference must have been, as it were, in no more than a nebulous state and could not constitute a complete system of defense. Freud's genius showed itself in his ability to realize how great was the scientific advantage that could be derived from this embryonic idea and to bring its elaboration to fruition through his subsequent research.

From the Transference to the Sexual Etiology of the Neuroses and Self-Analysis

It was therefore, in our opinion, at the time of the above-mentioned episode that the concept of transference took root in Freud's mind. It may perhaps be not unreasonable to suppose that the idea of the sexual etiology of the neuroses also occurred, or became clearer, to him on this same occasion. As he himself later observed: "The fact of the emergence of the transference in its crudely sexual form, whether affectionate or hostile, in every treatment of a neurosis, although this is neither desired nor induced by either doctor or patient, has always seemed to me the most irrefragable proof that the source of the driving forces of neurosis lies in sexual life" (Freud, 1914, p. 12).

It remains that Freud did not proffer any precise date in respect of his conception of the sexual etiology of the neuroses, as he had done in the case of his theory of dreams. It may nevertheless be assumed that it occurred fairly soon after the discovery of the transference. For the incident which determined the latter must be situated, as we have seen, shortly before June, 1892, while the first draft of the etiology of the neuroses is an undated manuscript which would seem to have been written towards the end of 1892 (Freud, 1950, pp. 177-178). One can only suppose that the discovery of the transference removed the last of Freud's inhibitions before he asserted the sexual nature of the neuroses.

With regard to this second discovery (sexual etiology), Jones states that it came as a "great shock" to Freud and that this could not have been otherwise in a man who was so "puritanical" (Jones, 1953, pp. 12, 298). All the more so, we may add, in that Freud suffered from neurotic disorders, and the very conception of his theory suddenly confronted him with his own sexuality. According to Jones (1953, pp. 334-337), these disorders assumed a serious nature around 1890, the period when Freud was regularly practicing hypnosis. These symptoms entered a critical stage in 1895, but eventually disappeared in 1900 or thereabouts. It seems probable that this exacerbation was due to the shock to which we have referred.

To be sure, the discovery of the transference might have set his mind at rest as to the nature of his patients' emotional demands or transports. But possibly, insofar as the actual basis of his own desires was concerned, he did not feel altogether reassured—whence a conflict with his superego, which combined with other factors to give rise to intense repercussions in his unconscious. It is with a view to investigating this conflict, probably in order to cure himself, that Freud decided in 1897 to undertake his self-analysis, which brought him greater stability. Jones very rightly points out that "it was just in the years when the neurosis was at its height, 1897-1900, that Freud did his most original work." And, as he states, "The neurotic symptoms must have been one of the ways in which the unconscious material was indirectly trying to emerge" (Jones, 1953, p. 335).

While psychoanalytic literature does not hesitate to extol Anna O. because of her role in the development of psychoanalysis, it might well pay equal tribute to the anonymous patient who, in throwing her arms one day around Freud's neck, thus initiated a series of discoveries of prime importance.

But—somewhat ironically—it is clear that the patient would have restrained her emotional impulse had Freud observed the practice (which was current in his day) of treating cases in the presence of a third person.

As to this being the precise origin of the discovery of the transference, the hypothesis advanced by one of the authors (Chertok, 1968b) is not inconsistent with Eissler's views (1971, p. 305). For the latter describes the episode as "crucial" to the birth of psychoanalysis and believes that, from then on, Freud "was bound to discover transference and its nature." In passing, he recalls a phrase of Freud's ("I was modest enough* not to attribute the event to my own irresistible personal attraction . . .") and, by way of a question, poses a problem of interpretation: "But how many men," he asks, "would have had the strength of character to resist that temptation? Even at present, when analysts learn throughout their training about the nature of transference, and should therefore be prepared for what they will have to expect, there is a substantial number who ascribe the patient's positive statements to their own excellence, and the negative ones only to transference."

What exactly does Eissler understand by "temptation"? Is it the temptation for Freud to respond to his patient's advances? Or else, the temptation to attribute to himself the role of seducer? This formulation and the use of the word "temptation" are at the least a source of ambiguity. (Be that as it may, we for our part feel certain that Eissler intends to convey the second of these hypotheses.)

At all events, it can hardly be doubted that in this connection Freud was a genius, as Eissler reiterates. But is it necessary to make him a superman? If Eissler wished to imply that Freud consciously rejected his patient's advances, then it must be admitted that Freud the physician had no great merit in so doing. If, on the other hand, it is a question of his diffidence in regarding himself as a Don Juan,

---

* We feel that *"nüchtern genug"* is better rendered by "sufficiently cool" or "cool-headed," rather than by the *Standard Edition*'s translation, "modest enough" (which Eissler reproduces).

one must, in our view, return to a somewhat less "lyrical" plane: Freud, considered as a male (at this period—and before his self-analysis), simply lacked self-confidence; this, as we have seen, was one of his personality traits.

It can be said, moreover, that a woman patient does not fling her arms around her physician's neck without some reason. It may be that Freud developed a "strong countertransference" and that he felt, unconsciously, a certain attraction toward his patient—which she in turn unconsciously perceived.*

If such was indeed the case, it would certainly not detract from Freud's genius. Would it not, in fact, be precisely the paradoxical but true mark of his genius to have made in his own case an error of interpretation—a providential error leading to the discovery of the transference? We shall presently reexamine these hypotheses.

Problems Raised by the Transference

Szasz (1963) has drawn attention to the value of the transference as a defense for the therapist and mentions, as we have here, the example of Breuer's being reassured by Freud's explanation. He sees in this precisely the occasion of Freud's discovery, without, however,

---

* Temptation as well as abuse (acting out) have always existed—and Bailly's Report (Rapport, 1784c) had already drawn attention to these dangers. They are undoubtedly still to be met with today. But there are those (might it be a manifestation of the permissive society?) who advocate, in certain cases and for the good of the patient, a systematic "love treatment." For such is the title which Dr. Martin Shepard (1971) has given to the book which he devotes to "sexual intimacy between patients and psychotherapists"—a title which is not without recalling the *Magnétiseur amoureux* of De Villers (but there any comparison between the two works ends).

It contains an account of eleven "cases" (in none of which its author is himself involved) where sexual relations occurred, and indeed continued, between patient and therapist—with no therapeutic intention. From these data Shepard first draws up a balance sheet: in six cases, the effect allegedly proved beneficial; in another three, harmful; and in the remaining two, negligible. He then has no hesitation in proceeding to formulate certain rules of "therapeutic conduct" in the matter.

Masters and Johnson (1970), call upon voluntary and carefully screened "partner surrogates" in a few cases of unmarried men. These provide the patients with practical help and "work" in sexual (and social) relations. But both of these authors, on being interviewed by Shepard (1971, pp. 7-8), expressed extreme skepticism with regard to his theory on the place of "love treatment" in psychotherapy. In fact, they make some highly relevant comments on the unfortunate consequences of "therapeutic malpractice" in this field, which they have by no means uncommonly encountered in their case histories (Masters and Johnson, 1970, pp. 385-391).

explaining how the latter arrived at this idea. He states only that Freud, as observer and not as actor, found himself in a position of scientific detachment: "I have tried to show," writes Szasz, "that because Anna O. was not Freud's patient it was easier for him to assume an observing role toward her sexual communications than if they had been directed towards himself" (p. 441).

The Breuer-Anna O. episode must undoubtedly have worried Freud and caused him to reflect upon the role of the physician in relation to his female patient. But in our opinion, the concept of transference actually arose in Freud's mind only at the time of his own misadventure, when, from his position of observer, he had become the actor. For if, as Szasz maintains, the transference is intended to ward off the "threat of the patient's eroticism," it is probable that Freud conceived his idea in a situation where he happened to be personally threatened.

It is obvious that, in the absence of definite biographical data, every explanation must necessarily remain purely hypothetical. In basing our own explanation on an episode which was actually experienced, we believe, however, that it remains in the direct line of psychoanalytic epistemology. Was it not indeed in his famous dream known as "Irma's injection," on the memorable date of July 24, 1895, that Freud found confirmation of the idea that the fulfillment of a hidden wish is the essence of a dream?

While it was through his practice of hypnosis that Freud conceived the idea of transference, he nonetheless decided immediately afterwards to abandon the use of hypnotism. The transference, constituting as it does a superior defense for the therapist, should in fact have reassured him (unless some doubt lingered in Freud's unconscious—perhaps the subject's love for her hypnotist was not exclusively transference-love?).* It should be remembered, on the other hand, that in Freud's view the transference had the disadvantage of presenting an obstacle to treatment, a resistance to the recovery of memories, as he observed in his *Studies on Hysteria* in 1895. However, in practicing his new technique, it was not long before Freud again en-

---

* See the following section on "Love and transference."

countered the transference. Although this surprised him, he was now able to convert the obstacle into an instrument; the analysis of resistances and of the transference has become the essential element of analytical treatment.

While we consider that the origin of the discovery of the transference can be traced to Freud's misadventure, it cannot be denied that the interpretation of this incident still presents not a few problems. We have already inquired into Freud's possible feelings toward his patient. But conversely, what was the meaning of this emotion with which a woman approached her physician? It is by no means certain that the feelings she evinced towards Freud were not in fact addressed to him personally. More particularly is this so since his practice of massage at the time brought him into close physical proximity to his female patients. The hypnotic procedures themselves at that period involved a direct contact more frequently than is the case with the techniques employed today* (by the very fact that the existence of transference relationships was still unknown). It is, therefore, not impossible that Freud's patient had been erotically aroused by direct physical excitation, instead of being brought by hypnosis to a state of regression favorable to the emergence of transference feelings.

All things considered, one cannot rule out the possibility that, from his personal case, Freud may have evolved an erroneous interpretation which, paradoxically, would have led him to one of his most fruitful discoveries. But is it not in consequence of an error of judgment that he came to make other discoveries? Is it not his credulity, when faced with certain patients supposedly seduced by their father, which put him on the track of the theories of psychical reality, infantile sexuality, and the Oedipus complex? The history of science, as we have already seen in connection with Charcot, doubtless provides more than one example of this kind of process based on a "providential error."

This problem of interpretation, together with others which have

---

* We know from Freud's article, *Psychische Behandlung* (1890), that he sometimes made use of passes at a short distance above the patient's face and body for the induction of hypnosis. In his article, *Hypnose* (1891b), he mentions a similar technique of passes which he used to deepen the trance.

previously been mentioned, compels us to admit that, on the theoretical plane, the concept of transference is far from being elucidated. It is nonetheless an operational concept of prime importance and one which constitutes the very center of all treatment. There are many other scientific concepts whose theoretical basis remains obscure, but whose practical effectiveness is incontestable.

In his well-known paper on "The problem of the transference," Lagache (1952) set forth the numerous and divergent interpretations of this concept that have been advanced. As to its mode of production, Ida Macalpine (1950) drew attention to the inadequacy of our knowledge in this respect. Finally, the more recent article by Szasz (1963), already cited and to which we shall return, provides a critical survey of the different definitions of the transference.

It is not proposed here to examine all the questions that still remain unsettled, but to confine ourselves to the period of the "genesis of the transference," when it was known solely in its libidinal form. In concluding this discussion, we would, therefore, wish to consider the much debated question of the nature of transference-love.

Love and Transference

Love in hypnosis is regarded as paradigmatic of transference-love. But Freud's meaning when he spoke of "the mysterious element that was at work behind hypnotism" (1925a, p. 27) is far from clear. The precise sense of the German word *"mystisch,"* as here employed by Freud, is already somewhat ambiguous. It may have not only a religious connotation, but also a wider meaning (but etymologically sound) of "hidden, inexplicable, obscure," etc.—as is indeed the case of the cognate words in English. In fact, it has been variously rendered in the English translation of Freud's works (*Standard Edition*), sometimes by "mysterious" (e.g. 1921, p. 115; 1925a, p. 27) and sometimes by "mystical" (e.g. 1910, p. 22), according to the context. It may be assumed that both interpretations coexisted in Freud's mind and that, in describing as *"mystisch"* the transference-love in hypnosis, he wished to emphasize at the same time its unusual as well as its idealistic aspect. He wrote: "The hypnotic relation is the unlimited devotion of someone in love, but with sexual satisfaction excluded" (Freud, 1921, p. 115).* He added that hypnosis "exhibits some features which are not met by the rational explanation we have hitherto given of it as a state of being in love, with the directly sexual trends excluded. There is still a great deal in it which we must recognize as unexplained and mysterious" (1921, p. 115).**

When Freud later encountered transference-love again in the course of analysis, he still invested it with the same impersonal quality and integrity as in the case of hypnosis. As he was to state in 1915, "the patient's falling in love is induced by the analytic situation and is not to be attributed to the charms of his [the physician's] own person" (Freud, 1915a, pp. 160-161).*** The therapist must, therefore, always exclude the physical aspect of this love. Thus does he find himself doubly insured against the erotic potential of the relationship: the patient's love is not directed towards him, nor is it in danger of leading to physical gratification. This, let us repeat, is a far cry from the image of a Freud accused of propagating a kind of "pansexualism": in fact Freud had, on the contrary, taken increasing precautions to safeguard himself against any such temptations and preserve his "purity."

In the same paper, Freud attempted to establish a difference between "genuine love" and "transference-love," although he did not arrive at any very clear-cut conclusions. First, after having specified that transference-love "consists of new editions of old traits and that it repeats infantile reactions" (1915a, p. 168), he added that "this is the essential character of every state of being in love" and "there

---

* Freud should have realized, from his personal experience, that it is incorrect to describe love in hypnosis as invariably platonic; the patient who threw her arms round his neck was clearly seeking physical gratification.

** As early as 1898, Janet had referred to the existence of a "very special kind" of love—without, however, seeing in it the slightest implication of a "mysterious/mystical" element.

*** Freud's andorocentrism is once again in evidence here—he speaks of *"Arzt"* (i.e. physician—masculine) and *"Patientin"* (feminine). Did he already have an inkling in 1915 (at which time he had only a few women pupils, including Lou Andreas-Salomé and Helene Deutsch; in 1919 there were five women in the Viennese group) that there would one day be many women analysts and that their patients would sometimes be men? It may be recalled, in this connection, that Deleuze mentions having been magnetized by a "demoiselle," and that Madame de R. was a "practicing adherent" of Puységur.

is no such state which does not reproduce infantile prototypes" (p. 168). He was consequently led to admit that "we have no right to dispute that the state of being in love which makes its appearance in the course of analytic treatment has the character of a 'genuine' love" (p. 168). He nevertheless noted that transference-love is characterized by certain specific features and, in particular, "is lacking to a high degree in a regard for reality" (pp. 168-169), a fact which would differentiate it from "normal love." But, thereupon, he immediately added: "We should not forget, however, that these departures from the norm constitute precisely what is essential about being in love" (p. 169).

It is perhaps because of the practical impossibility of distinguishing between what is "real" and what is not in transference-love that Freud advised, not without wisdom, that a patient be not shown out of hand the illusory nature of her love for the physician. For it is above all important not to send back into repression the instinctual drive which "emerges."

Szasz (1963), in the previously mentioned article, emphasized the complexity of the question. The distinction between what is attributable to reality and unreality, respectively, is very largely a matter of evaluative judgments on the part of the two persons involved, but the analyst's judgment and the patient's experience are not necessarily concordant. There is, generally speaking, no sure way of ascertaining whose impression, of the two, more closely approximates to "truth."

In 1966 Christian David published an interesting paper entitled "Metapsychological considerations on the state of being in love." In the course of his examination in general terms of the state of being in love, he, too, was led to investigate the same problem we ourselves have posed. He asked himself whether, in regarding love as essentially based on a "repetition of infantile reactions," one is not thereby reduced to adopting a somewhat oversimplified approach. He very brilliantly set about demonstrating that genuine love comprises not only elements which are outside the transference relationship and not subject to repetition, but also trends which are not regressive, but progressive. He wrote: "The state of being in love represents a rebirth, not merely a repetition, and as it were, the transposed melody of a forgotten experience" (David, 1966, p. 217). With regard to love, he placed emphasis on "innovation and not on repetition, on synthesis and not on dissociation" (p. 218). We have already noted that in every relationship, in every "exchange," strictly original elements come into play.

We do not propose to discuss here the theories advanced by David. For if one allows, as he does, that there is a distinct difference between the two kinds of love, it may well be asked by what criteria it will be possible to assign to one or the other of these the love that the patient undergoing analysis or hypnosis entertains for her physician. The author, however, provides no answer to this question. Indeed, some degree of confusion is liable to arise in the reader's mind from the fact that, in dealing with the phenomenological description of the "classical" state of being in love, David takes as a model love in hypnosis, i.e. the very kind of love which is generally regarded as the preeminent example of transference-love.

We may wonder whether this confusion might not be attributable precisely to that method which seeks to explain love from the starting point of hypnosis. Indeed, David believes, together with Freud, that "it would be more to the point to explain being in love by means of hypnosis than the other way round" (Freud, 1921, p. 114). But such a method, whereby it is attempted to explain one mysterious phenomenon by another which is no less so, in our opinion could not possibly lead to any satisfactory results; as we shall see, the two phenomena require different modes of investigation.

Freud's conception of hypnosis at the period of id-psychology has, moreover, evolved at the hands of those who succeeded him, in particular among the adherents of ego psychology. It is unnecessary here to consider at any length the ego-psychological theory of hypnosis expounded in the writings of Gill and Brenman (1959). Suffice it to say that, in order to explain hypnosis, we should not restrict ourselves to research in the instinctual field alone, but should pursue other lines of investigation in the somatic, "sensorimotor" field (Kubie and Margolin, 1944). According to Gill and Brenman, "hypnosis is a particular kind of regressive process which may be initiated either by sensorimotor-ideational deprivation or by the stimulation of an archaic relationship to the hypnotist" (1959, pp. xix-xx). The actual role of the transference is the subject of controversy. Whereas for Gill and Brenman it still constitutes an integral part of the hypnotic process, Kubie (1961) regards the transference (as also regression) as an epiphenomenon—as the consequence and not the cause of the hypnotic state. As already mentioned, in Kubie's opinion there is, from the psychological point of view, no feature that is specific to hypnosis. Its originality would then be situated principally in the psychophysiological setting; therefore, the solution of the enigma must be sought in a psychophysiological elucidation.

As to love, its particular mysterious character requires, so we believe, to be studied on a purely psychological, instinctual plane (the physiological aspect of physical love is obviously not taken into consideration here). Thus, the hypnotic state* and that of being in love are situated at two specific levels of consciousness. While transference factors may come into play in the one as in the other, the essential nature of these two states does not lie on an identical plane; in order to explain them respectively, one should employ different methods of research. Assuming that certain aspects of both love and hypnosis may lie outside the transference situation, hypnosis itself may present, in addition, some aspects extrinsic to interpersonal relations. However that may be, the hypnotic relationship is not necessarily "the unlimited devotion of someone in love"; the hypnotic relationship is no longer regarded, as in former times, predominantly as a libidinal submission of a masochistic type on the subject's part. An English psychoanalyst, Harold Stewart (1963), in fact considers that the hypnotized subject both loves and hates the hypnotist at the same time, and that it is his hostility which constitutes the most important aspect of the situation.

From the various hypotheses that have been advanced, it appears that erotism is not a strictly specific component of hypnosis.** We

---

* A state, be it remembered, whose actual existence remains the subject of controversy.

** Gill and Brenman (1959, p. 29) consider that erotic phantasies are not specific to hypnosis and do not occur any more frequently in the hypnotic relationship than in any other deep psychotherapeutic relationship. Such also is the opinion of Josephine Hilgard (1970) who states that the hypnotic relation does not necessarily comprise an erotic element and may in some cases even be impersonal. We may wonder whether Janet's varied ideas on "the very special kind of love," "the need of mental direction," "the need to love and to be loved," might not be more deeply investigated. They are not so far removed from Freud's ideas on "a state of being in love, with the directly sexual trends excluded." Might it be a "fusion" relationship at a "pre-object" level that is involved?

would again emphasize that the nature of hypnosis remains unknown. It is, no doubt, an induced regressive state, in the course of which there may emerge infantile emotional reactions of all kinds, both libidinal and aggressive, with a transference character. The same situation is to be found in the analytic relationship. As Ida Macalpine stated, "analytic transference manifestations are a slow motion picture of hypnotic transference manifestations: they take some time to develop, unfold slowly and gradually, and not all at once as in hypnosis" (1950, p. 519).

It must not be forgotten, moreover, that in analysis as in hypnosis (and even more so in the latter, because of a usually closer proximity) there also exists a *real encounter* between two persons, sometimes of opposite sex, and as Bailly had already observed: ". . . Whatever the illness may be, it does not deprive us of our sex" (Rapport, 1784c, p. 279). Thus, the part of the "real" and that of the "unreal," of the "present" and of the "past," are closely intermingled, and the problem of the true nature of transference-love is inextricable.

Visit to Nancy

If Freud's relations with hypnosis are examined, one cannot fail to recognize the part played by the experimentation with posthypnotic suggestion, a role not unlike that of the experimental paralyses to which we have already referred. It is probably at Nancy that the seeds implanted in his mind by the study of these paralyses (as also of major hysteria) really germinated and became integrated in the mainstream of ideas which would lead him to the elaboration of his own concept of the unconscious. It is there, as he later recorded, that he "received the profoundest impression of the possibility that there could be powerful mental processes which nevertheless remained hidden from the consciousness of men" (Freud, 1925a, p. 17). (On the subject of posthypnotic suggestion, see Chapter IV of the present work.)

Enriched by all that he had learned at the Salpêtrière, Freud now turned his attention toward the Nancy School and in 1888 produced a German translation of Bernheim's book *De la Suggestion* (Bernheim, 1888b). While he had already seen in Paris what rich experimental prospects are opened up by hypnosis, he made similar observations at Nancy on witnessing experiments in which orders, suggested under hypnosis, were carried out by the patient on awakening. He was thus led to state later that, "now for the first time, in the phenomena of hypnotism, it [the unconscious] became something actual, tangible and subject to experiment" (Freud, 1924, p. 192).

He was already acquainted with these experiments through Bernheim's book, but he was also able to witness them personally with Liébeault and Bernheim in 1889. In this respect he asserted: "If the work of Liébeault and his pupils had produced nothing more than the knowledge of these remarkable, though at the same time everyday, phenomena [of posthypnotic suggestion and suggestion in the waking state] and this enrichment of psychology by a new experimental method, . . . they would already be assured of a prominent place among the scientific discoveries of this century" (Freud, 1889, p. 99).

These lines appeared in the *Wiener medizinische Wochenschrift* of November 23, 1889, in Freud's review of Auguste Forel's book, *Der Hypnotismus.* The first part of this review had appeared in the number for July 13 of the same year. Freud's visit to Nancy took place, therefore, between the publication of the two parts of this review. Did he, even before his visit, intuitively sense the importance of posthypnotic suggestion for the development of his future discoveries (an intuition subsequently confirmed by the experiments which he witnessed with Bernheim) —or else, might he have added to an earlier text his praise of Liébeault (cited above), after having met the latter?

On several occasions in the course of his career, Freud would proffer the phenomenon of posthypnotic suggestion as evidence of the existence of the unconscious. Half a century after his visit to Nancy, in his last (unfinished) manuscript, dated October 20, 1938, with the title in English, "Some Elementary Lessons in Psychoanalysis" (Freud, 1938), he gave a detailed account of an experiment which he had witnessed: The subject is instructed, under hypnosis, to open an umbrella on awaking and hold it over the doctor's head— an order which he duly carries out. On being thereupon asked to give the reason for his action, he replies uncertainly that, as it is raining outside, he thought the doctor would wish to open his umbrella before going out. Being in ignorance of the real motive for his behavior, the subject therefore makes up an explanation out of hand, which is an obvious rationalization. Freud put forward this experiment as one of three examples selected to demonstrate the existence of the unconscious—the other two being the unreasond solution of a problem and the parapraxes (Freud, 1938, pp. 283-285).

Another experiment should also be mentioned here, concerning posthypnotic amnesia. It is of historical significance and was for Freud, who had often witnessed it while he was with Bernheim, the starting point of a complete transformation of his psychotherapeutic technique. When the subjects awoke from a state of hypnotic somnambulism, they could remember nothing of what had happened while they were asleep. But by insisting and, if necessary, laying his hand on their forehead, Bernheim succeeded in causing the "return to the surface" of the subjects' memories of what they had lived through in hypnosis. Freud, believing that his own patients, even without being hypnotized, "must in fact 'know' all the things which had hitherto only been made accessible to them in hypnosis," decided to adopt this method with a view to "forcing the forgotten facts and connections into consciousness" (Freud, 1925a, pp. 27-28). He then abandoned hypnotism and, later, the laying on of hands and switched over to the technique of free association; he retained, however, his practice of requiring the patient to lie down.

Let us consider, incidentally, the notion of "artificial," which may perhaps lead to one mode of the evolution of Freud's thought: posthypnotic amnesia is just as completely *artificial* as the paralyses induced by Charcot. In both cases, as Freud was able to observe, something was "done and undone" by the power of *idea* alone. But, while in the first case it was a physical symptom (paralysis), in the second it was a psychical phenomenon (amnesia), that was produced.

The very fact that it is possible to "do and undo" an amnesic state is clear proof that one can "manipulate" the memory, the recall—in short, the state of consciousness (*"Bewusstsein"*).

Freud derived benefit from the teachings of both French schools; and it should be remembered that he retained a hesitant attitude towards the controversy which existed between them, although he is commonly said to have sided with Nancy. Referring to Freud's interest in the theory of hypnotism and suggestion, James Strachey (1966, pp. 67-68) has shown that Freud oscillated somewhat with regard to the Charcot-Bernheim dispute. While he has noted five instances between 1888 and 1921 in which the master of psychoanalysis adopted a position opposing Bernheim, he has found only one instance where Freud defended Bernheim's views in part. Indeed, in his obituary notice on Charcot, written in 1893—influenced, so Strachey believes, by his visit to Nancy in 1889—Freud (1893b) supported Bernheim's concept of suggestion as the central point of hypnosis, while at the same time emphasizing the lack of precision of the term "suggestion" as employed by Bernheim. In conclusion, Strachey quotes a remark made by Freud in a letter to A. A. Roback in 1930 which seems to confirm his hesitation: ". . . over the question of hypnosis I sided against Charcot, even if not entirely with Bernheim" (Freud, 1960, p. 394).

Freud's doubts are in no way surprising since the controversy between the Schools of Nancy and the Salpêtrière centered around a phenomenon whose nature, as he was well aware, had not been elucidated.

It is, in fact, still impossible today to give a definitive verdict on the divergences between the somatic theories of the Salpêtrière and the psychological theories of Nancy. Each finds its historical justification and complements the other; and each has indeed contributed greatly to the advent of modern psychotherapy.

IV

The Unconscious in France
Before Freud:
Premises of a Discovery

WE CERTAINLY LAY NO CLAIM to being the first to
study the history of the unconscious before Freud. We do, however,
believe that our present inquiry is pursued within a strictly defined
perspective. Among all those who have dealt with the subject before
us, we may mention Whyte (1960), whose book extends very widely
into the realms of literature and philosophy. There is also the vast
synthesis by Ellenberger (1970) entitled *The Discovery of the Unconscious,* which in fact constitutes a textbook of universal history
of dynamic psychotherapy and psychiatry. In the USSR, following a
lengthy period during which the unconscious was disregarded, there
appeared an important work on the subject (Bassin, 1968) : while
remaining generally critical of Freud, it is nevertheless noteworthy
that the author concedes that here and there he does have some
merit (see the detailed review by Koupernik, 1969) . In addition, we
would refer to the book by Anzieu (1975) , *L'Auto-analyse de Freud*
("Freud's Self-Analysis") , which provides data of considerable interest on the development of Freud's thought.

The influence exerted on Freud by the German literature and
philosophy of the nineteenth century has often been stressed, and
rightly so. As Anzieu states, "the concept of the unconscious comes
as no surprise to someone who has been brought up in the Germanic

153

culture" (1975, I, p. 152). The idea of an unconscious instinctual
life, which reveals itself more particularly in dreams or in insanity,
is deeply rooted in the mind of the German Romantics. In the same
way, on reading Nietzsche or Schopenhauer, one cannot fail to be
impressed by the striking similarity between their theories and certain Freudian concepts. This is especially noticeable in regard to
Nietzsche; it is to him, for example, that we owe the term "Id" (in
its original German form, *"das Es"*) to designate the realm of the
instinctual drives and instincts. Freud was, moreover, so much aware
of this convergence that, on his own admission, for a long time he
avoided reading that author for fear of being too deeply influenced
by him (Freud, 1925a, p. 60).

In the field of psychology, Freud was very well acquainted with
the views of Johann Friedrich Herbart (1776-1841) whom both his
teachers, Brücke and Meynert, held in high esteem. He had, indeed,
long been familiar with this author, since G. A. Lindner's *Lehrbuch
der empirischen Psychologie* ("Textbook of Empirical Psychology,"
1858), which he had studied during his last year in high school, was
actually a compendium of the Herbartian conceptions. With Herbart
we already encounter the concepts of psychical conflict, the unconscious, and repression. These terms are employed, it is true, in the
context of an intellectualist psychology very different from the future
Freudian perspective. It nonetheless remains that for Freud a knowledge of Herbart no doubt played an important part in leading him
at a very early stage to conceive mental life as a system dominated
by the conflict between contradictory representations.

Many more non-French authors could be mentioned (such as, for
example, Theodor Lipps*), who also exerted an appreciable influence on Freud's elaboration of the concept of the unconscious. It is,
however, no accident that it was in Paris that Freud became definitively oriented toward the psychology of the neuroses and apprehended the first elements of his discovery. For he did not in fact
approach the unconscious as a theorist, but from the viewpoint of
medical practice. In this respect the French influence was for him

* On the influence of Theodor Lipps (1851-1914), who was Professor of Psychology
in Munich, see the letter to Fliess of August 26, 1898, and the footnote thereto
(Freud, 1954, pp. 260-261).

decisive. While French thought actually remained, on the whole, more firmly bound than German thought to the philosophy of consciousness inherited from Descartes, unconscious phenomena constituted in France, throughout the entire nineteenth century, the subject of experimental research which had no discernible counterpart at that period in the rest of Europe. For this reason it seemed to us interesting to retrace, within the framework of the present book, the emergence of the concept of the unconscious in French scientific discourse.

From earliest antiquity, philosophers have attached great importance to dreams and to altered or trance states, the latter implying more or less pronounced hypnotic states. They knew that in such states memories lost in the waking state could reappear and believed that the aptitude for "endoscopy" and telepathy was enhanced. They knew, too, that these states were concomitant with disorders of sensation (hypesthesiae and hyperesthesiae).

In some religions, the faculties of persons afflicted with these disorders came to be employed in foretelling the future. The trance states appeared just as sporadically and spontaneously in various collective religious neuroses—e.g., in the possessed nuns of Loudun (1633) or the mass ecstasy of those who assembled (around 1730) on the tomb of the beatified Jansenist deacon, François de Pâris. It may be noted, incidentally, that shamans and "medicine men" operate under similar conditions.

Until the end of the eighteenth century, these manifestations belonged to the realm of religious mysteries—or else they were regarded as epidemics of hysteria to which it was wiser not to attract attention. For a long time, and especially since Paracelsus, mystics had sought to heal psychosomatic disorders by placing the patients in a trance which rendered them more suggestible and so favored miraculous cures. The Freemasons, to whom Mesmer had adhered, carried out such cures in the secrecy of their lodges.

These practices and this knowledge remained esoteric. As already mentioned, through his quasi-paranoiac obstinacy Mesmer succeeded in attracting the attention of the academies (1784), the scientists and the physicians.

The concept of the unconscious thenceforth compelled recognition from three aspects:

1. The dream;
2. States of somnambulism, natural and induced;
3. Certain manifestations of mental illness.

Later it was realized that the unconscious plays a (sometimes decisive) part in the life and conscious actions of every one of us and that it is, on the whole, a constituent of our everyday life, and not a morbid state. Indeed there have ever been authors (Saint Augustine and Descartes among others) who emphasized the fact that memories from early infancy, which we had thought to be entirely lost, can reappear—and that our brain retains traces of all that we have previously experienced.

What, then, were the trends of thought during the nineteenth century, through which it became possible to define the concept of the unconscious?

1. *The Automatism of the Ideologists*

Under the leadership of Cabanis, the ideologist philosophers formed a circle of thinkers who gathered regularly around the widow of Helvétius at the beginning of the nineteenth century. Their aim was to analyze the mind while excluding all metaphysics. The group included Destutt de Tracy, Condorcet, Ampère, and others.* They based themselves on Condillac's view that in our decisions latent factors always intervene, which are more powerful than the motives we advance in explanation of our action. Maine de Biran (1802), for example, in his work on habit, used the term "automatism," although he did not employ the term "unconscious." He showed that a given action which at first requires some forethought does so decreasingly as it is repeated.

Not until the second half of the nineteenth century would this vague notion of the unconscious undergo any perceptible develop-

_____
* On the ideologists, see the works of Renouvier (1842) and Cousin (1828).

ment at the hands of the philosophers. Yet it is an important one to remember insofar as, subsequently, the French psychologists always evinced a tendency to regard the unconscious as an aggregation of automatisms rather than as a dynamic source which feeds our conscious thought.

2. *The Unconscious Studied by the Magnetists*

Mesmer's aphorisms, published by Caullet de Veaumorel (Mesmer, 1785), contain a description of somnambulism, albeit still a very sketchy one, for this state did not arouse in him the same curiosity as in Puységur. Here is the text of the two aphorisms concerned:

(Aphorism 261)—

"The unfortunate fact in regard to our opportunity of acquiring knowledge is that those persons who are subject to the crises almost always lose all memory of their impressions on regaining the ordinary state. Were it not so, and they were to retain a perfect idea of these, they would themselves provide us with all the observations that I place before you, more easily than I can; but as to that which these persons are unable to reproduce for us in the ordinary state, can we not learn it from them when they are in a state of crisis?"

(Aphorism 263) —

"I believe, therefore, that it is possible, by studying the nervous persons who are subject to the crises, to obtain from them personally an accurate account of the sensations they experience. I go so far as to say this: With care and perseverance, by exercising their inherent ability to describe what they feel, one can enhance their method of appreciating these new sensations, and so to speak, educate them for that state. It is with these subjects, trained in this way, that we can satisfactorily apply ourselves to acquiring knowledge of all the phenomena which are the result of the increased irritability of the senses."

There is no doubt whatever that Mesmer was here referring to somnambulistic states. While he did not give them this name, he pointed out that, on emerging from his "crisis," the patient remembered nothing of what had happened during it. Mesmer merely mentioned the fact without investigating it further, which is why it made no impression on his pupils. Diligent in his attendance at Mesmer's demonstrations, Puységur, for his part, was impressed when he saw his first patient enter into a state of deep sleep. As we have noted, Mesmer was probably afraid of this state which he did not know how to control. He used it to demonstrate to his pupils the state of "crisis," but failed to derive from it any therapeutic advantage for the exploration of the patient's past.

In this condition the subject was able to talk, to walk, and to act. Hence the name, magnetic somnambulism (as opposed to the natural somnambulism which may occur spontaneously in certain subjects) applied by Puységur to this state which had not been specifically described by Mesmer (Puységur, 1784).*

Puységur observed that, on being awakened, the patient had no recollection of what had happened in his somnambulistic state. From this he concluded that we have two memories; today we would say, one conscious, the other unconscious. It is, therefore, in 1784 that the study of the unconscious came into the sphere of psychology. On several occasions in the same work, Puységur pointed out that "presensation is so inherent in the *magnetic state*** that I have never found a single one of my Patients who, on regaining the natural state, was able to remember anything about what he had *done* and *predicted* during *his crisis*. I did what I could to relate their ideas in the transition from one state to the other, either on their entering *into a crisis*, or on emerging, but I found it impossible to do so. So great is the demarcation that one can regard these two states as two different existences. I have noticed, for example, that in the *magnetic* state they retain the idea and the memory of all they were doing in the *natural* state; whereas, in this [natural] state, they have no recollection whatever of all they were doing in the *magnetic state*: which fully confirms (in accordance with what I have already said) the existence of an additional *sensation* in this latter state" (Puységur, 1784, p. 90).

---

* Puységur later gave a detailed description of this difference (1811, chapter IV, pp. 73-91).
** Italics in original text, throughout this quotation and, unless stated, in the other quotations from the same author.

We have here a date and a description of such importance in the history of psychology, that it is surprising to find them so rarely mentioned. What struck the observers of this period was not the links which may exist between the two states, but indeed their complete separation. Thus, thirty-five years later, Deleuze would still write: "When he [the magnetized subject] regains the natural state, he loses entirely the memory of all the sensations and all the ideas which he had in the state of somnambulism; so much so that these two states are as unconnected with one another, as if the somnambulist and the man in the waking state were two different beings" (Deleuze, 1819a, I, pp. 186-187).

While the magnetists had been surprised at the difference between the two states, they had nevertheless had an inkling that the unconscious sometimes influences the conscious. Deleuze, although he accepted ideas which are now regarded as superseded, gave an interesting account of the unconscious when describing the somnambulistic state:

> He perceives the magnetic fluid. He sees or rather senses the interior of his body, and that of others; yet as a rule he notices there only those parts which are not in the natural state and which disturb the harmony. He rediscovers in his memory the recollection of things that he had forgotten in the waking state. He has spells of prescience and presensation which may on occasion prove erroneous, and are limited in their extent. He expresses himself with surprising facility. He is not wanting in vanity. He improves himself of his own accord for a certain time, if he is led wisely. He goes astray if he is wrongly directed (1819a, I, p. 186).

Somnambulism as described by the magnetists clearly reveals facts which are today regarded as characteristic of the unconscious. The skilled observers knew, moreover, that somnambulism does not perform miracles; it merely reactivates memory-traces. Thus, Deleuze pointed out that a peasant who only spoke a dialect was sometimes able, in a state of somnambulism, to speak correct French which he might have heard around him—but he could never speak Iroquoian. Just as Freud wrote that nothing is lost in the unconscious, so

Deleuze asserted that "all the sensations that we have experienced throughout our life have left traces in our brain. These traces are slight, and we are not aware of them, because present sensations prevent our being so; but they do exist, and often things that we had forgotten arise in our memory when an unforeseen circumstance excites our imagination" (1819a, I, p. 191).

Throughout the nineteenth century and until the Nancy School's experiments on hypnosis, this idea of a complete separation of the conscious from the unconscious will be seen to recur. As Baragnon wrote: "The forgetting of all that happened during the magnetic sleep is an invariable effect, without which there is no sleep" (1853, p. 173).

Even in the case of prolonged states, where for hours on end the somnambulist's behavior is as well "adapted" as in the waking state, if he had been put to sleep at the outset he retains no subsequent recollection of what he had been doing. Puységur had already kept some patients in a state of somnambulism for several days, with the purpose, however, of ascertaining what occurs in such conditions. A later observation by Janet on this type of prolonged experimentation may be quoted here:

One day, around two o'clock in the afternoon, I was about to put Léonie to sleep—she had already been in a state of somnambulism for some time—when I received a letter from Dr. Gilbert who, being unable to join me, asked me to bring Léonie to him. Instead of awaking the somnambulist, I showed her this letter and proposed that she come with me as she was. I am quite willing to do so, she replied, but I must first get dressed; you don't want me to go out like this. She went upstairs and dressed; and I then set off with her in a carriage, at which she was overjoyed like a child. She remained the whole evening in a state of somnambulism, was very vivacious and very gay, cooperated in various experiments that we wished to carry out, and between times talked of any number of things. It was not until about midnight that I accompanied her home, and there, in the same place that I had put her to sleep at two o'clock, I wakened her completely. After this lively session, here she was on awaking, calm and quiet, and convinced that she had not moved all day and had only just gone off to sleep. She was, however, dumbfounded to see that she had changed her dress, and I

was obliged to put her back to sleep and make various suggestions to prevent her worrying about this peculiarity (Janet,
1889, p. 74).

It is exceptional for the magnetists to record an observation where
the unconscious state influences the conscious. Puységur related that
his patient, Victor, when magnetized, had one day asked one of his
neighbors to keep in her cupboard a document by which his mother
left him her house as a reward for the unstinting care he had given
her. In the waking state, Victor feared that his sister might discover
this letter and destroy it. Puységur, finding that on being wakened
his patient did not seem so well as on the previous day and was
overwhelmed with despondency, asked him what was the matter.
Victor told him his worries: I searched in vain in my cupboard, he
said, for my mother's letter. Puységur told him what he had done
during his somnambulistic state. His consequent joy and two hours
spent in magnetic sleep entirely altered his mood (Puységur, 1784,
p. 38) .

Puységur was embarking on a new course—treatment by the acquisition of insight. Unfortunately, he failed to draw all the conclusions from an observation which could have provided him with
evidence of the action of the unconscious on the conscious. This is
not in fact an isolated observation; Abbé Faria (1819) , Bertrand
(1826) , and Charpignon (1841) noted that suggestions made during
magnetic sleep can, on his awakening, influence the patient, especially if he is informed that he will continue to experience emotions
which were induced during his somnambulism.

From all these phenomena we may single out that of "endoscopy"
—the faculty which somnambulists would seem to have possessed of
"seeing" inside their body. It is conceivable that a human being, in
a state of somnambulism or even simply by means of a dream during
natural sleep, might be able to perceive a symptom before it actually
presents in a "tangible" form.

The following examples were recorded by Macario (1857) . Galen
tells of a patient who, in a dream, saw himself with a stone leg—
and some time later was stricken with paralysis of one leg. The
scientist Conrad Gesner, having dreamed one night of being bitten

by a snake on the left side of the chest, was soon afterwards afflicted with a carbuncle at that site and within five days he was dead. The former minister of justice Teste, who died from an apoplectic fit, had dreamed three days earlier that he suffered an attack of this nature.

It is perhaps possible, therefore, to speak of a kind of foreknowledge or prescience of disease in dreams. These terms, as here employed, do not, however, imply any metapsychical connotation, nor a delusional idea as some skeptics believed, but specifically an unconscious perception of a physiological process that has already begun.* There may also be, concurrently, an unconscious perception (in dreams) of an affective conflict—a conflict manifesting itself in a delusion or a neurosis. We now know that the dream and the delusional state both have the same structure. For the authors of the nineteenth century, who generally assigned little importance to their patients' conflicts, it was the dream itself which induced the delusion.

Tissié devoted a chapter of a book (which incidentally is of little value) to the influence of dreams on the waking state. Having no idea whatever of the nature of unconscious conflicts, he gave an account of the following case:

> Mrs. B., an hysteric aged thirty-four, dreamed one night that she killed her husband and daughter with a large knife. In the morning, she made sure that this was not true, and said: "Oh, great heavens! What if I had killed them!" From that time on, she could never see a knife without being overcome by a terrible fear. She experienced intense distress and fainting fits if she was obliged to take hold of the sharp instrument: she was afraid of harming someone, especially her husband and her daughter whom she loved very much. She frequently had dreams about the knife: at night she tied her wrists together, for fear that she might get up and go and fetch one (Tissié, 1890, p. 160).

Instead of detecting the existence of an unconscious conflict, Tissié

---

* In this connection, see "The hypochondria of dreams" by Fedida (1972), who introduces his paper with the following quotation from Freud: "The 'diagnostic' capacity of dreams—a phenomenon which is generally acknowledged, but regarded as puzzling—becomes equally comprehensible, too. In dreams, incipient physical disease is often detected earlier and more clearly than in waking life, and all the current bodily sensations assume gigantic proportions" (Freud, 1917a, p. 223).

imagined that it was the dream which gave rise to the delusion. We may disregard this error of interpretation; what concerns us is the fact that, in the unconscious state, human beings are aware of things of which they have no knowledge in the waking state. Such was the case of this woman who, when asleep, knew that she was in conflict with her husband and daughter.

The first years of the scientific study of somnambulism produced but few works on the unconscious elaboration of thought—possibly because the use of the term "unconscious" was rare at the time. The previously mentioned treatise on magnetism by Julien Joseph Virey (1818) is one of the very few which touched upon the question. He wrote: "A certain feeling, a certain thought, which seemed to be forgotten during the day, because it is obfuscated by distractions, buries itself within us, but reappears, more brilliant and more elaborate, during night-time rest or somnambulistic concentration. The intermediate chain of reasoning having eluded us, or occurred without our knowledge, suddenly presents us with some striking truth; but as we do not perceive its source, it seems to have sprung from inspiration" (Virey, 1818, p. 75).

This elaboration of unconscious thought is also described in the work published by Faria in 1819:

> Whenever the impressions received by the internal organs from extreme contentment or intense sorrow remain smothered in the depths of the heart, they find in the inner calm induced by concentration the freedom to pursue their original course and to erupt in a violent way. He who experiences these effects is always compelled to abandon himself to their impetus, without being at all able to control them according to his wishes—more or less in the same way as no man is able, as soon as there is a sensation in the external organs, to prevent its perception in the mind; inasmuch as their cause, having passed into a man's intuitive state, becomes entirely independent of his sensible will (Faria, 1906 edition, p. 167).

Faria had well understood that this elaboration is not necessarily translated into thought, but that it sometimes appears in the form of a symptom:

It is this suppression of anxiety and sorrows, more often than of joy and contentment, which is the usual cause of the formation of those stones that are sometimes found by physicians on opening the bodies of persons of choleric and irascible temperament. . . . I think likewise that a large part of the women who suffer from swellings in the breasts, develop these swellings only from this same cause (Faria, 1906, p. 168).

Faria thus appears as a precursor in the psychosomatic field in connection with the formation of symptoms.

Already the idea advanced by Mesmer, of a universal fluid which should restore the equilibrium between the different organs, foreshadowed a dynamic psychophysiology. These hypotheses reappear in a far more developed form in the works of Faria, as well as Puységur, Bertrand (1823), and Charpignon (1841).

In summary, during the era of animal magnetism and up to the mid-nineteenth century, authors had made the following observations concerning the unconscious:

1. That it was a different state from the conscious, inasmuch as its "memory" was far more extensive.
2. That the somnambulist, once awakened, had no recollection of what had happened during his sleep.
3. That the intellectual faculties, if they were stimulated, were often enhanced [causing many magnetists to allow themselves to be deceived by their somnambulists' assertions as to their paranormal abilities].
4. That the unconscious involves a more acute perception of the autonomic nervous system than does the conscious—and that it can exert a direct influence on it.
5. That external sensibility is not the same as in the waking state. One can observe phenomena of hyperesthesia or hypesthesia, as well as anesthesia.
6. That one observes variations in muscle tone: flaccidity or rigidity of the limbs.
7. That the individual is more suggestible in the somnambulistic state. He tends to maintain a relationship with his magnetist alone.
8. That, all things considered, the unconscious can sometimes influence the conscious.

While precise observations continued to be made until about 1850, it remains that many magnetists were taken in by their somnambulists and purported to receive revelations from the other world, to be able to practice table-turning, etc., thus bringing magnetism into disrepute. The latter would, however, merely be reborn under another name: hypnotism.

3. *The Unconscious and the Psychologists*

Until the mid-nineteenth century, notwithstanding the successive reports of the academies, magnetism had remained on the fringe of science and had been integrated neither with psychology nor with medical science.

Charles Richet (1884) * not only demystified somnambulism, but initiated a new phase in its investigation through a series of experiments on the execution of posthypnotic commands; with originality, he drew valid conclusions for general psychology.

He showed that the phenomena produced under hypnosis are not so very "remote" from those encountered from day to day; that occurrences in an abnormal state only serve to give a clearer idea of those arising in everyday life. "What I would wish to bring to light," he wrote, "is that absolute unconsciousness which, even after a long period of time, causes a memory to persist, although the person who remembers is unaware of remembering. However strange the association of the two words may seem, it is an *unrecognized memory*" (Richet, 1884, pp. 254-255, 536-537). Richet was able to see that these memories are present to a high degree in the normal individual and that we are not conscious of them; we believe ourselves to be free whereas we are continually determined by our past.

"Let us suppose," said Richet, "that instead of a command given verbally, it is a question of a particular instinct. Let us, for example, take the cuckoo, which goes and deposits its eggs in neighboring nests. When the cuckoo does this, it thinks that it wants to do so, for it has doubtless never seen a bird of its species behaving in this way; . . . while it is ignorant of this cause, the latter is all-powerful and determines its actions" (Richet, 1884, p. 256) .

---

* An earlier work by Richet on somnambulism was published in 1875.

Richet explained this phenomenon of unrecognized memories (*"souvenirs ignorés"*) by the automatism of certain psychological reactions—in this respect initiating the ideas of Pierre Janet. He also recorded certain "dissociations" of the mind occurring in hypnotized subjects: it is suggested to a person that one of his teeth is being extracted and that this is very painful; he screams with pain but otherwise remains insensitive to all stimuli, such as pricking or pinching (cf. Richet, 1875, p. 357; 1884, p. 201).

All Richet's arguments are directed toward the elaboration of a psychology that is dynamic, not merely descriptive. For any given phenomenon he seeks the hidden causes. His aim is not solely to establish the reality of a fact, but to understand it by studying its concomitant causes and effects. It is this which distinguishes Richet from his contemporaries (especially those of the 1880's) and marks him as one of Freud's great precursors.

Richet was not alone in sensing how little the pathological differs from the normal phenomenon, the one being as susceptible as the other to control by unconscious processes. Many authors shared this view. Tarde, among others, observed:

> Yet by it [periodicity] we can learn that there are within us many invisible wheels which are turning unbeknown to us, in order to cause the periodical release of some terrible spring, to detonate some one of those internal explosive substances that we carry without knowing it. These countless and unceasing rotations, which are the unconscious life of our memories, our wishes, and our latent feelings, the continual repetition of everything that has once entered into us by way of an accidental impression, occur inside our brain cells. . . . The kind of enchanted and poignant melancholy, ever the same, which is invariably reawakened in many souls by the return of spring and which then compels them to suspend all work, has its source in the sorrows of love of their early youth. . . . But also, in those unfortunate people who, in their childhood or youth, suffered great deprivation, great humiliation, and ill-treatment, there are days when there seethes within them an inexplicable undertone of anger, a confused craving for hatred and vengeance, an envious cupidity (Tarde, 1889, p. 466).

Going beyond a simple description of facts, Taine showed that, within our unconscious, the classification of facts proceeds according to a certain dynamism:

> The sensation being revived in the image, the image returns more forcefully when the sensation has proved to be stronger. What was encountered in the first state is still met with in the second, since the second is but the revival of the first. Similarly, in the struggle for survival which is, at every moment, engaged between all our images, that one which was originally endowed with a greater energy retains in each conflict, by the very law of repetition which creates it, the capacity to repel [*refouler*] its rivals. This is why it immediately, and then frequently, rearises until the laws of progressive extinction and the sustained attack by the new impressions deprive it of its preponderance, and the competitors, left with a clear field, are able to develop in their turn (Taine, 1870, I, pp. 156-157).

Taine thus introduced the notion of repression (*refoulement*) which was to occupy a place of prime importance in Freudian psychopathology. These dynamics of the classification or organization of our ideas were to command increasing attention during the following years.*

In the mid-nineteenth century, investigation was no longer concerned only with the coexistence of two distinct memories in one and the same individual, but also with the dynamic organization of the emotions—an organization where nothing is lost and where the emotions experienced in infancy can set off in the unconscious upsurges of hatred, a craving for vengeance, of which the conscious remains ignorant.

Thus, there occurred a complete change in orientation. The mag-

---

* We know for certain that Freud had read Taine (Freud, 1954, p. 157) and Maury (Freud, 1900, p. 8). Yet he seems in general to have evinced a selective blindness toward a number of authors—assuming that he did in fact read them—who were "classical" at that period. For, in the *Studies on Hysteria,* he considered that his position differed from that of Breuer in that he ascribed a role to the mechanisms of defense. He spoke of repression (employed at that time in the same sense as "defense") as if he himself had introduced the term, whereas Taine and, as we shall see later, Maury and Maillet, also referred to it. It is true that these latter employed it generally to designate a mechanism of defense against unpleasant ideas, while Freud linked it to a whole theory of the neuroses.

netists for their part had applied themselves to inducing a state capable of stimulating the subject's "endoscopic" faculties and, where possible, to initiating in certain mediums phenomena of clairvoyance. Now, on the other hand, starting with the discoveries of Richet and Taine, the unconscious became an active part of the personality as well as a reservoir of the emotions and of forgotten or repressed facts. Tarde, in particular, showed that the unconscious loses none of its dynamism and that the past experiences of a child may in some cases influence his actions in adult life. We have here a very different conception of the unconscious, one which is remarkably close to the Freudian concept.

Richet seems to explain the pathological phenomena associated with the unconscious for the most part by states of distraction, whereas Tarde's theory is more dynamic; it clearly specifies that every unconscious idea (he does not use the term "repressed") tends to reappear in the form of some pathological state.

Since Maury in 1861, in his book *Le Sommeil et les Rêves* ("Sleep and Dreams"), showed that passions which are repressed in the waking state find expression in dreams, many authors came to propound a mixture of two theories. On the one hand, unconscious phenomena were explained as the result of a kind of distraction and a weakening of the control of reason. On the other hand, they offered a far more dynamic theory in which repression is involved.

The two explanations are often encountered side by side, in which childhood memories are held to play an important part. In this connection it is relevant to quote a few passages from a book that is today largely forgotten: *L'Essence des Passions* by Eugène Maillet (1877). Maillet proffered a dynamic explanation; without employing the terms "unconscious" and "conscious," he clearly expounded the notion of conflict between certain ideas, or rather certain emotions:

> These different states of the mind present a striking analogy to what takes place within us, albeit with a far more considerable intensity, during sleep. For then, nothing presents any further obstacle to the confused reappearance of the thoughts, dispositions and feelings, which formerly occupied our mind, but which reason has *repressed* [italics added]. In our dreams

these thoughts recur turbulently within us, and all the more so, the deeper our sleep and the more dulled our senses. Controlled in the waking state by the power of reason, they shake off their fetters and give themselves free rein, departing as far as possible from reality, reason and habit (Maillet, 1877, p. 57).

Elsewhere, Maillet argued more often from the states of distraction than from the power of the repressed ideas. Thus he wrote:

What is reverie, if not a state of mind in which we feel in ourselves a resurgence of an infinite number of images and ideas, an endless association of ideas . . . which take the place within us of existing thoughts and activities, especially when the lack of external excitations leaves us a prey to indolence and boredom? 1877, p. 56).

"Reverie" is here more or less the equivalent of "phantasies." The latter had not, however, really been studied at that time with regard to their significance, their content, or their organization.

Taking up the ideas of Moreau (1875), Maillet gave a good description of the regression that is seen in these states:

Pinel had already pointed out that one of the fundamental features of mental illness is that in it old ideas recur with such extreme vividness, that they greatly obfuscate the impressions of present objects. In consequence, the mental patient seems to live in a different world from that inhabited by other men. The psychological explanation of this remark of Pinel's is, we believe, that under the influence of the disintegration which occurs in the mind of this mental patient, the ideas which he had previously acquired, but which had become bound together and fused one with the other, are as it were *liberated*. They pass back from the organic state to the state of consciousness, and, by their disorderly affluence, smother the new ideas which the impression of external objects would at present tend to arouse (1877, p. 60).

It may be noted in passing that Maillet employed the term "organic" for the unconscious, a practice frequently repeated after Charcot's death, and one which Freud was to criticize in 1915 in his article on the unconscious (Freud, 1915b, p. 174).

An interesting work, which has already been mentioned, is that by Alfred Maury (1861), who oscillated between the concept of a psychological unconscious (which he called *"inscient"*) and that of a purely organic activity. This oscillation is well illustrated by the following excerpts:

> What I recorded, on p. 115, concerning the return in dreams of inscient memories, depends on the fact that, unbeknown to our mind, the memory may retain traces of impression. We then carry within us, without our being aware of it, a series of ideas which have been communicated to us or which we owed to some earlier work, and which are present in our mind without our suspecting it (Maury, 1861, p. 396).

> In every creation of our mind, there is a large part of memory, while there is but a small number of elements introduced through the work of reflection and of combination. As for that part constituted by the memory, we do not think it as large as it is in reality, because with us the memory is inscient for a host of facts; such in particular appears to be the nature of childhood memories (1861, p. 397).

While it is clear that for Maury dreaming involved cerebral activity and not merely experiencing sensations, the dream was in his view more a process of nervous excitation than a complex elaboration of our passions and inhibitions. He put forward, moreover, the very "intellectual" idea that nervous excitation is independent of our emotions:

> Nervous excitation sometimes accompanies sleep and induces dreams in which are freely displayed our passions, such as licentiousness, anger, hatred or fear, which may impart to our acts and our feelings a violent character that they do not possess in the waking state. The cause of this development of the passions then arises from the fact, not only that the will and other impressions are not there on the alert to restrain them, but that the sensibility is over-stimulated (Maury, 1861, p. 87).

The notion of conflict appears to have been entirely unknown to Maury. There are many authors of the nineteenth century who realized that it is not through suggestion alone, but also through dreams, that we can gain access to unconscious memories. Liégeois, among others, wrote:

> The dream remains, in the majority of men, an almost exclusively psychological phenomenon. Memories are reawakened in the mind, that we had thought extinct forever, sensations that we have previously experienced, griefs and joys that we have felt, pains from which we have suffered; we see again people now dead and they seem to us alive, absent friends and we believe they are near us; adversaries or enemies, and we think ourselves once more the object of their attacks or their plots. And also certain pictures that at some time or other in the past we have admired, of which we may indeed have caught but a glimpse, are renovated and reproduced in our mind's eye, with a vividness of color, a sharpness of outline, which cause us to take them for reality (Liégeois, 1889, p. 437).

With the advances in neurology, authors became increasingly reluctant to admit the idea of a psychological unconscious. So far as they were concerned, unconscious thought was strictly dependent on chance physical excitations. In other words, there was in the unconscious no organization whatever of our instincts and our emotions.

As an indication of the extent to which psychologists showed a resistance to using the term "the unconscious," it is noteworthy that Littré, in his Dictionary of the French Language (1874 edition), lists the word not as a substantive, but only as an adjective. It is perhaps for this reason that many authors hesitated to employ it. Simon, for example, did not use the term in his book *Le Monde des Rêves* ("The World of Dreams," 1882). And eighty years later, the encyclopedic French dictionary known as the "Grand Larousse" (1960 edition) remains in this respect as ambiguous as it is "traditionalist." As we are there informed (article "unconscious"), "The existence of unconscious states capable of exerting an influence on consciousness is undeniable (tendencies, automatic habits, urges, etc.). But these unconscious states cannot be called *psychological*: indeed they lack the subjective aspect without which there is no psychical fact (*see* Thought) ." The author of the same article previously observes: "A psychological fact being, by definition, a fact of consciousness, is there not a contradiction in the idea of *unconscious* psychological states? . . . Having but the objective aspect, they appertain to the physiology of the nervous system."

It is with scholastic arguments of the same order that Freud had to contend, being thereby obliged, notwithstanding the work of his predecessors, to defend the validity of the concept of a psychological unconscious.

While the proponents of one trend cling to the idea of a purely organic unconscious, those of another trend, developing the discoveries of Richet (1875, 1884), realize that psychology, whether conscious or unconscious, must be studied as a whole, as a science distinct from that which is concerned with investigating the connections between thought and cerebral function. From this point of view, the relations between the conscious and the unconscious are becoming the subject of increasingly fruitful research, whose field will be still further extended through the study of hypnotism.

4. *The Unconscious and Hypnosis*

For the psychologists of this second trend (one can even say, school), the unconscious is no longer a kind of phenomenon with occasional manifestations; it is for them an active and permanent part of the psyche. But we must first return to hypnosis itself and its own specific "value."

Hypnosis has given a new dimension to psychology, which remained purely "descriptive" before the reports that were drawn up by the Royal Commissioners (Rapports, 1784a, b, c). The latter endeavored to prove at that time, by a series of experiments, the existence or the non-existence of the fluid—for example, by getting subjects to walk about an orchard in which, unbeknown to them, this or that tree had been magnetized. However, the subjects went into a trance as readily beneath some non-magnetized tree as beneath any other. It was thus proved that the action was brought about not by the fluid but by the subject's imagination. It is unnecessary to describe here the numerous and well-known experiments of the Commissioners. Following up their work, Bertrand continued to experiment, seeking to ascertain whether suggestibility derived from a force emitted by the magnetist or from a natural disposition of the subject.

These experiments seem commonplace enough; yet they represent an important step forward in the history of psychology: the transition from a descriptive science to an experimental science.

A critical mind was wanting in many experimenters of the nineteenth century, who were often fanatics bent on exacting a recantation from the academies. Fortunately, this did not occur (for such recantation would have left a clear field to all the charlatans of the period). We need not dwell on these polemics, concerning which the reader is referred to the historical work by Burdin and Dubois (1841).

Following are some excerpts which we consider particularly cogent:

From Janet: ". . . the somnambulist, once awakened, retains nothing in his consciousness, or rather he preserves a latent association of ideas which does not require to be actually translated into a psychological phenomenon. We ourselves do not know all the latent associations that are present in our mind; the sight of a certain person perhaps must needs evoke in us a sad or happy thought of which we are not at present aware" (Janet, 1886a, p. 583).

From Bérillon: "If, however, during somnambulistic sleep, you order the hypnotized subject to retain on waking the memory of the actions he has performed, then the thinking machine, while it cannot, during hypnosis, avoid carrying out the acts of which you suggested to it the idea, will reassume its rights on waking. It will be indignant at the acts which it will have committed; it will repent, implore forgiveness, want to make amends for the harm it has done, and will beg you to help it do so with all your might, with all your authority. If you appear to hesitate, the thinking machine weeps, gets angry and threatens. The thinking machine has become once again the thinking, conscious, human being, and he is indignant at the way that you have abused his person" (Bérillon, 1886, pp. 33-41).

Bérillon emphasized clearly here the possibility of an antagonism between conscious and unconscious—a concept of conflict which was to reveal the mechanism of the neuroses and, at the same time, the appropriate therapy. This is well illustrated by Bourru and Burot's observation:

It is by causing her [the patient] to return to a period of her life where this dual state did not exist, by placing her again in a state of consciousness foreign to this somnambulistic life, that one could effect in her a favorable change (Bourru and Burot, 1888, p. 314).

Janet has clearly shown how the French psychologists had succeeded in developing the notion of an unconscious on the eve of the appearance of Freud's writings:

If such were the case, three-quarters of the phenomena observed in morbid, or even in normal, states would be inexplicable. All psychological laws appear erroneous if one seeks to apply them solely to conscious phenomena of which the individual is aware. We continually encounter facts, hallucinations or actions which seem inexplicable, because we cannot find the reason for them, or their origin in the other ideas recognized by consciousness; and, faced with these gaps, the psychologist is all too often inclined to declare himself incompetent, and to call upon physiology for assistance which it is hardly able to give him (Janet, 1889, pp. 223-224).

It can happen that the psychical automatism is not complete; that instead of governing the whole of conscious thought, it acts partially and controls but a small group of phenomena separate from the others, isolated from the individual's total consciousness, which continues to develop on its own account and in a different way. It must, however, be acknowledged that, under the impetus of the Nancy School, serious experimentation was undertaken with a view to establishing a link between the conscious and the unconscious. (In this the Nancy School was merely taking up a method whose first application goes back to 1784.)

Later, the Nancy School also experimented with posthypnotic commands (see also Chapters II and III of this book), in order to show how conflicts between conscious and unconscious can be created by giving the subject posthypnotic orders which are contrary to his moral sense. Liégeois made a special study of this aspect of the practice of hypnotism:

An hysterical young woman was presented by M. Dumont to

the Society of Medicine. While asleep she was commanded to go, after waking, and take the glass cylinder which surrounded the gas jet situated above the table, to place it in her pocket and carry it away on leaving. Once awakened, she approached the table timidly, seemed embarrassed to find all eyes fixed on her, and then, after some hesitation, climbed on to the table on her knees. She remained there for two minutes or so, apparently very much ashamed at her situation, glanced from one to another of the people who surrounded her and at the object that she must get hold of, stretched forth her hand, then withdrew it, and suddenly removed the glass, put it in her pocket, and departed hurriedly. Not until she had left the room did she agree to return the object (Liégeois, 1889, p. 197).

These experiments aimed at inducing artificial neuroses. And more than one physician would have wished to find the way to cross this barrier persisting between the conscious and the unconscious—a major obstacle to the understanding of repressed conflicts. Yet the experiments on posthypnotic commands had shed a little light on the problem, for the order was executed in a state analogous to that of artificial sleep.

Determined to overcome the obstacle, Delboeuf reasoned thus: In order that the command given shall be remembered, it is necessary that the action performed by the subject in his sleep be interrupted and that its repercussions persist on waking. Delboeuf has described, in this connection, a cogent experiment which he undertook, together with Dr. Féré, at the Salpêtrière:

There happened to be a basin full of water on the table. The woman W. [the patient] was put back to sleep. She was instructed to remember her dream when she wakened. I reproduce the dialogue faithfully. M. Féré had placed his arm around the young woman's neck. 'Do you feel well?' — 'Very well.' — 'I feel happy, too; I am near you; I am smoking an excellent cigar. What an aroma it has!' — 'Excellent!' — 'And how well it burns.' — 'Perfectly.' — 'Look at this ash burning at the tip.' — 'I see it.' — 'Oh, it has just fallen on your shawl, which is catching fire! Quick, soak it in water; there's a basin on the table!' In less time than it takes to tell, the patient had got up, removed her shawl, and plunged it in the basin. She urged M. Féré to help her put out the flames. 'Squeeze it, go on, squeeze it between your hands, and beat on it,' she cried, making the gesture. At this moment she was wakened. Her hands felt wet; she looked at them, then looked at us in consternation. She suddenly noticed that she was no longer wearing her shawl; she saw that M. Féré was holding it in his hands. 'Oh, what a hole!' she exclaimed. 'It's your cigar ash which did that!' — 'There we are,' said M. Féré, looking at me. 'I will mend it,' he went on, and unfolded the shawl before the fire in the hearth. — 'Leave it,' said the patient, 'I will mend it myself.' — 'No need. Look!' Seeing her shawl undamaged, she assumed the expression of someone awaking out of a far-off dream, and exclaimed (this was for me a solemn moment and her words are indelibly engraved in my memory) : 'Good heavens! It was all *a dream!* How strange. I remember absolutely everything. You were beside me; you were smoking; your cigar ash fell on my shawl which caught fire. I rushed to soak it in the water. You helped me; I even told you: Beat on it, beat on it hard (and she repeated her gesture) to put out the flames!' It was a brilliant demonstration (Delboeuf, 1886, pp. 446-447).

The fact was thenceforth established that, on the therapeutic level, it is useless to bring back under hypnosis the memory of a traumatic experience if the precaution is not taken to instruct the patient beforehand: "On waking you will remember everything you told me."

It is starting from the data provided by these experiments that Charcot discovered traumatic hysteria, and that new experiments would be attempted which gradually caused an increasing number of psychotherapists to recognize the importance of the unconscious in the production as in the cure of the neuroses. Of these many experiments, we shall only reproduce here that of which Pierre Janet published an account, some four years before the appearance in 1893 of the "Preliminary Communication" by Breuer and Freud (1895, pp. 1-17) :

Finally, I wished to investigate the blindness in the left eye, but Marie [the patient] objected when she was awake, saying that it had been like that from birth. It was easy to ascertain, by means of somnambulism, that she was mistaken: if she was transformed, by the usual procedures, into an infant of five years, she reassumed the sensibility which she had at that age,

and it was found that she could then see very well with both
eyes. It is, therefore, at the age of six years that she first became
blind. On what occasion? Marie persisted in saying, when awake,
that she had no idea. During somnambulism, and thanks to
successive transformations during which I got her to reenact
the principal scenes of that period of her life, I observed that
the blindness started at a certain moment, in connection with a
trivial incident. She had been forced, in spite of her cries, to
sleep with a child of her own age with *impetigo over the entire
left side of its face.* Some time afterwards, Marie developed im-
petiginous crusts which were almost identical in appearance,
and were situated *in the same place.* These crusts recurred for
several years at the same period, and then cleared up, but it was
not noticed that, from then on, *she had facial anesthesia on the
left side, and was blind in the left eye.* This anesthesia had persisted ever since; or at least, not to go beyond what could be
observed, to whatever later period I transported her by suggestion, she always had this same anesthesia, although at certain
times the rest of her body regained its sensibility completely.
Another attempt at a cure, similar to the previous one, was
made. I again brought her together with the child who filled her
with horror, and made her believe that it was a very nice child
and had not got impetigo. Of this she was only half convinced.
After twice repeating the scene, I won my case and she fondled
the imaginary child without fear. Sensation on the left side was
restored without difficulty and, when I wakened her, Marie
could see well with the left eye. It is now five months since
these experiments were undertaken. Marie has no longer shown
the slightest sign of hysteria, is in very good health, and above
all is growing much stronger. Her physical appearance has altered completely. I do not attribute to this cure any more importance than it deserves, and I do not know how long it will
last. But I considered this history of interest in showing the
importance of subconscious fixed ideas, and the part they play in
certain physical illnesses as well as in mental illnesses (Janet,
1889, pp. 439-440).

This was a new experiment; not only did Janet cause the initial
trauma to be relived under hypnosis, but by a series of suggestions,
still under hypnosis, he abolished the emotions that he had thus revived and which were at the root of the anesthesia. This experiment
—and others like it could be cited—shows that at this period the

elaboration of a theory on the origin of the neuroses and on their treatment was under way.

At the very beginning of his book, Janet had formulated an important distinction which was to shift the center of interest of experimentation toward therapy. "The great difference," he wrote, "which seems to exist between the states that we are comparing, is that during artificial catalepsy, the subject's movements and attitudes always originate externally in the modifications which are communicated to him; during the hysterical attack, on the contrary, the origin of the passionate attitudes seems to lie internally in the patient's memories" (1889, p. 51).

Many other passages of Janet's book show that he had a fairly precise idea of the dynamism of the unconscious, but nowhere did he take into account the importance of the transference. He understood the therapeutic value of hypnosis and the need to seek in the unconscious the causes of hysterical symptoms, but he remained more an experimenter than a physician. It was not until later that he became interested in therapy.

At various periods of the nineteenth century, authors seem to have more particularly directed their attention at times toward observation, and at other times toward therapy. Thus from 1889, following a period where interest had been principally focused on the action which the unconscious exerts on the conscious, it suddenly turned to personality changes and their explanation by distraction (understood as a kind of dissociation). Consequent on the publications of Azam of Bordeaux (1860), the discovery of multiple personalities diverted the interest then being shown in the experimental work of the Nancy School toward the phenomena of splitting of the personality.*

Abandoning experimentation to return to clinical observations, Charcot had emphasized the importance of psychical trauma in the

---

* Already in 1816, the description of these states of alternating personalities began with the case of Mary Reynolds (in 1811), known as "MacNish's American lady." We may also mention the famous cases of Félida, Louis V., etc. (Chertok, 1960, French version). In truth, it had to happen that the history of Anna O., merely one case among many, should by pure chance come to be reported to Freud, for this encounter, this convergence, to lead eventually to his discoveries.

etiology of the neuroses. In this line he was followed successfully by Pierre Janet. But the discovery of multiple personalities so impressed the imagination of the scientists of the period that even Janet turned aside from the path his teacher had indicated in order to devote himself to the explanation of dual personalities—phenomena which became a center of general interest, not to say a craze. It seemed likely that the states of distraction would be able to account for them, and they were studied by the best researchers of the time. It is hard for us to conceive today the extent to which minds were fascinated by this problem. Some idea of this may be conveyed by the introduction to Binet's book, *Les Altérations de la Personnalité* (1892):

> This seems to me a favorable opportunity to attempt this work of eclecticism. A rather curious occurrence is taking place at the present time. A large number of observers belonging neither to the same school nor to the same country, who are not experimenting on the same type of subject, who have not set themselves the same object of experiment, and who are sometimes completely unknown to one another, arrive at the same result, without being aware of the fact. And this result, which is reached by different routes, and constitutes the basis of a host of phenomena of mental life, is a particular form of personality change, a splitting, or rather a fragmentation, of the ego. One observes that in a large number of people, placed in the most diverse conditions, the normal unity of consciousness is disintegrated. Several distinct consciousnesses arise, each of which may have perceptions, a memory, and even a moral character, of its own. It is proposed to set out in detail the result of this recent research on personality changes (Binet, 1892, p. viii).

After recapitulating the experiments of Bourru and Burot, Binet stated:

> This method of suggestion, which enables us to return a person to earlier periods of his life will, I feel convinced, certainly find one day a number of medical applications. For, on the one hand, it will shed light on the diagnosis by enabling us to discover in its details the origin and the mode of production of an hysterical symptom; and on the other hand, we shall perhaps

find that by taking the patient back, by means of a mental artifice, to the very moment when the symptom first appeared, we may make that patient more amenable to a therapeutic suggestion.* In any event, it is an experiment worth trying.

From the purely psychological point of view, which alone interests us, retroactive suggestions teach us something new about the mechanism of the division of consciousness. They teach us in the first place that a host of older memories, which we believe to be dead as we are unable to evoke them at will, continue to live within us. Consequently, the limits of our personal and conscious memory are no more absolute limits than are those of our present consciousness. Beyond these lines there are memories, just as there are perceptions and reasoning processes, and what we know about ourselves is but a part, perhaps a very small part, of what we are.

The laws of the association of ideas, which, following the English psychologists, have been so much used and indeed abused to explain a host of phenomena of the mind, are here seen to be defective. They are incapable of telling us why and how preserved memories fail to revive at the call of the new impressions which are associated with them. Some particular episode of childhood, which no longer comes to our mind, but which may be restored to it by a retroactive suggestion, certainly did not lack opportunities in the course of normal life to rise again to the surface of consciousness; a great many similar events must have occurred since then. If, therefore, the mind did not respond to this call of similarity, it is because the action of the associations of ideas was insufficient to stimulate it, and consequently, is not a sufficient explanation of the development of our mental life. There is no doubt something other than these light bonds to link ideas together. Deeper causes, whose nature it is difficult for us to unravel, for they are unconscious, are working to distribute our ideas, our perceptions and memories, and all our states of consciousness, in autonomous and independent syntheses. When we are in one of these syntheses, we have difficulty in arousing an idea belonging to a different synthesis. In general, an association of ideas is not sufficient; but when several elements of this second synthesis have been revived for one reason or another, the entire synthesis reappears (Binet, 1892, pp. 242-244).

---

* Freud was to cite the last part of this sentence in *Studies on Hysteria* (Breuer and Freud, 1895, p. 7, footnote).

The above text dates from 1892; that of Breuer and Freud, where the latter placed emphasis on the mechanisms of defense and repression, dates from 1895.* It might almost seem that the whole of Freud's work was a reply to this paragraph of Binet's which he had certainly read. Binet was, however, too much imbued, especially at this period, with the theory of dissociations to be able to renounce it. Here is, moreover, the conclusion to his book:

> One must not, however, exaggerate the role of subconscious personages, or extend indiscriminately to normal life the conclusions of previous studies. As we have said, the original event is not the secondary personalities, but the disintegration of the psychological elements; it is only subsequently, and often through training and through suggestion, that these scattered elements become organized into new personalities (1892, p. 315).

It is noteworthy that, in these lengthy quotations from Binet, it is always the ideas, never the emotions, which are mentioned.

What strikes us as characterizing this last part of the nineteenth century in France, is that no prevalent theory came to the fore. On the one hand, a series of physicians experimented on the hypnotic phenomena; while compelled to concede that the unconscious exists and may determine a part of our conscious actions, they generally confined themselves to experimentation. From this some sought to draw conclusions as to the origin of the neuroses. Janet was the most eminent of the experimenters, but the dynamic aspect of the repressed escaped him. He remained attached to the theory outlined at the very beginning of the century by many alienists, namely, that of dissociation and distraction of the mind.

On the other hand, the psychologists were not to be held prisoners of hypnotic experimentation and had a good inkling that a large part of our psyche remains unconscious—but they pursued this line of thought no further. They tried to discover neither the laws of the

---

* At this period, the two terms were equivalent. In actual fact, there is a brief allusion to repression in the "Preliminary Communication" of 1893 (Breuer and Freud, 1895, p. 10). In "The Neuro-Psychoses of Defense" (Freud, 1894) the term "defense" makes its appearance, and its meaning is made clear.

unconscious nor those which govern the relations between the two states of our psyche: conscious and unconscious. Far less did they attempt to draw up an inventory of the unconscious. However pertinent their comments, concerning repression for instance, they did not lead to a general theory of the unconscious. It should, moreover, be remembered that, at this time, observations were made "from the outside." The psychologists of the nineteenth century scarcely allowed themselves to become personally involved and, with but rare exceptions (e.g., Maillet and Richet, who said "we"), spoke as if they themselves did not have an unconscious.

It is remarkable to note how little general psychology was influenced by the experiments of Beaunis (1886) or others. Ribot referred to an unconscious in connection with the memory (1881) or the personality (1885), but in his *Psychologie des Sentiments* (1896), although a later work, he disregarded it almost entirely.

While warning his readers that certain authors (unspecified) were employing the notion of an unconscious abusively, he conceded, without giving any example, that "the cause of some phobias lies in childhood experiences of which no memory has been retained" (Ribot, 1896, p. 213).

This work, it is true, appeared in 1896, that is, seven years after studies on hypnosis had reached their apogee. Although he was discussing affective memory, Ribot argued from the standpoint of an intellectualized psychology, based in particular on the association of ideas. This curious fact can, in our opinion, be explained as follows. The psychologists of the Nancy School were concerned above all with experiments on posthypnotic suggestion, but did not attempt to go any deeper into the problem of the content of the unconscious. To be sure, Richet, Taine, Tarde and a few others understood that the unconscious very largely dominates the conscious, and that we are beings who are not as free as we think, but they did not really try to discover what our unconscious comprises. Pierre Janet himself did not have the notion of a dynamic unconscious which conditions our conscious life. His thought and his investigations were unduly centered on states of distraction and multiple personalities. Nevertheless, by employing the regressive hypnotic method, he had succeeded in two different cases in uncovering the pathogenic emotions of his patients and at the same time the origin of their symptoms (Janet, 1889, p. 74). However, he had failed to draw from this the relevant inferences.*

5. *The Freudian Discovery*

One of Freud's achievements is that he furnished our unconscious with instincts, phantasies and unconscious memories, whose dynamic character he was able to demonstrate. He arrived at the concept of this hidden universe during his first stay in Paris in 1885-1886 and his subsequent visit to Bernheim in 1889.

In the *Studies on Hysteria* (Breuer and Freud, 1895), it was Breuer who compiled the theoretical chapter. It would indeed seem that it was after he had understood the importance of the transference (see the relevant section of Chapter III above) and after his self-analysis that Freud really endowed the unconscious with an actual content. It is not our purpose to summarize here the evolution of Freud's thought. However, with regard to the investigations on the unconscious, we would like to emphasize the decisive role which he fulfilled, in sharp contrast with the theories prevalent at the end of the nineteenth century.

In a certain sense it may be said that Freud invented nothing. The principal elements of his theory, the concept of an unconscious memory, repression, the role of sexuality, the significance of dreams and of childhood memories—all these phenomena were more or less known at the close of the nineteenth century. But they were not considered in relation to one another and consequently eluded any true understanding. Freud's greatness lies in his having succeeded in effecting their synthesis in such a way as to pass beyond the purely descriptive approach of his predecessors.

---

* That is, the inferences valid for any individual. For the researchers of the period —some of whom, such as Richet, had in fact sensed that the normal, no less than the pathological, is governed by the unconscious—the very concept of an unconscious remained "anchored," however lightly, to the notions of hysteria, hypnosis, and splitting of the personality—in short, to all that was commonly held to possess an "abnormal" character. No one, moreover, was prepared to "admit" to being an hysteric—a classical defense reaction, the refusal to dare face one's own unconscious. Freud, for his part, did so dare.

The attitude of the nineteenth-century psychologists toward the unconscious was indeed ambiguous. They knew of its existence and studied its manifestations; but at the same time, they excluded all possibility of understanding its mode of functioning, insofar as they refused to see in it anything but a process of disintegration of conscious thought, which latter remained for them the only conceivable model of psychical activity. In order to explain unconscious manifestations, they thus found themselves reduced to resorting to physiological theories—such as, for example, the notion of congenital weakness of the nervous system—which, in the absence of any observable phenomenon, had no scientific substance whatever. Moreover, while they had an inkling that the normal, as much as the pathological, is governed by the unconscious, the concept of an unconscious remained in their view essentially linked to that of a pathological state. This perspective excluded all generalization.

What the psychologists of the nineteenth century knew about the unconscious may be compared to what the medieval astronomers knew about the stars. The latter were familiar with a certain number of these and observed their motions in the sky, but were ignorant of the forces controlling their revolutions. It was the same with the psychologists' observations on dreams, hypnosis and the neuroses— all data which had not as yet led to one single constructive synthesis until the day Freud, discovering that every phantasy has a libidinal significance, succeeded in analyzing the structure and dynamics of the unconscious. It was, moreover, only by "stages" that Freud was able to analyze this structural component of our psyche.

At first, he attempted to reconstruct his patients' past by getting them to bring into consciousness their repressed memories. Later, he became aware of the special importance of phantasies—and that the fulfillment of our wishes, by means of dreams, reflected the actual organization of our unconscious. The latter was not the realm of arbitrary forces, but was structured according to a certain number of basic instincts. Since this discovery, the unconscious is no longer that dark well from whose depths one might, now and then, "fish up" some interesting phenomenon. It has indeed become an object that is accessible to scientific knowledge.

Conclusion

THROUGHOUT OUR INVESTIGATION, and with the help of historical and psychobiographical data, we have attempted to shed light on the origins of two fundamental psychoanalytic concepts: the unconscious and the transference. Needless to say, we do not pretend to have elucidated this subject in all its aspects. Apart from the possibility that new sources of information may eventually become available, it remains that Freud's genius, to which we owe these discoveries, in a certain sense (and paradoxically) eludes analysis, as does that of many a great innovator.

It was through his studies on hysteria that Freud was put on the track which led to psychoanalysis. This was in all probability no mere chance. We have seen how, in consequence of his personality, Freud became attracted by female hysterical patients. Moreover, situated, as it were, at the crossroads of soma and psyche, hysteria raised the problem of their interrelationship. It thus presented a most favorable field for seeking a scientific solution of this same problem, which would appear to have preoccupied Freud as it had obsessed the human mind since ancient times. Hypnosis is a meeting point of the same order, but was abandoned by Freud for the complex reasons which we have discussed.

It is while studying hysteria that Freud transferred his interest

185

from physiology to psychology in the course of the internal debate which we have retraced. In actual fact, he never ceased subsequently to be divided between the concern, respectively, to make sure of the "physiological bases" and to uphold the essential role of psychology, constantly seeking to reconcile these two requirements. Might one not regard as symbolic the fact that Freud bestowed on two of his sons the given names of his spiritual fathers, the physiologist Ernst Brücke and the "psychologist" Jean Martin Charcot?

This dichotomy and dualism are still discernible in the contemporary psychoanalytic movement, where some are above all concerned with the "biological foundations" while others wish to entrench themselves in the area of "pure psychology" and the rest seek to follow a middle way. It is not unreasonable to suppose that these divergent attitudes may in some degree become attenuated when further light has been cast upon the "psychobiological crossroads" that constitute hysteria. This basic neurosis, "the most enigmatic of all nervous diseases" as Freud termed it, is still far from having yielded all its secrets. The same may be said of hypnosis—another starting point of psychoanalysis—which involves a relationship so crudely revealing of unconscious motivations. In both fields a wide area remains open to further research and discovery.

We have shown how Freud derived inspiration from certain methods and concepts of the nineteenth century. But his creative spirit endowed them with a new meaning, with the result that everything he borrowed from the past assumed an unforeseen character. He organized them collectively into a coherent doctrine, one of such originality that psychoanalysis appears as a revolution in the realm of psychotherapy and in the understanding of the human mind.

Chronology

Antiquity. Knowledge of dreams and of "altered (trance) states" facilitating the reemergence of "forgotten memories."

16th Century. The suggestibility in trance states is used for the cure of illnesses (Paracelsus).

17th Century. Trance states are principally seen in cases of collective religious neuroses (possessed nuns of Loudun, etc.).

18th Century. The German Freemasons (to whom Mesmer adheres) employ suggestion in the secret practice of "miraculous" cures.

1734 Birth of Mesmer.

1751 Birth of Puységur, a disciple of Mesmer.

1778 Mesmer, aged 44, arrives in Paris and propagates the practice of animal magnetism (Convulsive "crises"; Theory of a fluid; Dynamic exchange between the therapist and the patient who is no longer treated as an inanimate object).

1784 Inquiries, and reports (secret and public) to the King on the "erotic dangers" in the practice of animal magnetism. Condemnation ("moral" in the secret report, and "scientific"—nonexistence of the fluid—in the public reports).

Puységur discovers artificial somnambulism; he observes that a somnambulist retains the ability to converse with the therapist (be-

ginning of verbal psychotherapy). Showing that man has two memories, one conscious and the other unconscious, he brings the study of the unconscious into the realm of psychology. Puységur, although a "fluidist," stresses the importance of the will to cure (on the therapist's part): introduction of the subjective element in the relationship. Puységur defends himself against erotic interference in the relationship.

1787 De Villers: Manipulation of the object relationship as a therapeutic factor.

1811 First reported case (published in 1816) of alternating personality (Mary Reynolds).

1813 Faria considers that in actual fact everything takes place in the subject's mind. Denial of the fluid.

1818 Virey sees in animal magnetism a "reciprocal influence" of an affective order. He is one of the first to suspect the nature of the process of elaboration of unconscious thought.

1819 Deleuze recognizes the danger of erotic complications, but seems to imply that certain feelings of affection can aid the magnetic cure. Faria, in the year of his death, publishes *De la Cause du Sommeil Lucide* ("On the Cause of Lucid Sleep"). He puts the subject to sleep by fixation of the gaze on a given point and by the command to sleep.

1820 Noizet, an "antifluidist," emphasizes the importance of mutual feelings of confidence between magnetist and subject.

1823 Birth of Liébeault.
    Bertrand publishes his *Traité du Somnambulisme*: the patient goes to sleep thinking of his magnetist, and therefore hears none but him during his sleep. Example of the mother who, asleep in the midst of noise, is wakened only by the cries of her child: this example will later be taken up by Pavlov in his theory of "waking points." Bertrand investigates the principle of posthypnotic suggestion.

1825 Birth of Charcot.

1837 Brodie publishes a study on "local nervous affections."

1840 Birth of Bernheim.

1856 Birth of Freud.

1882 Freud becomes engaged, and is apprised of the case of **Anna O.**

1841 Charpignon notes the importance of the repercussions on the patient of the magnetist's state of mind.

1843 Braid rejects fluidism and proffers a "psycho-neuro-physiological" theory. He refers everything back to cerebral mechanisms, and disregards "feelings"—but will later introduce the concept of suggestion.

1859 Birth of Janet.
Broca communicates to the Académie des Sciences the account of a surgical operation under hypnotic anesthesia (the recent appearance of chloroform was soon to put an end to research in this field).
Velpeau presents an account of Braid's work to the Académie des Sciences (which twenty years earlier had concluded that animal magnetism was nonexistent).

1860 Liébeault, a country doctor, establishes himself at Nancy as a simple philanthropic healer. For him, verbal suggestion is the key to Braidism.

1861 Maury shows that dreams express passions repressed in the waking state.

1863 Benedikt studies the correlation between hysteria and sexual disorders.

1866 Liébeault publishes *Du Sommeil et des États Analogues* ("On Sleep and Analogous States").

1869 Reynolds investigates psychical paralyses. Littré (French Dictionary) still lists the word "unconscious" as an adjective, and not as a noun.

1875 Earliest work of Richet on induced somnambulism. Experiments on posthypnotic suggestion.

1877 Maillet gives a superficial description of "reverie," which, however, foreshadows that of phantasy.

1878 Taine introduces the concept of repression.

1882 Charcot overcomes the opposition of the Académie des Sciences by presenting hypnosis as a somatic phenomenon, whereupon it will thenceforth be studied scientifically.

1884 (Jan.) Freud joins the neurological department of a general hospital where he understands "nothing about the neuroses."

1885 (June) Freud is granted a traveling scholarship to Paris.

(Oct.) Beginning of studies at the Salpêtrière, where Freud at first works in the laboratory of cerebral anatomy. He is "fascinated" by the lectures of Charcot (who, in teaching, at that time dissociates hysteria and sexuality, but in private shows flashes of etiological intuition on *"la chose génitale"*). Freud witnesses in particular the experiments of reproducing, by hypnotic suggestion, paralyses or other hysterical symptoms.

(Dec. 3) Freud appears discouraged, feels himself isolated in Paris, and wishes to leave the anatomical laboratory.

(Dec. 9) He writes to his fiancée that he has asked Charcot's permission to translate his *Lectures on the Diseases of the Nervous System.*

(Dec. 12) Letter to his fiancée: Charcot has given his consent. Freud's complete change of mind: there is no longer any question of his leaving Paris before the end of his scholarship.

1886 (Feb.) Freud takes his leave of Charcot, who agrees to the publication of a comparative study on organic and hysterical paralyses.

(Oct. 15) Freud's lecture before the Society of Medicine in Vienna. The hysterical nature of post-traumatic (accident) neurosis is contested by his audience. Freud apparently does not mention the experimental paralyses—but is probably already convinced, be it unconsciously, that they prove the psychical etiology of hysterical neurosis. All in all, he feels himself "forced into the Opposition."

1887 Freud employs hypnosis in private practice in the form of direct suggestion.

1888 Freud: A "characteristic of hysterical disorders is that they do not in any way present a copy of the anatomical conditions of the nervous system."

1889 (May) Freud begins to employ the cathartic method.

(July) Visit to Nancy: Freud discovers the significance of posthypnotic suggestion as proof of the existence of the unconscious; also, the lifting of posthypnotic amnesia by a process of insistence on the practitioner's part.

1884 Bernheim, introduced to hypnotism by Liébeault, publishes *De la Suggestion dans l'État Hypnotique et dans l'État de Veille* ("On Suggestion in the Hypnotic State and in the Waking State").

Richet (theory of unrecognized memories, elaboration of a dynamic psychology) appears as a precursor of Freud.

1885 (March) Charcot expounds the controversy on the "post-traumatic neuroses" which he for his part regards as hysterical. Experimental paralyses.

1886 Bernheim (Nancy School) publishes *De la Suggestion et de ses Applications à la Thérapeutique*. Krafft-Ebing publishes his *Psychopathia Sexualis*.

1888 Bourru and Burot, in *Les Variations de la Personnalité*, refer to a method of treatment comprising the recall of a memory and abreaction.

1889 Janet, four years before the publication of Breuer and Freud's "Preliminary Communication," describes a case of the reliving under hypnosis of an early trauma and, through repeated suggestions, effects the cure of a unilateral hysterical blindness (case of Marie).

1890 Publication of Freud's *Psychische Behandlung* ("Psychical Treatment")—which deals principally with hypnosis, but without any reference to the transference.

1891 Neither does Freud's article *Hypnose* make any mention of the transference, properly speaking.

At this period, Freud advises against the presence of a third person during hypnotization.

1891-1892 Episode of the hypnotized female patient who, on waking, flings her arms round Freud's neck.

1892 Freud tells Breuer of his misadventure and explains it by a "transference phenomenon." In his footnotes to his translation of Charcot's *Tuesday Lectures,* he emphasizes the notion of *the reliving of a memory* as the core of any hysterical attack.

In the autumn, for the first time he treats a patient (Elisabeth von R.) without hypnosis and will restrict its use increasingly, while elaborating (until 1898) the method of free association.

Around December, Freud sketches the first outline of the sexual etiology of the neuroses.

1893 (Jan.) Publication of the "Preliminary Communication." Guidelines on repression and abreaction.

(July) Comparative study on the paralyses in which Freud returns to the idea of the noncorrespondence of hysterical paralysis with anatomical localization.

Reference to the principle of constancy.

1895 *Studies on Hysteria.* First definition of the transference.

(July) Dream known as "Irma's injection"; Freud finds confirmation of the idea that the dream is the fulfilment of a hidden wish.

1897 Freud undertakes his self-analysis, confronting his own unconscious.

1900 Publication of *The Interpretation of Dreams.*

1909 Freud speaks of the "leap" from the psychical to the somatic as an unsolved enigma.

1921 Freud states that hypnosis remains for the most part incomprehensible.

1892 The fashion for studies on personality changes reaches its apogee. The "dynamic" aspect of the repressed eludes the researchers, who speak, moreover, as if they themselves did not have an unconscious.

1893 Death of Charcot.
     Notwithstanding the victory of the theories of the Nancy School, decline of studies on hypnosis.

1896 Ribot (*Psychologie des Sentiments*) practically ignores the concept of an unconscious.

Bibliography

N.B. — Where both a French book and its English translation are listed, * precedes the edition to which the page reference in the text is given. Quotations from the original French work are newly translated.

S.E. = Standard Edition of Freud's Works.

ACKERKNECHT, E. H. (1959) *A Short History of Psychiatry* (transl. from German). Hafner Publ. Co., New York & London.

ALEXANDER, F. G., & SELESNICK, S. T. (1966) *The History of Psychiatry.* Harper & Row, New York; Allen & Unwin, London, 1967.

AMERICAN MEDICAL ASSOCIATION. *Standard Nomenclature of Diseases and Operations.* 4th ed. Blakiston, Philadelphia, 1952. 5th ed. McGraw-Hill, New York, 1961.

ANDERSSON, O. (1962) *Studies in the Prehistory of Psychoanalysis—The Etiology of Psychoneuroses and some related themes in Sigmund Freud's scientific writings and letters, 1886-1896.* [Thesis, Univ. Uppsala] Svenska Bokförlaget, Stockholm, (Studia scientiae paedagogicae Upsaliensia, 3.)

ANDERSSON, O. (1965) [Paper presented to Int. Congress of Psychoanalysis, Amsterdam, 1965—Unpublished.] — We are indebted to Mr. Andersson for very kindly placing his MS at our disposal.

ANZIEU, D. (1975) *L'Auto-analyse de Freud.* Presses Univ. de France, Paris. 2 vols.

AZAM, E. (1860) Note sur le sommeil nerveux ou hypnotisme. In: *Archives générales de médecine,* janvier 1860, pp. 5-24.

BABINSKI, J. F. F. (1889) La suggestion dans l'hypnotisme. [Paper presented to 1er Congrès Int. de Psychologie Physiologique, Paris, 1889.] Report in: *Congrès International de Psychologie, 1889,* op. cit., pp. 131-136.

BABINSKI, J. F. F. (1909) *Démembrement de l'Hystérie traditionnelle; Pithiatisme.* Impr. Semaine Médicale, Paris.

BACHELARD, G. (1965) *La Formation de l'Esprit scientifique.* 4th ed. Vrin, Paris.

BALINT, M. (1957) *The Doctor, His Patient and the Illness.* Pitman, London; Int. Universities Press, New York. (2nd ed., revised and enlarged, 1964.)

BALINT, M. (1966) Psychoanalysis and medical practice. *Int. J. Psychoanal.,* 47:54-62.

BARAGNON, P. P. (*pseud.* Petrus) (1853) *Étude du Magnétisme Animal sous le point de vue d'une exacte pratique, suivie d'un mot sur la rotation des tables.* 2nd ed. Germer-Baillière, Paris.

BARBER, T. X. (1969) *Hypnosis: A Scientific Approach.* Van Nostrand, New York.

BARRUCAND, D. (1967) *Histoire de l'Hypnose en France.* Presses Univ. de France, Paris.

BASSIN, F. V. (1968) *Problema bessoznatel'nogo* [Problems of the Unconscious]. "Meditsina," Moscow. (In Russian.)

BEARD, G. M. (1869) Neurasthenia, or nervous exhaustion. *Boston med. surg. J.,* N.S., 80:217-221.

BEARD, G. M. (1884, 1885) *Die sexuelle Neurasthenie, ihre Hygiene, Aetiologie* . . . (authorized German ed.) Toeplitz & Deuticke, Vienna, 1885.—
Original American ed.: *Sexual Neurasthenia* (Posthumous MS). Treat, New York, 1884.

BEAUNIS, H. E. (1886) *Le Sommeil provoqué: Études physiologiques et psychologiques.* Baillière, Paris.

BENEDIKT, M. (1863) Beobachtungen über Hysterie. *Öst. Zschr. prakt. Heilkunde,* 9, Nr. 40:711-714.

BENEDIKT, M. (1889) Aus der Pariser Kongresszeit: Erinnerungen und Betrachtungen. *Int. klin. Rundschau,* 1889: 1531 seq. [Taken up in part in Benedikt (1894).]

BENEDIKT, M. (1891) Ueber Neuralgien und neuralgische Affektionen und deren Behandlung. *Klin. Zeit- u. Streitfragen,* 6, Nr. 3:68 seq.

BENEDIKT, M. (1894) *Hypnotismus und Suggestion: Eine klinisch-psychologische Studie.* Breitenstein, Vienna. [Takes up in part Benedikt (1889).]

BENEDIKT, M. (1895) *Die Seelenkunde des Menschen als reine Erfahrungswissenschaft.* Reisland, Leipzig. — (5. Anhang: Die Frauenfrage; pp. 181-188.)

BERGASSE, N. (1784) *Considérations sur le Magnétisme Animal, ou sur la théorie du monde et des êtres organisés, d'après les principes de M. Mesmer.* La Haye (The Hague).

[BÉRILLON, E.] (1886) L'École de Paris et l'École de Nancy. *Rev. Hypnotisme exp. thér.,* 1:33-41. [Anonymous article, with introductory superscription signed "E.B."]

BERNHEIM, H. (1884) *De la Suggestion dans l'État Hypnotique et dans l'État de Veille.* Doin, Paris.

BERNHEIM, H. (1886) **De la Suggestion et de ses Applications à la Thérapeutique.* Doin, Paris. [Foreword states: "The 1st part of this book was already published in 1884. I have revised it, adding some new facts. . . . The 2nd part, which is entirely new, is concerned with *suggestive therapy.*"]
—*German* transl.: *see* Bernheim (1888b).
—*English* transl.: *Suggestive Therapeutics: A Treatise on the Nature and Uses of Hypnotism.* G. P. Putnam's Sons, New York & London, 1889. (*Reissued* by Associated Booksellers, Westport, Conn., 1957.) *Same* transl. *reissued with different title: Hypnosis and Suggestion in Psychotherapy* [same subtitle] (with introd. by E. R. Hilgard). University Books, New Hyde Park, N. Y., 1964.

BERNHEIM, H. (1888a) *De la Suggestion et de ses Applications à la Thérapeutique.* 2nd ed., revised and enlarged. Doin, Paris. [Contains "Preface to the new edition," dated Nov. 1887.]

BERNHEIM, H. (1888b) *Die Suggestion und ihre Heilwirkung* (Suggestion and its Therapeutic Effects) — (authorized German transl. with preface by S. Freud). Deuticke, Leipzig & Vienna. [Though the title-page bears the date '1888,' publication was delayed, as stated in "Translator's postscript" dated Jan. 1889. It is a transl. of Part I of 1st French ed. (1886), and of preface of Nov. 1887 to 2nd French ed. — (Part II was translated by O. von Springer).] — *English* transl. of Freud's preface, with Editor's note, in: *S.E.* 1:71-87.

BERNHEIM, H. (1889) Valeur relative des divers procédés destinés à provoquer l'hypnose et à augmenter la suggestibilité au point de vue thérapeutique. In: *Congrès International de l'Hypnotisme, Paris, 1889,* op. cit., pp. 79-111.

BERNHEIM, H. (1907) Le Docteur Liébeault et la doctrine de la suggestion (Conférence faite sous les auspices de la Société des Amis de l'Université de Nancy, le 12 déc. 1906). *Rev. méd. de l'Est*, 39:36-51, 70-82.

BERTRAND, A. J. F. (1823) *Traité du Somnambulisme et des différentes modifications qu'il présente*. Dentu, Paris.

BERTRAND, A. J. F. (1826) *Du Magnétisme Animal en France*. Baillière, Paris.

BINET, A. (1888) *Études de Psychologie expérimentale*. Doin, Paris.

BINET, A. (1892) *Les Altérations de la Personnalité*. Alcan, Paris.

BINET, A., & FÉRÉ, C. (1887) *Le Magnétisme Animal*. Alcon, Paris.
—*English* transl.: *Animal Magnetism*. Appleton, New York, 1888.

BOURGUIGNON, A. (1971) La crise de la médecine contemporaine. *Rev. Méd. psychosom.*, 13:123-140.

BOURRU, H., & BUROT, P. (1887) *La Suggestion mentale et l'Action à distance des Substances toxiques et médicamenteuses*. Baillière, Paris.

BOURRU, H., & BUROT, P. (1888) *Variations de la Personnalité*. Baillière, Paris.

BRAID, J. (1843) *Neurypnology; or, the Rationale of Nervous Sleep, considered in relation with Animal Magnetism. Illustrated by numerous cases of its successful application in the relief and cure of disease*. Churchill, London.

BRAID, J. (1860) [*Original MS on Hypnotism* — Braid's last work written in Jan. 1860, for presentation to the Académie des Sciences, Paris. *English text* no longer extant and never published.]
—*First published in German transl.*, as appendix to: *T. W. Preyer, Die Entdeckung des Hypnotismus*. Gebrüder Paetel, Berlin, 1881.
—*Transl. from German into French*, as appendix to French transl. of *Neurypnology: *Neurypnologie: Traité du Sommeil Nerveux ou Hypnotisme* (transl. Jules Simon). Delahaye & Lecrosnier, Paris, 1883
—"Chapitre additionnel," pp. 222-262. [Page refs. are to *French* version, from which quotations are retranslated into English.]

BRENMAN, M., GILL, M. M., & KNIGHT, R. P. P. (1952) Spontaneous fluctuations in depth of hypnosis and their implications for ego-function. *Int. J. Psychoanal.*, 33:22-33.

BREUER, J., & FREUD, S. (1895) *Studies on Hysteria*. S.E. 2. (*Includes*: "On the psychical mechanism of hysterical phenomena: Preliminary Communication"—first published in 1893. S.E. 2:1-17.)

BRIQUET, P. (1859) *Traité clinique et thérapeutique de l'Hystérie*. Baillière, Paris.

BRODIE, B. C. (1837) *Lectures illustrative of certain Local Nervous Affections.* Longman, London.

BROWNE, THOMAS (1646) *Pseudodoxia Epidemica: or, Enquiries into Very Many Received Tenents, and Commonly Presumed Truths.* [1st ed.] Printed by T. H. for Edward Dod, London. [Running title: "Enquiries into Vulgar and Common Errors."]

BURDIN JEUNE, C., & DUBOIS, F. (1841) *Histoire académique du Magnétisme Animal.* Baillière, Paris.

BURQ, V. (1882) *Des Origines de la Métallothérapie—Part qui doit être faite au magnétisme animal dans sa découverte.* Delahaye, Paris. [Date on cover—1883.]

CHARCOT, J. M. (1877) *Leçons sur les Maladies du Système Nerveux faites à la Salpêtrière.* Vol. 1, 3rd ed. (ed. Bourneville). Delahaye, Paris.
—English transl.: *Clinical Lectures on Diseases of the Nervous System.* Vol. 1. New Sydenham Soc., London, 1877.

CHARCOT, J. M. (1882) Sur les divers états nerveux déterminés par l'hypnotisation chez les hystériques. *C. R. Acad. Sci., Paris,* 94:403-405.

CHARCOT, J. M. (1886) *Neue Vorlesungen über die Krankheiten des Nervensystems, insbesondere über Hysterie* (New Lectures on the Diseases of the Nervous System, particularly on Hysteria) — (authorized German transl. of Vol. 3 of Charcot (1887), with preface by S. Freud). Toeplitz & Deuticke, Leipzig & Vienna, 1886 [The transl. was published before the original French version.]
—English transl. of Freud's preface, with Editor's note, in: S. E. 1: 17-22.

CHARCOT, J. M. (1887) *Leçons sur les Maladies du Système Nerveux faites à la Salpêtrière.* Vol. 3 (eds. Babinski, Bernard & Féré). Delahaye, Paris. (Publications du *Progrès médical.*)
—German transl.: *see* Charcot (1886).
—English transl.: *see* Charcot (1889).

CHARCOT, J. M. (1889) *Clinical Lectures on Diseases of the Nervous System* (English transl.). Vol. 3. New Sydenham Soc., London.

CHARPIGNON, L. J. J. (1841) *Physiologie, Médecine et Métaphysique du Magnétisme.* Pesty, Orléans; Baillière, Paris.

CHERTOK, L. (1954) Sommeil hypnotique prolongé. In: G. Nora & M. Sapir (eds.), *La Cure de Sommeil.* Masson, Paris, pp. 57-70.

CHERTOK, L. (1960) *A propos de la découverte de la méthode cathartique. *Bull. Psychol.,* numéro spécial en hommage à P. Janet, 5 nov. 1960: 33-37. — (*Abridged English version*: On the discovery of the cathartic method. *Int. J. Psychoanal.,* 1961, 42:284-287.)

CHERTOK, L. (1966a) An introduction to the study of tensions among psychotherapists [Paper read at 6th Int. Congress of Psychotherapy, London, 1964]. *Brit. J. med. Psychol.,* 39:237-243.

CHERTOK, L. (1966b) **Hypnosis* (English transl. from expanded version of 3rd French ed.). Pergamon Press, Oxford, London & New York, 1966. — *(French editions*: *L'Hypnose,* 3rd ed., Masson, Paris, 1963; and 3rd ed. revised and enlarged, Payot, Paris, 1965.)

CHERTOK, L. (1967) Theory of hypnosis since the First International Congress, 1889. *Amer. J. Psychother.,* 21:62-73.

CHERTOK, L. (1968a) From suggestion to metapsychology: Centenary of the publication of Liébeault's "Du Sommeil et des États Analogues." *Brit. J. med. Psychol.,* 41:95-116.

CHERTOK, L. (1968b) The discovery of the transference: Towards an epistemological interpretation. *Int. J. Psychoanal.,* 49:560-577.

CHERTOK, L. (1970) Freud in Paris: A crucial stage. *Int. J. Psychoanal.,* 51:511-520.

CHERTOK, L. (1971) On objectivity in the history of psychotherapy: the dawn of dynamic psychology. *J. nerv. ment. Dis.,* 153:71-80.

CHERTOK, L. (1972) Mania operativa: Surgical addiction. *Psychiatry in Medicine,* 3:105-118.

CLAVREUL, J. (1970) Aspects cliniques des perversions. In: *Sexualité humaine;* Aubier-Montaine, Paris (Centre d'Études Laënnec—Collection Recherches économiques et sociales); pp. 193-213.

CODET, H., & LAFORGUE, R. (1925) L'influence de Charcot sur Freud. *Progrès médical,* 1925: 801-802.

COLLOQUE (XIIIe) de Psychologie Médicale de Langue française (Liège, 25-27 mars 1971). *Psychol. méd. et Sci. humaines appl. à la Santé,* 1971, 3, Nos. 2 & 3.

CONGRÈS (Premier) International de l'Hypnotisme expérimental et thérapeutique (tenu à l'Hôtel-Dieu de Paris, 8-12 août 1889). *Comptes rendus* (ed. E. Bérillon). Doin, Paris, 1889.

CONGRÈS International de Psychologie physiologique. Première session (Paris, 1890 [*sic* for 1889]). *Compte rendu* (présenté par la Soc. de Psychol. physiol. de Paris). Bureau des Revues, Paris, 1890.

COUÉ, E. (1913) De la suggestion et de ses applications. *Bull. Soc. lorraine Psychol. appliquée,* 1, No. 1. [Original ed.—Lecture delivered at Chaumont, 1912; Nancy, 1913, 1915, 1917.]

COUSIN, V. (1828-1829) *Cours de Philosophie.* Pichon & Didier, Paris. 3 tom. in 2 vols.

CRANEFIELD, P. F. (1970) Some problems in writing the history of psychoanalysis. In: G. Mora & J. L. Brand (eds.), *Psychiatry and its His-*

tory: Methodological Problems in Research. C. C Thomas, Springfield, Ill., pp. 41-55.

DAVID, C. (1966) Réflexions métapsychologiques concernant l'état amoureux. *Rev. franç. Psychanal.,* 30:195-218.

DEJERINE, J., & GAUCKLER, E. (1911) *Les Manifestations fonctionnelles des Psychonévroses; leur Traitement par la Psychothérapie.* Masson, Paris.
—*English* transl.: **The Psychoneuroses and their Treatment by Psychotherapy.* Lippincott, Philadelphia & London, 1913.

DELBOEUF, J. R. L. (1886) La mémoire chez les hypnotisés. *Rev. philos. France et Étranger,* 1886, 1er semestre: 446-447.

DELBOEUF, J. R. L. (1890) *Magnétiseurs et Médecins.* Alcan, Paris.

DELEUZE, J. P. F. (1819a) *Histoire critique du Magnétisme Animal.* 2nd ed. Belin-Leprieur, Paris. 2 vols. [1st ed.: Mame, Paris, 1813. 2 vols.]

DELEUZE, J. P. F. (1819b) *Défense du Magnétisme Animal contre les attaques dont il est l'objet dans le Dictionnaire des Sciences Médicales.* Belin-Leprieur, Paris.

DELEUZE, J. P. F. (1825) *Instruction pratique sur le Magnétisme Animal, suivie d'une lettre écrite à l'auteur par un médecin étranger.* Dentu, Paris.

DUBOIS, P. C. (1904) *Les Psychonévroses et leur Traitement moral.* Masson, Paris. [The authors refer to 3rd ed., 1909.]
—*English* transl.: **The Psychic Treatment of Nervous Disorders.* Funk & Wagnalls, New York & London, 1905.

DUMONTPALLIER, A. (1889) [Opening address, Aug. 8, 1889] In: *Congrès International de l'Hypnotisme, Paris, 1889,* op. cit., pp. 21-26.

DU PREL, K. (1899) Die ödische Individualität des Menschen. *Übersinnliche Welt, Monatsschrift,* 3, Nr. 3.

EISSLER, K. R. (1971) *Talent and Genius: The Fictitious Case of Tausk contra Freud.* Quadrangle Books, New York.

ELLENBERGER, H. F. (1965) Charcot and the Salpêtrière School. *Amer. J. Psychother.,* 19:253-367.

ELLENBERGER, H. F. (1968) La conférence de Freud sur l'hystérie masculine (15 octobre 1886) : Étude critique. *Information psychiat.,* 1968: 921-930.

ELLENBERGER, H. F. (1970) *The Discovery of the Unconscious: The history and evolution of dynamic psychiatry.* Basic Books, New York.

ELLENBERGER, H. F. (1972) L'histoire d' "Anna O.": Étude critique avec documents nouveaux. *Évolution psychiat.,* 1972: 693-717.

ERBEN, S. (1890) Die nicht stofflichen Krankheiten des Nervensystems (Neurosen). In: *Die Gesundheit*, ed. R. Kossmann & J. Weiss, 2: 315-338. Union Deutsche Verlagsgesellschaft, Stuttgart.

ERNST, M. (1884) Über den "Iliacalschmerz." *Wiener med. Blätter*, 1884, Nr. 28:866-871; Nr. 29:903-906; Nr. 30:935-937.

FARIA, ABBÉ J. C. DE (1819) *De la Cause du Sommeil Lucide*. Mme Horiac, Paris, 1819 (tome I). — Reissued (with preface and introd. by D. G. Dalgado). Jouve, Paris, 1906.

FEDIDA, P. (1972) L'hypocondrie du rêve. *Nouv. Rev. Psychanal.*, 1972: 225-238.

FERENCZI, S. (1909) Introjection and transference (English transl. by Ernest Jones). In: *Sex in Psycho-Analysis;* Basic Books, New York, 1950; and: *First Contributions to Psycho-Analysis;* Hogarth Press, London, 1952; pp. 35-93. [Different titles, but identical text and page numbers.]

FOREL, A. (1889) *Der Hypnotismus, seine Bedeutung und seine Handhabung*. Enke, Stuttgart.

FOVILLE, A. (1867) "Du Sommeil et des États analogues" par le Dr Liébeault [Review]. *Ann médico-psychol.*, 25:339-342.

FREUD, S. — *Collected Works*:
—*Gesammelte Schriften*. 12 vols. Internationaler Psychoanalytischer Verlag, Vienna, 1924-1934.
—*Gesammelte Werke*. 18 vols. — Vols. 1-17: Imago Publishing Co., London, 1940-1952; Vol. 18: S. Fischer Verlag, Frankfurt a/M., 1968. — (The whole edition published since 1960 by S. Fischer, Frankfurt a/M.)
—*The Standard Edition of the Complete Psychological Works of Sigmund Freud (English transl.* — General editor, James Strachey; in collaboration with Anna Freud, assisted by Alix Strachey and Alan Tyson; editorial assistant, Angela Richards). 24 vols. Hogarth Press, London, 1953-1974. [Abbreviated as *S.E.* in present bibliography.]

FREUD, S. (1886a) Report on my studies in Paris and Berlin [cited as "Paris Report"]. S.E. 1:1-15.

FREUD, S. (1886b) Observation of a severe case of hemi-anaesthesia in a hysterical male. S.E. 1:23-31.

FREUD, S. (1888) Hysteria [Article *Hysterie,* in: *Handwörterbuch der gesamten Medizin,* ed. A. Villaret, vol. 1, Stuttgart]. S.E. 1:37-59.

FREUD, S. (1889) Review of August Forel's *Hypnotism*. S.E. 1:89-102.

FREUD, S. (1890) Psychical (or mental) treatment [Article *Psychische Behandlung (Seelenbehandlung),* in: *Die Gesundheit,* ed. R. Kossmann & J. Weiss, 1:368-384, Stuttgart]. S.E. 7:281-302. — [On date of publication, *see*: Strachey (1966), op. cit., pp. 63-64.]

FREUD, S., & RIE, O. (1891a) Klinische Studie über die halbseitige Cerebrallähmung der Kinder (*Beiträge zur Kinderheilkunde*, Heft III). M. Perles, Vienna.

—*English transl. of Freud's abstract*: Clinical study of the unilateral cerebral palsies of children. S.E. 3:241-242.

FREUD, S. (1891b) Hypnosis [Article *Hypnose*, in: Anton Bum's *Therapeutisches Lexikon*, Vienna]. S.E. 1:103-114.

FREUD, S. (1892) On the theory of hysterical attacks [In: Sketches for the "Preliminary Communication" of 1893]. S.E. 1:151-154. — [First published in 1940.]

FREUD, S. (1892-1894) Preface and footnotes to the translation of Charcot's *Tuesday Lectures*. S.E. 1:129-143.

FREUD, S. (1893a) Quelques considérations pour une étude comparative des paralysies motrices organiques et hystériques. *Arch. Neurol., Paris*, 26:29-43.

—*English* transl.: *Some points for a comparative study of organic and hysterical motor paralyses. S.E. 1:155-172.

FREUD, S. (1893b) Charcot. S.E. 3:7-23.

FREUD, S. (1894) The neuro-psychoses of defence. S.E. 3:41-68.

FREUD, S., & BREUER, J. (1895) See: Breuer, J., & Freud, S. (1895).

FREUD, S. (1896a) Further remarks on the neuro-psychoses of defence. S.E. 3:157-185.

FREUD, S. (1896b) The aetiology of hysteria. S.E. 3:187-221.

FREUD, S. (1900) *The Interpretation of Dreams*. S.E. 4 and 5.

FREUD, S. (1904) Freud's psychoanalytic procedure. S.E. 7:247-254.

FREUD, S. (1905a) On psychotherapy. S.E. 7:255-268.

FREUD, S. (1905b) *Three Essays on the Theory of Sexuality*. S.E. 7:123-245.

FREUD, S. (1905c) Fragment of an analysis of a case of hysteria. S.E. 7:1-122.

FREUD, S. (1909) Notes upon a case of obsessional neurosis. S.E. 10:151-257.

FREUD, S. (1910) Five Lectures on Psychoanalysis. S.E. 11:1-56.

FREUD, S. (1912) Contributions to a discussion on masturbation. S.E. 12:239-254.

FREUD, S. (1913) On beginning the treatment (Further recommendations on the technique of psychoanalysis I.) S.E. 12:121-144.

FREUD, S. (1914) On the History of the Psychoanalytic Movement. S.E. 14:1-66.

FREUD, S. (1915a) Observations on transference-love. S.E. 12:157-171.

FREUD, S. (1915b) The unconscious. S.E. 14:159-215.

FREUD, S. (1917a) A metapsychological supplement to the theory of dreams. S.E. 14:217-235.

FREUD, S. (1917b) *Introductory Lectures on Psycho-Analysis*—Part III: General Theory of the Neuroses. S.E. 16.

FREUD, S. (1919) Lines of advance in psychoanalytic therapy. S.E. 17: 157-168.

FREUD, S. (1921) *Group Psychology and the Analysis of the Ego*. S.E. 18:65-143.

FREUD, S. (1924) A short account of psychoanalysis. S.E. 19:189-209.

FREUD, S. (1925a) *An Autobiographical Study*. S.E. 20:1-74.

FREUD, S. (1925b) Josef Breuer. S.E. 19:277-280.

FREUD, S. (1938) Some elementary lessons in psychoanalysis. S.E. 23: 279-286. [First published in 1940.]

FREUD, S. [1950] Extracts from the Fliess Papers. [Selected extracts from Freud [1954] — *translation entirely revised* by J. Strachey.] S.E. 1: 173-280.

FREUD, S. [1954] *The Origins of Psycho-Analysis—Letters to Wilhelm Fliess, Drafts and Notes: 1887-1902* (ed. M. Bonaparte, A. Freud & E. Kris—English transl.). Imago Publishing Co., London; Basic Books, New York; 1954.

FREUD, S. [1960] *Letters of Sigmund Freud, 1873-1939* (selected and ed. E. L. Freud—English transl.). Basic Books, New York, 1960; Hogarth Press, London, 1961.

GENIL-PERRIN, G. (1913) *Histoire des Origines et de l'Évolution de l'Idée de Dégénérescence en Médecine Mentale*. A. Leclerc, Paris.

GICKLHORN, J., & GICKLHORN, R. (1960) *Sigmund Freuds akademische Laufbahn im Lichte der Dokumente*. Urban & Schwarzenberg, Vienna & Innsbruck.

GILL, M. M., & BRENMAN, M. (1959) *Hypnosis and Related States: Psychoanalytic Studies in Regression*. Int. Universities Press, New York. (Austen Riggs Center Monograph No. 2.)

GOSHEN, C. E. (1952) The original case material of psychoanalysis. *Amer. J. Psychiat.*, 108:829-834.

GREENSON, R. R. & WEXLER, M. (1969) The nontransference relationship in the psychoanalytic situation. *Int. J. Psychoanal.*, 50:27-39.

GRUHLE, H. W. (1932) I. Geschichtliches. In: O. Bumke's *Handbuch der Geisteskrankheiten,* Vol. 9, Pt. 5:1-30. Springer, Berlin.

GUILLAIN, G. (1955) **J. M. Charcot, 1825-1893: Sa Vie, son Oeuvre.* Masson, Paris.
—*English* transl.: *J. M. Charcot, 1825-1893: His Life, His Work,* Hoeber, New York, 1959.

GUZE, S. B. (1970) The role of follow-up studies: their contribution to diagnostic classification as applied to hysteria. *Seminars in Psychiatry,* 2:392-402.

HEIDENHAIN, R. P. H. (1880) *Der sogenannte thierische Magnetismus: Physiologische Beobachtungen.* [Lecture before the Schlesische Gesellschaft für vaterländische Kultur; General meeting, Jan. 19, 1880.] Breitkopf & Härtel, Leipzig.

HELD, R. (1952) Psychopathologie du regard. [Lecture before the Groupe de l'Évolution Psychiatrique, Jan. 1952.] *Évolution psychiat.,* 1952: 221-255.

HILGARD, E. R. (1965) *Hypnotic Susceptibility* (with a chapter by J. R. Hilgard). Harcourt, New York.

HILGARD, E. R. (1970) Review of: Barber, "Hypnosis: A Scientific Approach." *Amer. J. clin. Hypnosis,* 12:272-274.

HILGARD, J. R. (1970) *Personality and Hypnosis: A Study of Imaginative Involvement.* Univ. Chicago Press, Chicago.

HOLT, R. R. (1965) A review of some of Freud's biological assumptions and their influences on his theories. In: N. S. Greenfield & W. C. Lewis (eds.), *Psychoanalysis and Current Biological Thought.* Univ. Wisconsin Press, Madison, pp. 93-124.

JANET, P. M. F. (1886a) Les actes inconscients et le dédoublement de la personnalité pendant le somnambulisme provoqué. *Rev. philos. France et Étranger,* 1886, 2e semestre: 583.

JANET, P. M. F. (1886b) Note sur quelques phénomènes de somnambulisme [Lecture before the Soc. de Psychologie physiologique, Nov. 1885—Chairman: Charcot.] *Rev. philos. France et Étranger,* 1886, 1er semestre: 190-198.

JANET, P. M. F. (1887) L'anesthésie systématisée et la dissociation des phénomènes psychologiques. *Rev. philos. France et Étranger,* 1887, 1er semestre: 449-472.

JANET, P. M. F. (1889) *L'Automatisme psychologique: Essai de Psychologie expérimentale.* Alcan, Paris.

JANET, P. M. F. (1892) L'anesthésie hystérique [Lecture at the Salpêtrière, March 1892.] *Arch Neurol., Paris,* 23:323-352.

JANET, P. M. F. (1898) *Névroses et Idées fixes. I. Études expérimentales sur les troubles de la volonté, de l'attention, de la mémoire, sur les émotions, les idées obsédantes et leur traitement.* Alcan, Paris. (Travaux du Laboratoire de Psychologie de la Clinique de la Salpêtrière, 1re série.)

JANET, P. M. F. (1919) *Les Médications Psychologiques: Études historiques, psychologiques et cliniques sur les méthodes de la psychothérapie.* Vol. 1: *L'Action morale, l'utilisation de l'automatisme.* Alcan, Paris.
—*English* transl.: **Psychological Healing: A Historical and Clinical Study.* Vol. 1. Allen & Unwin, London; Macmillan, New York; 1925. [In Vol. 1 of transl., Part I—"Search for Mental and Moral Action"; Part II—"Utilization of the Patient's Automatism."]

JONES, E. (1923) *Papers on Psycho-Analysis.* 3rd ed. Baillière, Tindall & Cox, London. — *See especially*: The action of suggestion in psychotherapy, pp. 340-381; and: The nature of autosuggestion, pp. 382-403.

JONES, E. (1953-1957) *Sigmund Freud: Life and Work.* Hogarth Press, London. 3 vols. — 1 (1953) : *The Young Freud, 1856-1900;* 2 (1955) : *Years of Maturity, 1901-1919;* 3 (1957) : *The Last Phase, 1919-1939.*

KONSTORUM, S. I. (1959) *Opyt prakticheskoj Psikhoterapij* (Practical Psychotherapy) , Moscow. (Trudy Gos. N.i.i. psikhiatrij, T. 21.) [Publ. Min. Health RSFSR, Inst. Psychiatry, Vol. 21.] (In Russian)

KOUPERNIK, C. (1969) À propos du livre de Ph. Bassine: "Les Problèmes de l'Inconscient". *Rev. Méd. psychosom.,* 11:523-533. [*See*: Bassin (1968) .]

KRAFFT-EBING, R. VON (1879) *Lehrbuch der Psychiatrie.* Enke, Stuttgart, 1879-1880. 3 vols.

KRAFFT-EBING, R. VON (1886) *Psychopathia Sexualis: Eine klinische-forensische Studie.* Enke, Stuttgart.

KRAFFT-EBING, R. VON (1888) *Eine experimentelle Studie auf dem Gebiete des Hypnotismus.* Enke, Stuttgart.

KRAFFT-EBING, R. VON (1893) *Hypnotische Experimente.* 2nd, enlarged ed. Enke, Stuttgart.

KUBIE, L. S. (1961) Hypnotism: A focus for psychophysiological and psychoanalytic investigations. *Arch. general Psychiat.,* 4:40-54.

KUBIE, L. S., & MARGOLIN, S. G. (1944) The process of hypnotism and the nature of the hypnotic state. *Amer. J. Psychiat.,* 100:611-622.

LAGACHE, D. (1952) Le problème du transfert. *Rev. franç. Psychanal.,* 16:5-115.

LANTERI-LAURA, G. (19970) *Histoire de la Phrénologie: L'Homme et son Cerveau selon F. J. Gall.* Presses Univ. de France, Paris.

LAPLANCHE, J., & PONTALIS, J.-B. (1973) **The Language of Psycho-Analysis* (English transl.). Hogarth Press, London. (Translation of: *Vocabulaire de la Psychanalyse.* Presses Univ. de France, Paris, 1971.)

LAROUSSE (1962) *Grand Larousse encyclopédique en dix volumes.* Larousse, Paris. Vol. 6, 1962 [*siv.* "inconscient" ("unconscious")].

LEBEDINSKIJ, M. S. (1959) *Ocherki Psikhoterapij* (Handbook of Psychotherapy). Medgiz, Moscow. (2nd ed., 1971) (In Russian)

LIÉBEAULT, A. A. (1866) *Du Sommeil et des États Analogues considérés surtout au point de vue de l'action du moral sur le physique.* Masson, Paris.

LIÉBEAULT, A. A. (1886) Confession d'un médecin hypnotiseur. *Rev. Hypnotisme exp. thér.,* 1:105-110, 143-148.

LIÉGEOIS, J. (1889) *De la Suggestion et du Somnambulisme dans leurs rapports avec la Jurisprudence et la Médecine Légale.* Doin, Paris.

LITTRÉ, E. *Dictionnaire de la Langue française.* Hachette, Paris. [*s.v.* "inconscient" ("unconscious")] — Original ed., Vol. 2, 1869: "in sleep there are unconscious acts." — 1874 and 1882 editions: ditto. — Supplement, 1877: "*Add:* Part of the natural actions which have no consciousness [French = "*conscience*"] of themselves."

MACALPINE, I. (1950) The development of transference. *Psychoanal. Quart.,* 19:501-539.

MACARIO, M. M. A. (1857) *Du Sommeil, des Rêves et du Somnambulisme dans l'état de santé et de maladie.* Périsse, Lyon & Paris.

MAILLET, E. (1877) *De l'Essence des Passions: Étude psychologique et morale.* (Thèse) Hachette, Paris.

MAINE DE BIRAN, M. F. P. (1802-1803) *Influence de l'Habitude sur la Faculté de Penser.* Hinrichs, Paris, an XI [=1802-1803].

MANNONI, O. (1971) *Freud: The Theory of the Unconscious* (transl. from French). New Left Books, London.

MARGOLIN, S. G. (1954) Psychotherapeutic principles in psychosomatic practice. In: E. D. Wittkower & R. A. Cleghorn (eds.), *Recent Developments in Psychosomatic Medicine;* Pitman & Sons, London; Lippincott, Philadelphia; pp. 134-153.

MARIE, P. (1925) Éloge de J. M. Charcot [prononcé à l'Académie de Médecine, 26 mai 1925 — Centenaire de Charcot et 25e Anniversaire de la Société de Neurologie de Paris.] *Rev. neurol.,* 1925: 731-745.

MASTERS, W. H., & JOHNSON, V. E. (1970) Human Sexual Inadequacy. Little, Brown & Co., Boston.

MAURY, L. F. A. (1861) Le Sommeil et les Rêves: Études psychologiques. Didier, Paris.

MESMER, F. A. (1781) Précis historique des Faits relatifs au Magnétisme Animal, jusques en avril 1781 (ouvrage traduit de l'allemand). Londres. — [Reproduced in extenso, with introd. and notes, in: Mesmer (1971), pp. 89-202.]

MESMER, F. A. (1785) *[Caullet de Veaumorel:] Aphorismes de M. Mesmer dictés à l'assemblée de ses élèves (Ouvrage mis à jour par M. C. de V. . . .). Quinquet, Paris, 1785. — Idem, 3e éd. revue, corrigée et . . . dans laquelle on trouve les moyens de magnétiser d'intention. Bertrand, Paris, 1785.
—English transl.: Maxims on Animal Magnetism (with introd. by J. Eden). Eden Press, Mt. Vernon, N. Y., 1958.

MESMER, F. A. [1971] Le Magnétisme Animal: Oeuvres (ed. R. Amadou, with commentaries and notes by F. A. Pattie and J. Vinchon). Payot, Paris.

MEYNERT, T. (1888) Ueber hypnotische Erscheinungen. Wiener klin. Wochenschr., 1:451-453, 473-476, 495-498.

MILLER, J. A., ET AL. (1969) Some aspects of Charcot's influence on Freud. J. Amer. Psychoanal. Ass., 17:608-623.

MOLL, A. (1888) [Contributions to Discussion at Berlin Soc. of Medicine] Report in: Rev. Hypnotisme exp. thér., 2:180, 187.

MOREAU, J. J. (1845) Du Hachisch et de l'Aliénation mentale: Études psychologiques. Fortin, Masson & Cie., Paris.
—English transl.: Hashish and Mental Illness (ed. H. Peters & G. G. Nahas). Raven Press, New York, 1973.

MOREL, B. A. (1857) Traité des Dégénérescences physiques, intellectuelles et morales de l'Espèce humaine et des causes qui produisent ces variétés maladives. Baillière, Paris (with Atlas).

NACHT, S. (1957) [Address delivered at the Salpêtrière, during the celebration of the centenary of Freud's birth.] Rev. franç. Psychanal., 21: 319-320.

NACHT, S. (1963) La Présence du Psychanalyste. Presses Univ. de France, Paris.

NOIZET, F. J. (1854) Mémoire sur le Somnambulisme et le Magnétisme Animal (adressé en 1820 à l'Académie royale de Berlin, et publié en 1854). Plon, Paris.

O'Connell, D. N., & Orne, M. T. (1968) Endosomatic electrodermal correlates of hypnotic depth and susceptibility. *J. psychiat. Res.,* 6: 1-12.

Olivier, J. (1849) *Traité du Magnétisme, suivi des Paroles d'un Somnambule, et d'un Recueil de Traitements magnétiques.* Jougle, Toulouse.

Orne, M. T. (1971) The simulation of hypnosis. *Int. J. clin. exp. Hypnosis,* 19; No. 4:183. [This number contains various other articles on the simulation of hypnosis.]

Orne, M. T., Sheehan, P. W., & Evans, F. J. (1968) Occurrence of posthypnotic behavior outside the experimental setting. *J. Personality soc. Psychol.,* 9:189-196.

Pribram, K. (1965) Freud's project: an open biologically based model for psychoanalysis. In: N. S. Greenfield & W. C. Lewis (eds.), *Psychoanalysis and Current Biological Thought*; Univ. Wisconsin Press, Madison; pp. 81-92.

Puységur, A. M. J. de (1784-1785) *Mémoires pour servir à l'Histoire et à Établissement du Magnétisme Animal. S. l.,* 1784. — *Suite des Mémoires. . . .* Londres, 1785. — (2 vols.)

Puységur, A. M. J. de (1807) *Du Magnétisme Animal, considéré dans ses rapports avec diverses branches de la physique générale.* Desenne, Paris.

Puységur, A. M. J. de (1811) *Recherches, Expériences et Observations physiologiques sur l'Homme dans l'État du Somnambulisme naturel, et dans le Somnambulisme provoqué par l'Acte magnétique.* Dentu, Paris.

Puységur, A. M. J. de (1813) *Appel aux savans Observateurs du dix-neuvième Siècle, de la Décision portée par leurs Prédécesseurs contre le Magnétisme Animal, et fin du traitement du jeune Hébert.* Dentu, Paris.

Rapports (1784) :—
— (1784a) *Rapport des Commissaires chargés par le Roi de l'examen du magnétisme animal. Imprimé par ordre du Roi.* [Public Report by members appointed from the Academy of Sciences and Faculty of Medicine. — Benjamin Franklin, Chairman; J. S. Bailly, Reporter. — Aug. 11, 1784.] Imprimerie royale, Paris, 1784.
—*English* translation: Report of Dr. Benjamin Franklin and other Commissioners, charged by the King of France with the examination of the animal magnetism, as now practised at Paris. Translated from the French. J. Johnson, London and Philadelphia, 1785.

—(1784b) Rapport des Commissaires de la Société royale de médecine, nommés par le Roi pour faire l'examen du magnétisme animal. Imprimé par ordre du Roi. [Public Report by members appointed from the Royal Society of Medicine. — Aug. 16, 1784.] Imprimerie royale, Paris, 1784.

—(1784c) *Rapport secret des Commissaires. . . . [This Secret Report to the King was of course not published at the time. It was drawn up by the Commissioners who wrote Report (1784a). J. S. Bailly, Reporter. — Aug. 11, 1784.]

The text was *first published* in *Le Conservateur* (a collection of previously unpublished historical and other documents), Imprimerie de Crapelet, Paris, an VIII [= 1799-1800], Tome I, pp. 146-155. It is this, the most accurate text available, that is reproduced *in extenso* in: *Mesmer (1971), op. cit., App. 1, pp. 278-281. [It has been reproduced elsewhere from time to time, with varying degrees of accuracy, e.g., in: A. Bertrand (1826), op. cit., pp. 511-516; also, in: Burdin & Dubois (1841), and Binet & Féré (1887).]

—*English* transl.: Secret Report on Mesmerism, or Animal Magnetism; in: Binet & Féré (transl.: 1888), op. cit., pp. 18-25; reprinted in: R. E. Shor & M. T. Orne (eds.), *The Nature of Hypnosis: Selected Basic Readings*, Holt, Rinehart & Winston, New York, 1965, pp. 3-7.

REICHARD, S. (1956) A re-examination of "Studies in Hysteria." *Psychoanal. Quart.*, 1956: 155-177.

RENOUVIER, C. B. J. (1842) *Manuel de Philosophie moderne*. Paulin, Paris.

RÉSIMONT, C. C. DE (1843) *Le Magnétisme Animal considéré comme moyen thérapeutique; son application au traitement de deux cas remarquables de névropathie*. Germer-Baillière, Paris.

REYNOLDS, J. R. (1869) Remarks on paralysis and other disorders of motion and sensation dependent on idea. *Brit. med. J.*, 1869, 2:483-485.

RIBOT, T. (1881) *Les Maladies de la Mémoire*. Baillière, Paris.

RIBOT, T. (1885) *Les Maladies de la Personnalité*. Alcan, Paris.

RIBOT, T. (1896) *La Psychologie des Sentiments*. Alcan, Paris.

RICHER, P. (1885) *Études Cliniques sur la Grande Hystérie ou Hystéro-Épilepsie* (with Lettre-Préface by J. M. Charcot). 2nd ed., enlarged. Delahaye, Paris.

RICHET, C. (1875) Du somnambulisme provoqué. *J. Anat. Physiol. norm. et pathol. Homme et Animaux*, 11:348-378.

RICHET, C. (1884) *L'Homme et l'Intelligence: Fragments de Physiologie et de Psychologie*. Alcan, Paris.

ROAZEN, P. (1969) *Brother Animal: The Story of Freud and Tausk*. A. A. Knopf, New York.

ROBERT, M. (1964) *Psychoanalytic Revolution*. George Allen & Unwin Ltd., London.

ROSENTHAL, M. (1875) *Klinik der Nervenkrankheiten, nach seinen an der Wiener Universität gehaltenen Vorträgen*. (2nd ed. of his *Handbuch*, completely rewritten.) Enke, Stuttgart, 1875. — [1st ed.: *Handbuch der Diagnostik und Therapie der Nerven-Krankheiten*. Erlangen, 1870].

ROSENTHAL, M. (1878) *Traité clinique des Maladies du Système Nerveux* (French transl. from 2nd German ed. — revised by the author, with preface by Prof. Charcot). Masson, Paris.

SACHS, H. (1944) *Freud, Master and Friend*. Harvard Univ. Press, Cambridge, Mass. — Imago Publishing Co., London, 1945.

SAPIR, M. (1972) *La Formation psychologique du Médecin, à partir de Michael Balint* (Prefaces by Mrs. E. Balint and Prof. H. Péquignot). Payot, Paris.

SAUSSURE, R. DE (1922) *La Méthode Psychanalytique* (with preface by S. Freud). Payot, Lausanne & Geneva.
—*English* transl. of Freud's preface in: S.E. 19:283-284.

SAUSSURE, R. DE (1968) La cure magnétique. *Information psychiat.*, 44: 903-909.

SAUSSURE, R. DE (1971) Le caractère de Mesmer. [Essay] in: J. Vinchon, *Mesmer et son Secret* (new ed. by R. de Saussure). Privat, Toulouse, pp. 9-19.

SCHNEIDER, P. B. (1968) Remarques sur les rapports de la psychanalyse avec la médecine psychosomatique. [Lecture before the Société Suisse de Psychanalyse, May 1967.] *Rev. franç. Psychanal.*, 32:645-677.

SCHUR, M. (1972) *Freud: Living and Dying*. Int. Universities Press, New York.

SHEPARD, M. (1971) *The Love Treatment: Sexual Intimacy between Patients and Psychotherapists*. P. H. Wyden, New York.

SHOR, R. E., & ORNE, E. C. (1962) *The Harvard Group Scale of Hypnotic Susceptibility, Form A*. Consulting Psychologists Press, Palo Alto, Calif.

SIMON, P. M. (1882) *Le Monde des Rêves*. Baillière, Paris, 1882. — 2nd ed., *ibid.*, 1888.

STEWART, H. (1963) A comment on the psychodynamics of the hypnotic state. *Int. J. Psychoanal.*, 44:372-374.

STONE, I. (1971) *The Passions of the Mind—A Novel of Sigmund Freud.* Doubleday, New York; Cassell, London.

STRACHEY, J. (1955) The chronology of the case of Frau Emmy von N. (Appendix A to *Studies on Hysteria*). S.E. 2:307-309. Hogarth Press, London.

STRACHEY, J. (1966) Editor's Introduction [to Freud's Papers on Hypnotism and Suggestion]. S.E. 1:63-69. Hogarth Press, London.

SVJADOSHCH, A. M. (1971) *Nevrozy i ikh Lechenie* (Neuroses and their Treatment). "Meditsina," Moscow. (In Russian)

SZASZ, T. S. (1963) The concept of transference. *Int. J. Psychoanal.*, 44: 432-443.

TAINE, H. A. (1870) *De l'Intelligence.* Hachette, Paris. 2 vols.

TARDE, J. G. DE (1889) Le crime et l'épilepsie. *Rev. philos. France et Étranger*, 1889: 449-469.

THOURET, M. A. (1784) *Recherches et Doutes sur le Magnétisme Animal.* Prault, Paris.

TICHO, E. A., & TICHO, G. R. (1972) Freud and the Viennese. *Int. J. Psychoanal.*, 53:301-306.

TISSIÉ, P. A. (1890) *Les Rêves: Physiologie et Pathologie* (Preface by Prof. Azam). Alcan, Paris.

TISSOT, S. A. A. D. (1758) *Dissertatio de Febribus biliosis. . . . Accedit Tentamen de Morbis ex Manustupratione.* [1st Latin ed.] M. M. Bousquet, Lausanne.

TISSOT, S. A. A. D. (1760) *L'Onanisme, ou Dissertation physique sur les Maladies produites par la Masturbation* (transl. from the Latin, and considerably enlarged). [1st French ed.] Impr. A. Chapuis, Lausanne.

TISSOT, S. A. A. D. (1766) *Onanism: or, a Treatise upon the Disorders produced by Masturbation* (transl. from the last Paris edition [in French] by A. Hume). [1st English ed.] The Translator, London.

TRAUGOTT, N. N. (1972) Preface to: L. Chertok, *Gipnoz* (Russian transl. of *L'Hypnose*). "Meditsina," Moscow.

ULETT, G., AKPINAR, S., & ITIL, C. (1972) Hypnosis: physiological, pharmacological reality. *Amer. J. Psychiat.*, 128:799-805.

VALABREGA, J.-P. (1962) *La Relation thérapeutique: Malade et Médecin.* Flammarion, Paris.

VALÉRY, P. (1928) *Les Cahiers—1926-1928.* Vol. 12, p. 905. (Mimeographed by Centre National de la Recherche Scientifique, at the Bibliothèque Nationale, Paris.)

VEITH, I. (1965) *Hysteria: The History of a Disease.* Univ. Chicago Press, Chicago.

[VILLERS, C. DE] (1787) *Le Magnétiseur amoureux, par un membre de la société harmonique du régiment de Metz.* "Genève" [= Besançon].

VINCHON, J. (1936) *Mesmer et son Secret.* A. Legrand, Paris, 1936. — *New edition* (ed., with introduction and essay "Le caractère de Mesmer," by R. de Saussure). Privat, Toulouse, 1971.

VIREY, J. J. (1818) *Examen impartial de la Médecine magnétique.* Panckoucke, Paris. — [Extract from:] *Dictionnaire des Sciences médicales,* par une société de médecins et de chirurgiens; Panckoucke, Paris, Vol. 29, pp. 463-558, art. "Magnétisme animal".

WEITZENHOFFER, A. M., & HILGARD, E. R. (1959) *Stanford Hypnotic Susceptibility Scale, Forms A and B.* Consulting Psychologists Press, Palo Alto, Calif.

WEITZENHOFFER, A. M., & HILGARD, E. R. (1962) *Stanford Hypnotic Susceptibility Scale, Form C.* Consulting Psychologists Press, Palo Alto, Calif.

WETTERSTRAND, O. G. (1888) *Om Hypnotismens användande i den praktiska Medicinen.* Seligmann, Stockholm, 1888 [Original ed. in Swedish.]
—German transl.: *Der Hypnotismus und seine Anwendung in der praktischen Medicin.* Urban & Schwarzenberg, Vienna & Leipzig, 1891.
—English transl. *from German: Hypnotism and its Application to Practical Medicine.* G. P. Putnam's Sons, New York & London, 1897.

WHYTE, L. L. (1960) *The Unconscious before Freud.* Basic Books, New York.

WITTELS, F. (1924) *Sigmund Freud: der Mann, die Lehre, die Schule.* E. P. Tal, Vienna.
—English transl.: *Sigmund Freud: His Personality, His Teaching and His School.* Dodd Mead, New York; Allen & Unwin, London; 1924.

WITTELS, F. (1933) Revision of a biography. *Psychoanal. Rev.,* 20:361-374.

ZILBOORG, G., & HENRY, G. W. (1941) *A History of Medical Psychology.* Norton, New York.

Index

Abreaction, 77 74n.
 and carthartic method, 121
 guidelines on, 194
Académie de médecine (Paris), 9, 155
Académie des Sciences (Paris), 9, 41-42, 191
Ackerknecht, E. H., 92n.
Acting out, 7
 cathartic value of, 35
 and Freud, rejection of, 30
 therapeutic danger in, 14ln.
 and transference, 34
Affective conversion, 84
Alexander, F. G., 57
Altérations de la Personnalité, Les (Binet), 136, 179
Amadou, R., 4n.
Ambroise, 42
American Medical Association, 133
American Psychoanalytic Association, 38, 133
Amnesia, 48, 151, 192. *See also* Suggestion
Ampère, 156
Andersson, O., 68, 75, 101, 107, 108, 118; 130, 131
Andreas-Salomé, L., 145n.
Anemia, functional, 70
Anesthesia:
 facial, 177
 hypnotism for, 41, 191
 and hysteria, 77
Animal magnetism, 3ff., 157-65. *See also* Hypnotism; Somnambulism

Bertrand, 28
Charpignon, 29
 dangers in, perceptions on, 187
Deleuze, 18-23, 26, 27, 145n.
De Villers, 23
 development of, vi, xi
 and emotions, 22-24, 61
 and eroticism, 18-20, 135
Faria, 28
 fluid transmission, 21-22
 and hypnosis, 4-9
 magnetists, catagories of, 31
Mesmer, 4-12
Noizet, 27-28
 process of, 34, 54-55
 and psychotherapy, development of, 4
 and Puységur, 12-17
 reciprocal influence in, 189
 regression in, 13-14, 16, 136
 scientific evaluation of, 9-12
 and suggestion, 25
 treatment dynamics, 30-33
Virey, 23
Anna O. case, 63-64, 67, 88, 118, 124n., 125, 129, 131, 139, 142, 178n., 190. *See also* Breuer, J.
Anxiety:
 and neurosis, 90
 suppression of, 164
Anzieu, D., 197
Aphonia, 133n.
Archives de Neurologie, 76, 77

217

Reizzustäude der Weiblichen Geschlecht-sorgane, 105
Renouvier, C. B. J., 156n.
Repetition compulsion, 82n.
Repression, 77, 167n., 181
  discovery of, 183
  and dreams, 191
  of Freud, 64
  guidelines on, 194
  and interpretation, 83
  term introduction, 167
Résimont, C. C. de, 31-32, 35
Resistance, and hypnosis, 122
Retina, and hypnotism, 39. *See also* Eye, human
Reverie, and phantasies, 169
Reviviscence, technique of, 121
Revue, française de Psychanalyse, v
Reynolds, M., 72, 72n., 178n., 189, 191
Ribot, T., 122, 182, 195
Richer, R., 54, 55, 56, 78, 79, 81, 168
Richet, C., 165, 166, 172, 182, 183n., 193
Richetti, 85
Rie, O., 137
Roazen, P., 93n., 101
Roback, A. A., 152
Roberts, R., 101
Rosenthal, M., 105-106, 108, 126n.
Russia, 5n., 79n. *See also* Soviet Union

Sachs, H., 101, 134
Sadism, term introduction, 97
Sadomasochism, and animal magnetism, 16, 35
Saint Augustine, 156
Salpêtrière school, 49-61, 78, 81ff., 104, 109, 110, 115, 116, 129, 135, 149, 152, 175, 192
Sapir, M., 100
Sardou, V., 85
Saussure, F. de, v, vi
Saussure, J. de, vii
Saussure, R., vi, vii, 30
Schizophrenia, diagnosis of, 131
Schneider, P. B., 69n.
Schopenhauer, 154
Schur, M., 68, 131, 134, 135
Secret Report to the King (Bailly), 9-11, 17, 18, 58
Seduction theory, 134, 140. *See also* Sexuality
Selesnick, S. T., 57
Sexuality. *See also* Masturbation
  and hypnosis, 13ff., 91, 134, 135, 148-49

and hysteria, 51, 62, 88, 96, 104, 105-106, 129n., 135, 191, 192
morality on, 64
and nervous disorder, 95-96
and psychotherapy, 127-28, 141n.
and transference, 99
in Victorian period, 97-98
Shepard, M., 141n.
Shor, R. E., 47
Sigmund Freud, Archives, New York, 101
Sigmund Freuds akademische Laufbahn, 112
Simmel, E., 118
Simon, J., 39n.
Simon, P. M., 171
Simpson, 41
Sleep, and hypnosis, 43
Sleep theory, 131n.
Société de Psychologie Médicale, 45n.
Society of Medicine, Vienna, 99, 192
Sommeil et les Rêves, Le (Maury), 168
Somnambulism, 6, 191. *See also* Animal magnetism; Hynotism
  and animal magnetism, 15, 17
  commitment in, 32
  discovery of, 189
  and disturbed mind, 29
  and hypnotism, 70
  and imagination, 28
  isolation in, 31-32
  and tactile stimulation, 55
  and theoretical rivalry, 38
  and unconscious, 156-65, 173-83
Sophrosis, as term, 37n.
Souffrances du jeune Hubert, 91-92
Soul, 27-28
Souvenirs ignorés, 166
Soviet Union:
  and hypnosis, 58-59
  sleep therapy, 131n.
  study of unconscious in, 153
Staël, de, v
Standard Nomenclature of Diseases (AMA), 133
Stewart, H., 148
Stone, I., 101
Strachey, J., 76, 77, 118n., 125, 152
Studies in the Prehistory of Psychoanalysis (Andersson), 68
Studies on Hysteria (Breuer and Freud), 84, 118n., 127, 136, 142, 167n., 180n., 183, 194
Suggestion, 54, 61, 62, 83. *See also* Hypnotism